Conversations on Servant-Leadership

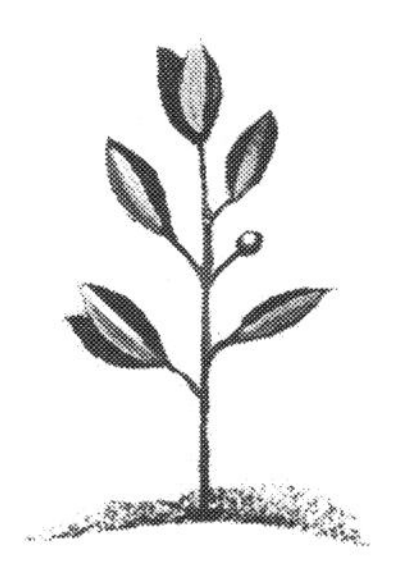

Conversations on Servant-Leadership

Insights on Human Courage in Life and Work

Edited by

Shann Ray Ferch

Larry C. Spears

Mary McFarland

Michael R. Carey

Published by State University of New York Press, Albany

Printed in the United States of America

For information, contact State University of New York Press, Albany, NY
www.sunypress.edu

Production, Ryan Morris
Marketing, Anne M. Valentine

Library of Congress Cataloging-in-Publication Data

Conversations on servant-leadership : insights on human courage in life and work / edited by Shann Ray Ferch, Larry C. Spears, Mary McFarland, and Michael R. Carey.
pages cm
Includes index.
ISBN 978-1-4384-5507-5 (hardcover : alk. paper)
ISBN 978-1-4384-5508-2 (pbk. : alk. paper)
ISBN 978-1-4384-5509-9 (ebook)
1. Servant leadership. I. Ferch, Shann R. (Shann Ray), 1967–

HM1261.C695 2015
658.4'092—dc23 2014012933

10 9 8 7 6 5 4 3 2 1

Contents

What Others Say About Servant-Leadership

"The servant-leader is servant first. Becoming a servant-leader begins with the natural feeling that one wants to serve, to serve first."

—Robert K. Greenleaf, "The Servant as Leader"

"The most difficult step, Greenleaf has written that any developing servant-leader must take, is to begin the personal journey toward wholeness and self-discovery."

—Joseph Jaworski, *Synchronicity*

"With its deeper resonances in our spiritual traditions, Greenleaf reminds us that the essence of leadership is service, and therefore the welfare of people. Anchored in this way, we can distinguish between the tools of influence, persuasion, and power from the orienting values defining leadership to which these tools are applied."

—Ronald Heifetz, Distinguished Professor,
Harvard University; *Leadership Without Easy Answers*

"Robert K. Greenleaf's work has struck a resonant chord in the minds and hearts of scholars and practitioners alike. His message lives through others, the true legacy of a servant-leader."

—Jim Kouzes, *The Leadership Challenge*

"Anyone can be a servant-leader. Any one of us can take initiative; it doesn't require that we be appointed a leader; but it does require that we operate from moral authority. The spirit of servant-leadership is the spirit of moral authority."

—Stephen R. Covey, *The 7 Habits of Highly Effective People*

"Servant-leadership is now part of the vocabulary of enlightened leadership. Bob Greenleaf, along with other notables such as McGregor, Drucker, and Follett, has created a new thought-world of leadership that contains such virtues as growth, responsibility, and love."

—Warren Bennis, Distinguished Professor,
Marshall School of Business,
University of Southern California; *On Leadership*

"I truly believe that servant-leadership has never been more applicable to the world of leadership than it is today."

—Ken Blanchard, *The Heart of Leadership*

"We are each indebted to Greenleaf for bringing spirit and values into the workplace. His ideas will have enduring value for every generation of leaders."

—Peter Block, *Stewardship*

"Servant-leadership teaches the value of building relationships, using persuasion in decision making, understanding the use of foresight, and other elements that are essential to creating meaning."

—Richard Leider, *Repacking Your Bags*
and *The Power of Purpose*

"Robert Greenleaf takes us beyond cynicism and cheap tricks and simplified techniques into the heart of the matter, into the spiritual lives of those who lead."

—Parker Palmer, *The Courage to Teach*

"Servant-leadership is more than a concept. As far as I'm concerned, it is a fact. I would simply define it by saying that any great leader, by which I also mean an ethical leader of any group, will see herself or himself primarily as a servant of that group and will act accordingly."

—M. Scott Peck, *The Road Less Traveled*

"No one in the past 30 years has had a more profound impact on thinking about leadership than Robert Greenleaf. If we sought an objective measure of the quality of leadership available to society, there would be none better than the number of people reading and studying his writings."

—Peter M. Senge, *The Fifth Discipline*

"Servant-leadership offers hope and wisdom for a new era in human development, and for the creation of better, more caring institutions."

—Larry C. Spears, president and CEO,
the Spears Center for Servant-Leadership;
editor/contributing author, *Insights on Leadership*

"I believe that Greenleaf knew so much when he said the criterion of successful servant-leadership is that those we serve are healthier and wiser and freer and more autonomous, and perhaps they even loved our leadership so much that they also want to serve others."

—Margaret Wheatley, *Leadership and the New Science*

"Despite all the buzz about modern leadership techniques, no one knows better than Greenleaf what really matters."

—*Working Woman* magazine

Preface

The Road from Darkness to Light

Shann Ray Ferch

In a world often brimming with disdain, what is hope? And where does hope reside? I grew up in Montana, a state that boasts miles of open land split by the rugged and sometimes brutal heights of one hundred mountain ranges. For me, hope is found in nature, in wilderness, and in the wilderness that exists inside people. Servant-leadership, a way of being that is characterized by wisdom, freedom, health, and autonomy; it is a source of hope in all the complexity and chaos of the present day. Contrary to the hyperspeed of the contemporary age, I've found there are those who walk toward the dawn, and having traversed the night's darkness they emerge unafraid. When we return from walking such roads we are never the same again.

The elegant and powerful collection of interviews you now hold delves deep into the heart of leadership, both the shadow side and the transcendent side, and emerges with profound answers to some of life's most perplexing and ultimate questions.

Who are those who enter the dark and come forth with light in their hands?

Where are these people?

Can I know them?

Will they welcome me?

From global servant-leader and former president of the Philippines Corazon Aquino to agents of exquisite social change Frances Hesselbein, Parker Palmer, and Meg Wheatley to profound leadership personas Ken Blanchard, John Carver, Larry Spears, and George Zimmer, *Conversations on Servant-Leadership* provides uncommon insight and a clear sense of the humility and courage needed to engage the human community in the work of individual and collective responsibility.

In contemporary life, irony is the breeding ground where we first begin to feel comfortable placing others, and the world we inhabit, under the cold eye of our contempt. We might say irony is the more raucous and less easily controlled brother of healthy skepticism, but without health we collude in our own collective inertia and inch forward until we fall like detritus over the lip of a great abyss and finally reach what Wallace Stegner famously referred to as our angle of repose. With the current rate of physical, emotional, and familial deficit, and with a deficit-economy equaled only by our immense spiritual poverty, where do we look to find a sense of hope? When speaking of America, Mother Teresa gave an indictment more barbed than we might imagine: she said America is the poorest country in the world because America's poverty is a spiritual poverty. The same criticism might also be leveled at the Western postcolonial world as a whole, a world where debt, rampant abuse of capitalism, and the degradation of the least privileged of society often goes unchecked. Into this void of consumerism, lack of integrity, and lack of intimacy, a voice of hope is needed.

Hope.

We find it in the least likely places. At dusk when the sky's burden moves from blue to black. At dawn when as if from far below, the vault is filled with light. Or sometimes we find hope down one of those high country roads we knew we needed to walk but were afraid to for fear of what we might find.

I am reminded of the kind of humanity that is the result of such hope, and so I want to close this introduction with a brief description of the servant-leadership that rises in the midst of despair. The healing work of the Nez Perce gives a bright echo to the narratives of hope found in the interviews in this book.

Ten miles west of Wisdom, Montana, there are miracles of topography dazzling to the eye. The Canadian border is not far away. The Rocky Mountain front runs north to south and in late autumn, if we have the will, we might walk together into the night. The night is long and the path uneven and often precarious. In the predawn blackness the grand fortresses of rock are ominous, and forests shroud the land around us. When at last the sun begins to light the world, the mountains look strange and otherworldly, black against a sky filled with open air and refracted light. Soon the towering sculptures of stone come clear, carved as if from an extraordinary excess of materials. Above and to the east a red swath burns on the jagged edge of the earth, and when the sun finally breaks the horizon our bodies tilt and our faces turn gold.

And ten miles west of Wisdom, Montana, there are miracles of friendship and grace to marvel the miracles of the sky. Robbie Paul, a modern-day Nez Perce, Nimi'ipuu, woman who knew the depths of atrocity her people experienced leads us. Consider her story, a woman whose family suffered nearly insurmountable loss, and who discovered the only road out was to pass through a heart-wrenching encounter with the history of genocide endured by her people.

Intuitively, she knew she needed to walk that road hand in hand with her father.

In this, a time fraught with violent upheavals in America and across the globe, if we listen to Robbie's story, we are led to a place of right feeling again. In a world harried by human atrocity, waste, and war, there are those who speak a reverberating truth. Robbie Paul is a descendent of Chief Joseph, the man who spoke his words of grief and resignation on the trail of tears: "I will fight no more forever." The Nez Perce are a people of uncommon tenacity in the unfolding of United States history. The Nez Perce are also a sovereign nation who now hold reconciliation ceremonies at the site of the Big Hole Massacre, ten miles west of Wisdom, Montana, where little more than a century ago, Nez Perce women and children were cut down and destroyed by U.S. Cavalry.

Unimaginable if it weren't for the fact that it's true, today the descendants of those who were massacred meet with the descendants of the Cavalry who committed the massacre. A ceremony of peace is performed. The Nez Perce invite reconciliation. Despite every right to be hateful or violent, the Nez Perce forgive and lead the human race into a necessary engagement with our own darkness. They take the veil from our eyes and let us see.

Robbie Paul, a scholar with a doctorate in leadership studies, traced five generations of Nez Perce servant-leaders in her own family, from the advent of first white contact to today. In her research, she recorded the resilience of her people. She also found in her people the road to healing in the face of genocide, and she found that this road requires our most essential will. At the end of this road she took her father's hand and walked with him into the heart of the mountains, where she sat down together with the descendants of those who had massacred her people and her father's people.

There she offered not cynicism, or contempt, or ruin.

She and her father offered peace.

In the symphony of voices in *Conversations on Servant-Leadership*, leaders honestly consider the darkness of the age and help us emerge with light, hope, and courage in our hands. From this example, we can walk forth and seek to fulfill the beautiful call of Robert K. Greenleaf, envisioning and embodying a leadership that serves others in a way that together we become more wise, more free, more healthy, and more autonomous, and the least privileged among us are benefited, or at least not further deprived.

Introduction to Servant-Leadership

LARRY C. SPEARS

> The servant-leader is servant first. It begins with the natural feeling that one wants to serve. Then conscious choice brings one to aspire to lead. The best test is: do those served grow as persons; do they, while being served, become healthier, wiser, freer, more autonomous, more likely themselves to become servants?
>
> —Robert K. Greenleaf

Glancing Backward

It has been forty-five years since Robert K. Greenleaf coined the term *servant-leader*, and first wrote about it in his classic essay, "The Servant as Leader." And, it has been twenty-five years since I began my own journey in helping to carry the message of servant-leadership, first as CEO of the Greenleaf Center (1990–2007), then as both CEO of the Spears Center for Servant-Leadership (2008–present) and as Servant-Leadership Scholar with Gonzaga University's School for Professional Studies (2010–present). This book, and those milestones, prompts me to begin by sharing some insights regarding servant-leadership literature, followed by a look at the understanding and practices of contemporary servant-leadership.

Starting in 1970, Robert Greenleaf began to pen what became a dozen essays and two books published during his lifetime. The 1970 publication of "The Servant as Leader" essay was followed in 1972 by "The Institution as Servant," and the 1974 publication, "Trustees as Servants." In 1977, Paulist Press published those first three essays, plus other writings by Greenleaf, in the book, *Servant Leadership: A Journey into the Nature of Legitimate Power and Greatness*. Then, in 1979, Paulist Press published a second book by Greenleaf titled, *Teacher as Servant*. Greenleaf continued to write essays on servant-leadership into the mid-1980s, when a series of strokes made it increasingly difficult for him to write. Bob Greenleaf died in 1990 at the age of eighty-six.

I first encountered the term *servant-leader* in the early 1980s, while working on the staff of *Friends Journal*, a Quaker magazine, published in Philadelphia. More than thirty years later, I still recall having one of those "aha" moments—the realization that the term *servant-leader* had named something to which I aspired, but for which I had not had a name until reading it in the manuscript that had arrived in the *Friends Journal* office. The author who had sent us his article was Robert K. Greenleaf.

In December 1989, I was living in the Philadelphia area and working at Bryn Mawr College when my wife and I learned that we were expecting a second child. This got us thinking and talking about several things related to our parents living in Indiana, and we and our children living relatively far away in Philadelphia. A series of conversations that my wife and I had led us to decide within the space of a week or two that if I could find a position in Indianapolis that seemed like a good fit, we would make the move back to Indiana after living in the Philadelphia area for thirteen years.

I ordered a subscription to Sunday edition of the *Indianapolis Star* to be sent to me at our home in Ardmore, Pennsylvania. When the first issue arrived, I opened the paper and began to read the Help Wanted ads. One of the very first listings that I read was for the position of executive director of the Robert K. Greenleaf Center for Servant-Leadership. As it turned out, this was also the final placement in a series of three notices that had been run in the Sunday editions of the *Indianapolis Star*. I was excited to read the description, and even more excited by the feeling that what was being described was something that I had to offer. I wrote a long letter, sent it along with my résumé, and was invited to come to Indianapolis for an interview.

At the interview, I learned that a decision had been made to move the Greenleaf Center from Newton Centre, Massachusetts to Indianapolis. What was initially described as a one-hour meeting soon stretched into a much longer meeting, after which I was offered the position as executive director by the Greenleaf Center's hiring committee, which included Jim Tatum (Tatum Motors, Neosho, Missouri), Sister Joel Read (Alverno College, Milwaukee, Wisconsin), and Jack Lowe Jr. (TDIndustries, Dallas, Texas). We shook hands, and eight weeks later, I moved back to Indianapolis with my family. Several days after that, a moving truck showed up with the contents of the Greenleaf Center's office that had been loaded up in Massachusetts and brought to Indianapolis. In 1990, we began the Greenleaf Center's operations with a two-room office, a staff consisting of myself and a part-time bookkeeper, and an operational budget of ninety thousand dollars—most of which was in the form of a final operational grant that had been given to the Greenleaf Center by Lilly Endowment (located in Indianapolis). The small tree that was the Greenleaf Center at that time had been transplanted in Indianapolis, where it would soon take root and begin to grow in many remarkable ways.

Robert Greenleaf died shortly after I was hired to lead the Greenleaf Center, and we spent just one morning together. I am eternally grateful to have had the few hours that we spent together at Crosslands, the Quaker retirement center located in Kennett Square, Pennsylvania. Elsewhere, I have written of my one visit with Bob Greenleaf. I recall how he chuckled when I told him that our second son had been born on Greenleaf's own birthday: July 14 (Bastille Day)!

In my early months at the Greenleaf Center, I spoke with the board members and others and eventually developed a plan aimed at stabilizing and then growing the center into a stronger entity. The combination of collaboration, hard work, and good fortune quickly began to pay off, and over time, the Greenleaf Center thrived as an organization. This, in turn, helped us in our primary goal of encouraging a better world through the understanding and practice of servant-leadership.

From the age of ten on, I have felt a calling as a writer and editor, and I have consistently focused a good portion of my energies toward using those gifts and skills on behalf of those causes I believe in, and to which I have devoted my own life's work. Starting in 1990, I worked to further our mission through writing and editing in many different ways, including the creation of newsletters, correspondence, grant proposals, articles, membership letters, display advertisements, essays, and much more. Nearly everything that I did in this vein was done with the goal of furthering our message and mission.

Several months after Bob Greenleaf's death, his family sent me a number of boxes containing a vast array of papers that they had found in his home files. The day the boxes arrived, I pulled up a chair next to the boxes and began to go through the contents. By that time, I had read all of Robert Greenleaf's published work and was familiar with it. However, as I began to go through the boxes, from time-to-time I would come across a file folder that contained a piece of writing by Bob Greenleaf. Most of these folders had a title written across the top in Bob's handwriting. These appeared to be things that Bob Greenleaf had written, though in most instances I did not recognize them as anything that was found in his published work. At first, there were five folders, then a dozen, then fifty. At the end of that day, I had made a cursory pass through all of the boxes that I had received, set aside the file folders that contained writings by Bob that I did not recognize as being among his published work, and I began to count the number of folders, which totaled about ninety. Some of these folders held pieces of writing as short as a single page. One folder held about one hundred pages of what appeared to have been an uncompleted book project. Most of the folders held articles and reflections that varied in length from two to twenty pages. The hair on the back of my neck was standing up as I came to the realization that Robert Greenleaf had privately written dozens and dozens of articles and essays, stretching over a fifty-year period. It seemed clear that he had done this mostly as an aid to his own developmental thinking on various topics. It also appeared that he had done so without any expectation of publishing what he had written.

I had uncovered a treasure trove of largely unknown writings by Bob Greenleaf. This, in turn, would shape my own work in a profound way for years to come. With support from the Lilly Endowment, and together with Don Frick and Anne Fraker, we published many of the works in two new books.

Starting in 1990, and almost every day since then, I have made it a point to write or edit something in furtherance of encouraging a more servant-led world. On days when my spirit and energies have been high, I have sometimes written or edited a broad range of things in a single day (articles, correspondence, grant proposals, newsletters, books, etc.). On days when my spirit or energies have been low, I have made a point of at least responding to my e-mail, or reaching out to someone who I have wanted to encourage in their own work as a servant-leader. Whether it was ten minutes one day, or ten hours another day, my personal sense of calling to this kind of work, plus a deep feeling of persistence, has led me to write and edit others writings on servant leadership on a daily basis. Each passing week, month, year, and decade has created a longer paper trail of published work. Here at the twenty-five-year mark, this has resulted in more than a dozen books that I have created with the help of others, plus another dozen books to which I have contributed chapters. Since 2005, I have had the great joy of working with Shann Ferch on the annual *International Journal of Servant-Leadership*. Shann serves as editor and I serve as senior advisory editor. I have also written over 300 articles on servant-leadership.

From 1996 to 2003, I cocreated a series of five books of writings by Robert Greenleaf. They are: *On Becoming a Servant-Leader* (1996), *Seeker and Servant* (1996), *The Power of Servant-Leadership* (1998), *Servant Leadership:*

25th Anniversary Edition (2002), and, *The Servant-Leader Within* (2003). *On Becoming a Servant-Leader* and *Seeker and Servant* are collections of Bob's writings that I found among the boxes in 1990. *Servant Leadership* and *The Power of Servant-Leadership* are collections made up mostly of the series of a dozen articles that Bob had published through the Center for Applied Ethics (the name was changed to the Greenleaf Center in 1985). In addition, *The Servant-Leader Within* contains his 1979 book, *Teacher as Servant,* plus some other content. As I have said on more than one occasion to aspiring writers: Even one's own death need not be an impediment to becoming a published author. You just need someone who has an interest in your writings and a commitment to seeing that they are published.

As both an editor and as a writer, I have maintained a dual commitment that I have tried to serve in equal measure. One commitment has been to ensure that Robert Greenleaf's own ideas and writings were made available and continue to be made available. I view his thinking on servant-leadership as being of critical importance to our understanding of the servant-as-leader idea. As such, about half of the books that I have cocreated, and about half of the articles that I have written have focused on Robert Greenleaf's writings or ideas.

The second commitment that I have had is to encourage the development of many other voices in the servant-leadership choir, and help writers to share their ideas with others. This has led me to cocreate a series of Servant-Leadership Anthologies, which include: *Reflections on Leadership* (1995), *Insights on Leadership* (1998), *Focus on Leadership* (2002), *Practicing Servant-Leadership* (2004), and *The Spirit of Servant-Leadership* (2011). In some ways, the book that you are now holding is the latest servant-leadership anthology—though this one is in the form of interviews with thought-leaders on servant-leadership. Roughly half of the articles that I have written have focused on trying to expand the edges of our understanding about servant-leadership and covered a lot of ground as I have examined servant-leadership in relation to people, organizations, places, and ideas. In recent years I have written or cowritten articles on servant-leadership in conjunction with service-learning, Myers-Briggs, aging, meditation, the Council of Equals, Bruce Springsteen, spirituality, King Arthur and the Knights of the Roundtable, organizational practices, personal development, philanthropy, and other topics. The single thread running throughout all of this has been a belief that servant-leadership has something to offer in these and many other areas.

These two strands of my work—helping to ensure that Robert Greenleaf's ideas and writings are encouraged and understood, and simultaneously helping to ensure that servant-leadership continues to grow in new and unexpected directions through the varied writings of others, and myself, have served as a consistent two-pronged approach for me for the past twenty-five years. While I leave it to history to determine how effective this strategy has been, from my own perspective it has offered the best of both worlds of maintaining the solid core of Greenleaf's ideas while expanding outward the scope of servant-leadership in how it is understood and practiced.

The Johnny Appleseed Approach to Servant-Leadership

Since 1970, roughly one million people have read either an essay or book on servant-leadership growing out of the work that Bob Greenleaf and/or I have done in collaboration with others. Articles and television appearances have been read or viewed by another fifteen million people. As I look back, I begin to see each article, essay, book, and television appearance as seeds that have been planted. Some have fallen on hard soil, been left unwatered, and blown away in the wind. Others have been dropped in good soil, been cared for, and have bloomed into a beautiful array of people and organizations currently practicing servant-leadership. Many other seeds have been planted and are simply waiting for the right set of conditions to come together and to trigger still more growth.

It is in that way that I have come to see the writings of Robert Greenleaf, the authors interviewed in this book, the hundreds of contributing authors to the various servant-leadership anthologies and to the International Journal of Servant-Leadership, untold numbers of others, and my own work, as representing a kind of Johnny Appleseed approach to servant-leadership.

When taking the long view of things, a servant's heart and a pocketful of seeds may help in the creation of a better, more caring world. I hope so. No, I believe it is so.

Understanding Servant-Leadership and the Ten Characteristics of Servant-Leadership

The servant-leader concept continues to grow in its influence and impact. In fact, we have witnessed an unparalleled explosion of interest and practice of servant-leadership in the past fifteen years. In many ways, it can truly be said that the times are only now beginning to catch up with Robert Greenleaf's visionary call to servant-leadership.

The idea of servant-leadership, now in its fifth decade as a concept bearing that name, continues to create a quiet revolution in workplaces around the world. This Introduction is intended to provide a broad overview of the growing influence this inspiring idea is having on people and their workplaces.

In countless for-profit and not-for-profit organizations today we are seeing traditional, autocratic, and hierarchical modes of leadership yielding to a different way of working—one based on teamwork and community, one that seeks to involve others in decision making, one strongly based in ethical and caring behavior, and one that is attempting to enhance the personal growth of workers while improving the caring and quality of our many institutions. This emerging approach to leadership and service is called *servant-leadership*.

The words *servant* and *leader* are usually thought of as being opposites. When two opposites are brought together in a creative and meaningful way, a paradox emerges. And so the words *servant* and *leader* have been brought together to create the paradoxical idea of servant-leadership. The basic idea of servant-leadership is both logical and intuitive. Since the time of the industrial revolution, managers have tended to view people as objects; institutions have considered workers as cogs within a machine. In the past few decades, we have witnessed a shift in that long-held view. Standard practices are rapidly shifting toward the ideas put forward by Robert Greenleaf, Peter Block, Stephen Covey, Peter Senge, Max DePree, Margaret Wheatley, Ken Blanchard, Richard Leider, Shann Ray Ferch, James Autry, and many, many others who suggest that there is a better way to lead and manage our organizations. Robert Greenleaf's writings on the subject of servant-leadership helped to get this movement started, and his views have had a profound and growing effect on many.

Robert K. Greenleaf

> Despite all the buzz about modern leadership techniques, no one knows better than Greenleaf what really matters.
>
> —*Working Woman* magazine

The term *servant-leadership* was first coined in a 1970 essay by Robert K. Greenleaf (1904–1990), titled "The Servant as Leader." Greenleaf, born in Terre Haute, Indiana, spent most of his organizational life in the field of management research, development, and education at AT&T. Following a forty-year career at AT&T, Greenleaf enjoyed a second career that lasted twenty-five years, during which time he served as an influential consultant to a number of major institutions, including Ohio University, MIT, Ford Foundation, R. K. Mellon Foundation, the Mead Corporation, the American Foundation for Management Research, and Lilly Endowment. In 1964 Greenleaf also founded the Center for Applied Ethics, which was renamed the Robert K. Greenleaf Center in 1985, and is now headquartered in Westfield, Indiana.

I was blessed to have met Bob Greenleaf, and to have served as president and CEO of the Greenleaf Center from 1990 to 2007. In 2008, I launched the Spears Center, where I continue to carry forward the idea of servant-leadership as first described by Greenleaf.

As a lifelong student of how things get done in organizations, Greenleaf distilled his observations in a series of essays and books on the theme of the servant as leader—the objective of which was to stimulate thought and action for building a better, more caring society.

The Servant as Leader Idea

The idea of the servant as leader came partly out of Greenleaf's half century of experience in working to shape large institutions. However, the event that crystallized Greenleaf's thinking came in the 1960s, when he read Hermann Hesse's short novel *Journey to the East*—an account of a mythical journey by a group of people on a spiritual quest.

After reading this story, Greenleaf concluded that the central meaning of it was that the great leader is first experienced as a servant to others, and that this simple fact is central to his or her greatness. True leadership emerges from those whose primary motivation is a deep desire to help others.

In 1970, at the age of sixty-six, Greenleaf published "The Servant as Leader," the first of a dozen essays and books on servant-leadership. Since that time, more than a half-million copies of his books and essays have been sold worldwide. Slowly but surely, Greenleaf's servant-leadership writings have made a deep, lasting impression on leaders, educators, and many others who are concerned with issues of leadership, management, service, and personal growth.

What Is Servant-Leadership?

In his works, Greenleaf discusses the need for a better approach to leadership, one that puts serving others—including employees, customers, and community—as the number one priority. Servant-leadership emphasizes increased service to others, a holistic approach to work, promoting a sense of community, and the sharing of power in decision making.

Who *is* a servant-leader? Greenleaf said that the servant-leader is one who is a servant first. In "The Servant as Leader" he wrote, "It begins with the natural feeling that one wants to serve, to serve first. Then conscious choice brings one to aspire to lead. The difference manifests itself in the care taken by the servant—first to make sure that other people's highest priority needs are being served. The best test is: Do those served grow as persons; do they, while being served, become healthier, wiser, freer, more autonomous, more likely themselves to become servants? And, what is the effect on the least privileged in society? Will they benefit or at least not be further deprived?"

It is important to stress that servant-leadership is *not* a "quick-fix" approach. Nor is it something that can be quickly instilled within an institution. At its core, servant-leadership is a long-term, transformational approach to life and work—in essence, a way of being—that has the potential for creating positive change throughout our society.

Characteristics of the Servant-Leader

> Servant leadership deals with the reality of power in everyday life—its legitimacy, the ethical restraints upon it and the beneficial results that can be attained through the appropriate use of power.
>
> —*New York Times*

I have spent many years carefully considering Greenleaf's original writings, and from them I have extracted a set of ten characteristics of the servant-leader that I view as being of critical importance. The following characteristics are central to the development of servant-leaders:

Listening: Leaders have traditionally been valued for their communication and decision-making skills. While these are also important skills for the servant-leader, they need to be reinforced by a deep commitment to listening intently to others. The servant-leader seeks to identify the will of a group and helps clarify that will. He or she seeks to listen receptively to what is being said (and not said!). Listening also encompasses getting in touch with one's own inner voice and seeking to understand what one's body, spirit, and mind are communicating. Listening, coupled with regular periods of reflection, is essential to the growth of the servant-leader.

Empathy: The servant-leader strives to understand and empathize with others. People need to be accepted and recognized for their special and unique spirits. One assumes the good intentions of coworkers and does not reject them as people, even while refusing to accept their behavior or performance. The most successful servant-leaders are those who have become skilled empathetic listeners.

Healing: Learning to heal is a powerful force for transformation and integration. One of the great strengths of servant-leadership is the potential for healing one's self and others. Many people have broken spirits and have suffered from a variety of emotional hurts. Although this is a part of being human, servant-leaders recognize that they have an opportunity to "help make whole" those with whom they come in contact. In "The Servant as Leader" Greenleaf writes: "There is something subtle communicated to one who is being served and led if, implicit in the compact between servant-leader and led, is the understanding that the search for wholeness is something they share."

Awareness: General awareness, and especially self-awareness, strengthens the servant-leader. Making a commitment to foster awareness can be scary—you never know what you may discover. Awareness also aids one in understanding issues involving ethics and values. It lends itself to being able to view most situations from a more integrated, holistic position. As Greenleaf observed: "Awareness is not a giver of solace—it is just the opposite. It is a disturber and an awakener. Able leaders are usually sharply awake and reasonably disturbed. They are not seekers after solace. They have their own inner serenity."

Persuasion: Another characteristic of servant-leaders is a primary reliance on persuasion, rather than using one's positional authority, in making decisions within an organization. The servant-leader seeks to convince others, rather than coerce compliance. This particular element offers one of the clearest distinctions between the traditional authoritarian model and that of servant-leadership. The servant-leader is effective at building consensus within groups. This emphasis on persuasion over coercion probably has its roots within the beliefs of the Religious Society of Friends (Quakers), the denomination with which Robert Greenleaf himself was most closely allied.

Conceptualization: Servant-leaders seek to nurture their abilities to "dream great dreams." The ability to look at a problem (or an organization) from a conceptualizing perspective means that one must think beyond day-to-day realities. For many managers this is a characteristic that requires discipline and practice. The traditional manager is focused on the need to achieve short-term operational goals. The manager who wishes also to be a servant-leader must stretch his or her thinking to encompass broader-based conceptual thinking. Within organizations, conceptualization is also the proper role of boards of trustees or directors. Unfortunately, boards can sometimes become involved in the day-today operations and fail to provide the visionary concept for an institution. Trustees need to be mostly conceptual in their orientation, staffs need to be mostly operational in their perspective, and the most effective CEOs and leaders probably need to develop both perspectives. Servant-leaders are called to seek a delicate balance between conceptual thinking and a day-to-day focused approach.

Foresight: Closely related to conceptualization, the ability to foresee the likely outcome of a situation is hard to define, but easy to identify. One knows it when one sees it. Foresight is a characteristic that enables the servant-leader to understand the lessons from the past, the realities of the present, and the likely consequence of a decision for the future. It is also deeply rooted within the intuitive mind. As such, one can conjecture that foresight is the one servant-leader characteristic with which one may be born. All other characteristics can be consciously developed. There has not been a great deal written on foresight. It remains a largely unexplored area in leadership studies, but one most deserving of careful attention.

Stewardship: Peter Block (author of *Stewardship* and *The Empowered Manager*) has defined stewardship as "holding something in trust for another." Robert Greenleaf's view of all institutions was one in which CEOs, staffs, and trustees all played significant roles in holding their institutions in trust for the greater good of society. Servant-leadership, like stewardship, assumes first a commitment to serving the needs of others. It also emphasizes the use of openness and persuasion rather than control.

Commitment to the growth of people: Servant-leaders believe that people have an intrinsic value beyond their tangible contributions as workers. As such, the servant-leader is deeply committed to the growth of every individual within his or her institution. The servant-leader recognizes the tremendous responsibility to do everything within his or her power to nurture the personal, professional, and spiritual growth of employees. In practice, this can include (but is not limited to) concrete actions such as making available funds for personal and professional development, taking a personal interest in the ideas and suggestions from everyone, encouraging worker involvement in decision making, and actively assisting laid-off workers to find other employment.

Building community: The servant-leader senses that much has been lost in recent human history as a result of the shift from local communities to large institutions as the primary shaper of human lives. This awareness causes the servant-leader to seek to identify some means for building community among those who work within a given institution. Servant-leadership suggests that true community can be created among those who work in businesses and other institutions. Greenleaf said, "All that is needed to rebuild community as a viable life form for large numbers of people is for enough servant-leaders to show the way, not by mass movements, but by each servant-leader demonstrating his own unlimited liability for a quite specific community-related group."

These ten characteristics of servant-leadership are by no means exhaustive. However, I believe that the ones listed serve to communicate the power and promise that this concept offers to those who are open to its invitation and challenge.

Servant-Leadership in Practice

> Servant-leadership has emerged as one of the dominant philosophies being discussed in the world today.
>
> —*Indianapolis Business Journal*

The domains and applications for the purposeful presence of servant-leadership today are many. Servant-leadership principles are being applied in significant ways in many different areas. The first area has to do with servant-leadership as an institutional philosophy and model.

1. Servant-Leadership as an Institutional Model

Servant-leadership crosses all boundaries and is being applied by a wide variety of people working with for-profit businesses; not-for-profit corporations; and churches, universities, health care, and foundations.

Servant-leadership advocates a group-oriented approach to analysis and decision making as a means of strengthening institutions and improving society. It also emphasizes the power of persuasion and seeking consensus, over the old top-down form of leadership. Some people have likened this to turning the hierarchical pyramid upside down. Servant-leadership holds that the primary purpose of a business should be to create a positive impact on its employees and community, rather than using profit as the sole motive.

Many individuals within institutions have adopted servant-leadership as a guiding philosophy. An increasing number of companies have adopted servant-leadership as part of their corporate philosophy or as a foundation for their mission statement. Among these are Synovus Financial Corporation (Columbus, Georgia), ServiceMaster Company (Downers Grove, Illinois), the Men's Wearhouse (Fremont, California), Southwest Airlines (Dallas, Texas), Starbucks (Seattle, Washington), and TDIndustries (Dallas, Texas).

TDIndustries (TD), one of the earliest practitioners of servant-leadership in the corporate setting, is a Dallas-based heating and plumbing contracting firm that has consistently ranked in the top ten of *Fortune* magazine's *100 Best Companies to Work for in America.* TD's founder, Jack Lowe Sr., came upon "The Servant as Leader" essay in the early 1970s, and began to distribute copies of it to his employees. They were invited to read the essay and then to gather in small groups to discuss its meaning. The belief that managers should serve their employees became an important value for TDIndustries.

Forty years later, TDIndustries continues to use servant-leadership as the guiding philosophy. Even today, any TDPartner who supervises at least one person must go through training in servant-leadership. In addition, all new employees continue to receive a copy of "The Servant as Leader" essay, and TD has developed elaborate training modules designed to encourage the understanding and practice of servant-leadership.

Some businesses have begun to view servant-leadership as an important framework that is helpful (and necessary) for ensuring the long-term effects of related management and leadership approaches, such as continuous quality improvement and systems thinking. It is suggested that institutions that want to create meaningful change may be best served in starting with servant-leadership as the foundational understanding and then building on it through any number of related approaches.

Servant-leadership has influenced many noted writers, thinkers, and leaders. Max DePree, former chair of the Herman Miller Company and author of *Leadership Is an Art* and *Leadership Jazz* has said, "The servanthood of leadership needs to be felt, understood, believed, and practiced." In addition, Peter Senge, author of *The Fifth Discipline,* has said that he tells people "not to bother reading any other book about leadership until you first read Robert Greenleaf's book, *Servant-Leadership.* I believe it is the most singular and useful statement on leadership I've come across." In recent years, a growing number of leaders and readers have "rediscovered" Robert Greenleaf's own writings through books by DePree, Senge, Covey, Wheatley, Autry, and many other popular writers.

2. *Education and Training of Not-for-Profit Trustees*

A second major application of servant-leadership is its pivotal role as the theoretical and ethical basis for "trustee education." Greenleaf wrote extensively on servant-leadership as it applies to the roles of boards of directors and trustees within institutions. His essays on these applications are widely distributed among directors of for-profit and nonprofit organizations. In his essay, "Trustees as Servants," Greenleaf urged trustees to ask themselves two central questions: "Whom do you serve?" and "For what purpose?"

Servant-leadership suggests that boards of trustees need to undergo a radical shift in how they approach their roles. Trustees who seek to act as servant-leaders can help to create institutions of great depth and quality. Historically, two of America's largest grant-making foundations (Lilly Endowment and the W. K. Kellogg Foundation) have sought to encourage the development of programs designed to educate and train not-for-profit boards of trustees to function as servant-leaders. John Carver, the noted author on board governance, has also done much to raise awareness of servant-leadership in relation to trustee boards.

3. *Community Leadership Programs*

A third application of servant-leadership concerns its deepening role in community leadership organizations across the country. A growing number of community leadership groups are using Greenleaf Center resources as part of their own education and training efforts. Some have been doing so for more than thirty years.

M. Scott Peck, who wrote about the importance of building true community, said the following in *A World Waiting to Be Born*: "In his work on servant-leadership, Greenleaf posited that the world will be saved if it can develop just three truly well-managed, large institutions—one in the private sector, one in the public sector, and one in the nonprofit sector. He believed—and I know—that such excellence in management will be achieved through an organizational culture of civility routinely utilizing the model of community."

4. *Service-Learning Programs*

A fourth application involves servant-leadership and experiential education. During the past thirty years experiential education programs of all sorts have sprung up in virtually every college and university—and, increasingly, in secondary schools, too. Experiential education, or "learning by doing," is now a part of most students' educational experience.

Around 1980, a number of educators began to write about the linkage between the servant-leader concept and experiential learning under a new term called *service-learning*. It is service-learning that has become a major focus for some experiential education programs in the past two decades.

The National Society for Experiential Education (NSEE) has service-learning as one of its major program areas. In 1990, NSEE published a massive three-volume work called *Combining Service and Learning*, which brought together many articles and papers about service-learning—several dozen of which discuss servant-leadership as the philosophical basis for experiential learning programs.

5. *Leadership Education*

A fifth application of servant-leadership concerns its use in both formal and informal education and training programs. This is taking place through leadership and management courses in colleges and universities, as well as through corporate training programs. A number of undergraduate and graduate courses on management and leadership incorporate servant-leadership within their course curricula. Several colleges and universities now offer specific courses on servant-leadership. Since 2005, I have personally collaborated with Gonzaga University around the creation and teaching of graduate courses in servant-leadership, and in the creation of the annual *International Journal of Servant-Leadership*. From my collaboration with Gonzaga University, this book emerged, and it is my great honor to present interviews of several of my Gonzaga colleagues here alongside more well-known thought leaders. My experience of my Gonzaga colleagues has been profound, and the text of their interviews here confirms exceptional servant-leaders exist be they more or less famous, more or less published, or more or less positioned to influence a national or international audience.

In addition to educational institutions promoting servant-leadership, a number of noted leadership authors, including Peter Block, Ken Blanchard, Max DePree, and Peter Senge, have all acclaimed the servant-leader concept as an overarching framework that is compatible with, and enhancing of, other leadership and management models such as total quality management, systems thinking, and community-building.

In the area of corporate education and training programs, dozens of management and leadership consultants now utilize servant-leadership materials as part of their ongoing work with corporations. Among these companies are U.S. Cellular, Synovus Financial, and Southwest Airlines. A number of consultants and educators are now touting the benefits to be gained in building a total quality management approach on a servant-leadership foundation. Through internal training and education, institutions are discovering that servant-leadership can truly improve how business is developed and conducted, while still successfully turning a profit.

6. *Personal Transformation*

A sixth application of servant-leadership involves its use in programs relating to personal growth and transformation. Servant-leadership operates at both the institutional and personal levels. For individuals it offers a means to personal growth—spiritually, professionally, emotionally, and intellectually. It has ties to the ideas of M. Scott Peck (*The Road Less Traveled*), Parker Palmer (*The Active Life*), and others who have written on expanding human potential. A particular strength of servant-leadership is that it encourages everyone to seek opportunities to both serve and lead others, thereby setting up the potential for raising the quality of life throughout society. In recent years, there has been growing attention paid to the ways in which servant-leadership and Myers-Briggs Type Indicator are mutually strengthening of each other.

7. *Servant-Leadership and Diversity*

For some people, the word *servant* may prompt an initial negative connotation due to the oppression that many people—especially women and people of color—have historically endured. However, on closer analysis many come to appreciate the inherent spiritual nature of what Greenleaf intended by the pairing of *servant* and *leader*. The startling paradox of the term *servant-leadership* serves to prompt new insights.

In an article titled, "Pluralistic Reflections on Servant-Leadership," Juana Bordas has written, "Many women, minorities, and people of color have long traditions of servant-leadership in their cultures. Servant-leadership has very old roots in many of the indigenous cultures. Cultures that were holistic, cooperative, communal, intuitive, and spiritual. These cultures centered on being guardians of the future and respecting the ancestors who walked before."

Women leaders and authors are writing and speaking about servant-leadership as a leadership philosophy that is most appropriate for both women and men to embrace. Patsy Sampson, a former president of Stephens College in Columbia, Missouri, was one such person. In an essay on women and servant-leadership, she writes, "So-called (service-oriented) feminine characteristics are exactly those which are consonant with the very best qualities of servant-leadership."

A Growing Movement

> Servant-leadership works like the consensus building that the Japanese are famous for. Yes, it takes a while on the front end; everyone's view is solicited, though everyone also understands that his view may not ultimately prevail. But once the consensus is forged, watch out: With everybody on board, your so called implementation proceeds wham-bam.
>
> —*Fortune Magazine*

Interest in the philosophy and practice of servant-leadership is now at an all-time high. Hundreds of articles on servant-leadership have appeared in various magazines, journals, and newspapers over the past decade. Many books on the general subject of leadership have been published that recommend servant-leadership as a more holistic way of being. In addition, there is a growing body of literature available on the understanding and practice of servant-leadership.

Both the Greenleaf Center (www.greenleaf.org) and the Spears Center for Servant-Leadership (www.spearscenter.org) are not-for-profit educational organizations whose missions focus on encouraging the understanding and practice of servant-leadership around the world.

Life is full of curious and meaningful paradoxes. Servant-leadership is one such paradox that has slowly but surely gained hundreds of thousands of adherents over the past thirty-five years. The seeds that have been planted have begun to sprout in many institutions, as well as in the hearts of many who long to improve the human condition. Servant-leadership is providing a framework from which many thousands of known and unknown individuals are helping to improve how we treat those who do the work within our many institutions. Servant-leadership truly offers hope and guidance for a new era in human development, and for the creation of better, more caring institutions. In the end, I believe that servant-leadership is the integrative system that unites the heart, mind, and spirit of many organizations today. Moreover, the interviewees in this book are some of the thought leaders who are helping to guide this quiet revolution of substance over style.

Chapter One

James A. Autry

Interviewed by Larry C. Spears and John Noble

James A. Autry is an author, poet, and consultant. Before retiring in 1991, he was president of Meredith Corporation's Magazine Group, a 500-million-dollar operation with more than 900 employees. During his thirty-two-year career, Autry served as a daily newspaper reporter, editor of a weekly newspaper, and editor and publisher of various books and magazines. He is the author of twelve books, including Love and Profit, Confessions of an Accidental Businessman, *and* The Servant-Leader, *as well as two collections of poetry,* Nights Under a Tin Roof *and* Life After Mississippi. *He has been a keynote speaker at the Greenleaf Center's annual international conference. Special thanks to John Noble, director of the Greenleaf Centre–United Kingdom, for his involvement in this interview.*

John Noble: Jim, you have had a profound effect on the attitudes and actions of huge numbers of people through your work. What were the markers in your life, the people and events that have helped shape your thinking?

James A. Autry: I feel that everything is connected, every experience and relationship is connected, and somehow they all point in the same direction. So I go back to people in my childhood who were people of good values who had a great influence on me in a very difficult situation—my parents were divorced, and I lived in a federal housing project in Memphis with my mother. These were some of the personal influences that shaped my values along the way.

And then I learned in the Air Force—which we all think of as a hierarchical structure—that the best leaders, the ones who seemed to achieve the best results, weren't the ramrod-straight, "kick 'em in the rear" sort, but the ones willing to get out among the people to identify with them. The best squadron commanders were the ones who regularly flew, who didn't just sit behind a desk, who mingled with the pilots and had a more personal relationship with them. I also found that they didn't have any more problems with discipline than the ramrod-straight ones did, and that had an influence on me.

Later, when I went into business, it was very clear to me that the people who were the most effective managers were those who were thought of as the weakest by higher management. This always troubled me, because if the objective was to achieve results, why was there such an emphasis on behaving a certain way? It was as if the results themselves were worthless if the managers didn't conform to what was perceived to be a management attitude. I think I learned from that. When I became a manager—at twenty-nine, I think I was the youngest managing editor in the history of *Better Homes and Gardens*—I thought the way to do it was to adopt the hierarchical attitude. It didn't work for me. I tried, but it wasn't me and it didn't work.

Then along came a man named Bob Burnett, the CEO of the Meredith Corporation. In 1968 he made a speech about self-renewal. This was a top corporate manager—one of the most courageous ones I ever saw—and he made a speech to the management group about self-renewal. As he went through the list of all the things about self-renewal, he said, "The most important thing is love." That was the first time I had ever heard the word *love* used in the context of corporate life. This was 1968, and he spoke of love—love of what we do together, love of ourselves, love of our customers, love of our products. He said we could not renew ourselves without love. The company really was in need of renewal, and I saw his leadership turn the company around. He became a mentor to me, and that probably marked the beginning of the end of my transformation.

That's when I completely let go of the old ways. In the next several years I tried to integrate that love into the corporate setting. And it just kept working: I kept getting results. We went from 160 million dollars in revenues to 500 million dollars; we went from four magazines to seventeen magazines during that period, and it was all about supporting people, being a resource to people and letting the vision evolve from the organization, rather than enforcing the "top-down" vision. These were my markers. They started with values. I'll tell you something else I've learned: there's something about being at the bottom of the economic totem pole, and it seems to me it goes one of several ways. With the grace of God, a good mother, and several other influences, I went in a good direction. I learned that if you can retain the feeling of what it feels like to be a "have not" in a society of "haves," to be down in the hierarchy, you can carry that with you into leadership positions.

I think it makes you a more effective leader. So don't forget where you came from. In *Love and Profit* there's an essay called "Management from the Roots."

Larry Spears: Can you tell us about three or four authors or books about leadership that you have found particularly useful?

JA: I'm not just saying this because you're here, but Robert Greenleaf's work has had a great influence on me. Before discovering that, I was influenced a good deal by Warren Bennis, not just by his writing but by the man himself, in his seminars and workshops. I'm taken by Peter Block and Peter Vaill, especially Vaill's book *Managing as a Performing Art.* These are the people that just jump to mind. I have a library full of leadership books. And it's interesting—I get something out of a lot of them, and yet I find that the totality of the work often doesn't appeal to me, but something in there does. But Warren Bennis's work, Peter Vaill, and, although it's a lot to work through, Peter Senge's *Fifth Discipline* and his whole learning organization work I've found very helpful. I've used some of the exercises in Senge's books to help achieve some honesty in a community setting. I've never met him, but I've seen videos of him, and he seems to be what his work reveals. I guess that's what jumps to my head. Oh! Of course! Margaret Wheatley for *Leadership and the New Science*, that whole notion of everything in relationships and everything affecting everything else, the model from quantum physics. And then there are people who've not written on leadership but whose work has had an influence on me, like Joan Borysenko and Scott Peck. I've enjoyed Joan's work, and Scott Peck's original *The Road Less Traveled*, and subsequently meeting him and working with him has been a very positive influence on some of the things I've done on leadership.

LS: Leadership concepts, including servant-leadership, values-based management, learning organizations, and similar ideas are being learned, taught, and practiced more than ever before. What do you see as the cultural changes that have caused these ideas to be more widely accepted?

JA: Well, we have to qualify the answer by saying that there are still some industries where none of this is being done, like in Detroit, the oil industry, and some of the heavier manufacturing industries. I don't think it's because they have union people; I think it's just that the culture hasn't shifted. Now, it may be that within departments or within groups you'll find these values. I work all the time in companies you wouldn't think of as being particularly servant-leader oriented or values-based oriented, and yet within a group it's very much alive. So I see it as a positive virus in these businesses. But there are companies that are wholly committed. I am not a sociologist, only an amateur social observer, and anything I say on the subject will be obvious, but clearly one of the cultural shifts has been the increasing number of women in the workforce. There are two factors that come into play. One is the impact of motherhood and women's need to balance this, and the other is scientifically based, the idea that women socialize by affiliation, whereas men socialize by separation. That makes a profound difference on how their work styles will be manifested. These are generalizations, of course. You will find women who are hard-edged and tough, and men who are sensitive and supportive, so I don't want to overgeneralize, but I do think these differences have had a major impact in the development of workplace culture, especially in helping to create a medium in which concepts that are more affiliative and communal and more supportive of workers and less hierarchical can grow. I think the presence and influence of women is certainly a factor.

I think another factor is that so many people have seen that the old ways simply don't work as well as this stuff. There's been a feeling of frustration that "I can't get the results that I want to get" that leads to an openness to writings and influences from the media about another way to do it, so that's been a factor. The challenge of how to get results has permeated management generally as compensation systems have shifted for CEOs and have created a downward pressure from CEOs to enhance stock price. *Stockholder value* has become the mantra, and in the end that is defined as stock price. So the emphasis on results has created fear and frustration, on the one hand, and a desire to try almost anything to get better results, on the other hand. And that creates an approach to change that's phony: "Well, I think I'll try the soft approach now and get them to work a lot harder." You have to be careful about that; it's got to really come from the inside of a person. But it does seem to me that society is more open to it.

Many company leaders are concerned about loyalty and turnover. This also creates an interest in values-based leadership. What's been proved over and over again is that people are not going to work where they feel driven or unhappy. They work hard (and I think people are working way too hard doing unnecessary things), they're putting in a lot of hours, but they're not doing it because managers are kicking them in the rear and making them do it. What does that mean if you're trying to hang onto people in a highly mobile culture? How do you create culture, how do you do things that bind them, that make them want to stay someplace? What works is creating community, even if people say, "Yeah, but they're not going to be here very long." This is a lesson I learned in the Air Force: people rotate in and out of squadrons and highly intensive settings all the time. Personnel are changing all the time; in fact, the most you get is a three-year tour. There's a very intense and intentional imperative toward creating a community, then people come into these communities, they're brought into it, and immediately become a part of it. They may be only there six months, but they're no less a member of this community and they feel no less committed to it. I have seen it work in that kind of setting, and I know that it can be done. And the businesses that are building community are the ones who are holding on to employees the longest, regardless of what the compensation structure might be.

JN: One situation I think we are familiar with is that in which the CEO of a company is very willing to make the change toward more values-based management. The junior managers are gung-ho for the whole idea, but it is in the ranks of middle management where the resistance, not surprisingly, exists. What advice or guidance do you offer companies in this situation?

JA: I think the situation starts with an analysis. Part of the analysis is this: the reason is fear. So what are the middle managers afraid of? They are afraid of the loss of power, perceived power, the loss of their jobs. If everything goes well, they might not be needed. In order to make this change, you have to address the fear issue in the middle manager. Let's face facts—in the great wave of white-collar layoffs, it was the middle managers who got the ax, so they've got good reason to be afraid in view of what's been happening in the last fifteen years or so. If the CEO is gung-ho on it, it's on the CEO to bring it about.

I think it has to be done by building a sense of community based on trust. The middle managers have to feel that they are a part of bringing this about, that it's not being foisted on them. It's a huge education process for them because a lot of them got where they are under the old ways. "The old ways worked for me; why change?" So there's a reeducation and a reorientation process needed, and at the same time there has to be a reaffirmation that they got there because of their knowledge and competence, not because of their management style, not because of authoritarianism. What we're going to change is the culture, the social architecture, the interpersonal relationships. We're not going to change the positions, the accountability. We're not going to change the results we want. But the fear has to be taken out, and that's an education process.

I've been involved in this in three companies and, I'll tell you, it's a tough nut to crack. Managers have been brought up in an atmosphere of—they don't trust people, they don't feel trusted, they don't trust the company.

It's a long process and it's a difficult challenge. I think it takes community building, it takes personal attention and commitment from the CEO, because on the one hand, he or she's saying, "I'm going to need these results," and on the other hand, he or she's saying, "We want to be this kind of company." The CEO's got to somehow communicate that "I think creating this kind of company is going to give us these even better results. Trust me on this—let's do it." This takes leadership from the top. You can't delegate this kind of cultural change.

JN: Thinking more about these young leaders, what are two skills or characteristics you would wish them to have?

JA: Let's call them characteristics, because I never try to tell people what to do—I try to tell them how to be. I think they have to be empathetic, that's one of the characteristics. Can I give you five? The five are: be authentic, be vulnerable, present, accepting, and useful. And by *useful* I mean, be servants. Those are the five characteristics. And underneath all that they have to be courageous, they have to show that vulnerability and authenticity, and empathize and listen—that's all part of it. One of the first things I say to groups when I speak to them is: "I'm not here to tell you what to do. You know what you should do much better than I could ever know."

JN: One of the things I often find myself talking to colleagues about is the joy of what you once called leaving work and being able to say, "I did it well today." What were the circumstances that usually led you to be able to say that?

JA: It's always been relationships. It's always been somehow if at the end of the day I've managed to create a sense of community, and have either resolved conflicts or created circumstances in which they got resolved. It's always been about personal relationships. Now, am I really happy when we start a new magazine, or we got a good sales result, or we turned the corner and made a profit? Yes, I really am, and that gives me an enormous sense of satisfaction. But I have always seen those results—even my own salary—as simply the tangible measurement of the real work. That's not the real work, making profits. This is one of the great distortions in American business life. The real work is not making profits; making profits is the result of the real work. So I get enormous satisfaction from that, and great satisfaction from the doing that's done. But when I felt *I did it well today*, it's always been relationships, even if it was just convening a good meeting filled with ideas and energy. That could make me feel good because I realize that people felt confident enough to be able to say things, knowing that they might not work, without fear of ridicule or fear of being shouted down.

Lately, in the last several years, the greatest feeling of satisfaction I've gotten is when I've been called to go into a company to resolve conflict between people. I've done a lot of what's now called executive coaching and counseling, and a lot of this is listening to people talk about the things that trouble them most deeply in their personal relationships. But conflict resolution is getting people who are at odds with one another—vociferously and sometimes angrily at odds with one another—bringing them together and getting them to make a human connection. You realize that underneath the differences in ideas, they are more similar than dissimilar. They have joys, fears, griefs, and celebrations that are more similar than dissimilar. Because they have different views of how the work has to be done does not make them enemies.

And it's that old dualism, and we fight the dualism all the time—you know, "If you're not for me, you're against me." We know from Biblical scholarship that's not exactly what Jesus meant, but it gets quoted all the time. "If you're not with me, you're against me." That dualism of defining myself by the other, by who I'm not, permeates business. People have disagreements over all kinds of things, like budgets or sales presentations. Some things that require disagreements, perhaps to shape them to the most effective way of doing business, turn into personal warfare. Well, it gives me an enormous sense of satisfaction to help people accept one another as human beings, even uneasily at first, and know that they can disagree about ideas without demonizing one another as fellow human beings. Sometimes I let these discussions become heated because it's necessary to get some of the feelings out on the table where they can be dealt with.

JN: I'd like to ask you about one of the old chestnuts, "I don't have to be liked to be an effective leader." What are your views on that?

JA: The way you hear it in America often is, "Look, management is not a popularity contest." When a manager would say that to me, I'd say, "Well, to a certain extent, it is." It's not that you have to be the jolly, well-liked, hail-fellow-well-met, but if people don't respect you—and that's the operative word—if they don't respect you and your abilities as a person, it's not going to work for you. What I think and what I've often said is, we don't really have to love one another to work together. In fact we really don't have to like one another. We don't have to walk out of the building and commingle, have drinks or party or anything. But in this kind of place we have to care about one another. That's kind of an interesting concept, to say we don't have to love one another, just care about one another. Because you have to care about what we do together, because what we do together is interdependent. We need to care about one another in the context of what we do together. That's a difficult concept sometimes for people. If people like one another and care about one another—genuinely—outside, then so much the better. I've always promoted that sort of personal connection. I've always been against the idea that "I have to remain aloof from the people, and it doesn't matter if they like me or not, because I might have to fire one of them." So I may use a different vocabulary in saying this, but respect and caring in the context of what we do together is essential. Whether you have personal likes or not is neither here nor there.

LS: In *Confessions of an Accidental Businessman* you wrote, "The commitment to act out beyond ego, to recognize when we are in denial, to retain humility, to correct our mistakes and to learn from others, regardless of their so-called status, is the commitment to grow personally and spiritually through the work we've chosen to do." To me that really captures the essence of servant-leadership, at least in my own understanding of what servant-leadership is about. Would you talk about how one goes about overcoming ego in a leadership position?

JA: That's a good question: How do you overcome ego? The first step toward overcoming acting out of ego, I think, is to recognize that you do it, and to be able to identify when you are doing it. I think the only way to get out of the ego is to get into yourself. You have to have some sort of spiritual discipline—meditation, prayer, yoga. I am always recommending to people that they do something to nurture the inner life, that they try to do something every day that is reflective or meditative, even if they do it while they're jogging or walking. In order to get out of the ego you have to somehow get deeper into your own inner life. And I think you do that through the spiritual disciplines of silence and prayer and meditation. Or by reflective and meditative action, and by that I mean you can jog meditatively. I do it. I walk that way. You could also do psychotherapy or counseling, or meet with groups or just meet sometimes like with these groups where high-level businesspeople meet to discuss their mutual problems.

Once you recognize it and begin to work on it, you have to stop throughout the day and examine what your actions are. In order to be able to admit mistakes and to learn from others, no matter what their status, the piece of advice I give to everybody—in fact, it's the same advice I offer every manager, new or old—is this: Whenever you attempt to make a statement, ask a question. Instead of saying "Here's what you should do," you say, "What do you think we should do?" That's a huge leap for a lot of people. It seems simple to say it, doesn't it? But it's difficult for us to fathom how challenging that is for some people who act out of ego. Because you are saying, "Put my ego in the drawer and I'm gonna ask how you think it should be done—you, who are seventeen layers down in the hierarchy from me."

The next step is to do that not just as a technique, but to recognize that you're open to learning, and that other person may know the thing to do. My attitude about this is, if an employee comes in and says, "Jim, here's the situation and this is the problem and I'm laying it out and what do you think we ought to do?" then I know that person already knows what to do. They've got the situation surrounded, they have the problem defined, and they, whether it's a group, or just a he or she, they know what to do—probably. If not, they've got a good first step. And I may know what to do, too, because I've been in this long enough, I can see all the pieces, it fits together, and I know what has to happen. And I know they have a step. They know that I know. But as soon as I fulfill the expectation that I'm going to be "Big Daddy"—you know, I'm going to make a pronouncement and they're gonna go do it—I've destroyed any possibility, one, to learn something from them and, two, to recognize their own power, which is their knowledge and their skill and which is real empowerment. Empowerment is not about "I take some of my power and give it to you." That's the myth. Real empowerment is recognizing that you, by your skill, your knowledge, your commitment, you already have power. What I'm trying to do is take the leashes that I've put on, off.

So by that simple technique of asking a question instead of making a pronouncement, we can start to come out of ego. Another step toward acting beyond ego is to let go of my solution and embrace someone else's. Any number of solutions may work. They may not work as well as I think mine would work, but if one will work and achieve the result, then let go of ego and embrace the other solution. All our management structure traditionally is built on the basis of the person up here who has all the answers. What I keep saying is, don't be the person who has all the answers; be the person who has the best questions. And then you'll get better answers!

LS: You mentioned doing work in the governor's office, and your wife is lieutenant governor of the state of Iowa. I was curious to know whether past experience, or even more recent experience, has led you to any sense regarding whether there are differences between leadership as practiced in politics versus business or organizations. You've written a great deal about effective leadership in the business setting. Do you see any differences when it comes to that kind of leadership within the political structure?

JA: I think leadership in public service is more difficult. It is a good place to practice servant-leadership. American people seem to want a field general in their leadership positions, yet the most effective leaders have been the ones who really practiced community and consensus building. It's really the only way to get anything done—I've learned that from the inside, just seeing this process. I realize that the most effective public servant-leaders are those who know how to get people together and build a consensus; who interpret and articulate what they are trying to accomplish; and who tell why and how they are doing it for the people, for the voters.

It's a much more challenging kind of leadership than in business, because in business, the objectives are very clearly defined. One, the most imperative objective is survival—not survival at any cost, not sacrificing your values for survival (though some have done that)—but survival. Second, you need to achieve the objectives of the business, which some people define as *stockholder value.* Once you define the objectives of the business, they are pretty concrete; they don't shift very much. There may be factors around market changes and things like that, but you're still trying to achieve these objectives. The constituency you have may be millions of stockholders, but they're represented by a board of directors of twelve or fourteen people, and they're the ones you have to convince. So finding the leadership of the employee group is, I think, less challenging in business because you have such flexible tools. You have compensation systems; you have hours and benefits; you can try all sorts of modes of structuring the office, from the virtual office to flextime. You find you have a vast array of tools that you can use, if you're courageous enough to use them and smart enough to use them.

In public service, all the employee rules have been set by legislation, and are managed by agencies and work under legislative oversight. It's a very complex management challenge. There are posts that the governor comes in and appoints, then these appointees hire more positions, and then agencies get permeated with people with one political philosophy. Legislation changes, political philosophy changes, and it's very difficult. We've heard that democracy's messy. Democracy's very messy! It's a good system—I like the checks and balances. I think that it generally serves the people, but it could serve them better if we could get better public perception and understanding of what the real objectives are, what we're really trying to accomplish, rather than all the peripheral things. And in that, I blame my old business, the media. They are forever doing an injustice to the system by jumping on things that are of relatively little consequence when it comes to governance and the objectives of society. So, yes, I think political leadership is far more difficult. Yet there are some good people on both sides of the aisle. They're good leaders, they're good about the vision, they're good about consensus, they don't let their egos paint them into a corner, and they don't demonize others.

In politics there's a lot of demonizing. Having grown up a fundamentalist Christian, I understand those folks and what they want. But, as I say to my relatives in Mississippi, the U.S. Constitution is about equality and justice and opportunity. It's not about righteousness. There was no intention for us to become a righteous nation, but a nation governed by people whose values, perhaps even whose righteousness, was based on their faith—probably. Wouldn't have to be. You can be moral without religious faith, you can be an atheist, but for the most part, these values are based on faith. But the objective of the Constitution is not to be a righteous country; even George Washington said that America is by no means a Christian nation. But these folks say America is a Christian nation. When this kind of thing happens—when the objective becomes righteousness and not good moral governance—we begin to demonize people who don't agree with us. To me that's the great malignancy in American politics. It's not new, of course, but it seems to be particularly virulent right now. I don't think they'd put up with that attitude in companies, because the governance is much more tightly focused. Yet because of that tight focus, it does allow egomaniacal top-down management to have free rein, whereas that only goes so far in politics before you throw them out. There are shadow sides to both!

LS: Do you recall when you first discovered Greenleaf's writings and what it was you first read?

JA: I think it was in the mid- to late 1980s, at the Foundation for Community Encouragement, which was Scott Peck's organization. I met several people, and one of them, Will Clarkson was his name, first recommended Greenleaf's work to me.

LS: Can you speak briefly to your understanding of servant-leadership and what it means to you?

JA: First, understand that when I talk about servant-leadership, I usually pair it—because I'm bringing it to business audiences who may have never heard of it before, who don't know The Greenleaf Center—I usually pair it with these terms: *being useful* and *being a resource.* The leader's responsibility, or one of them, is to ensure that the people have the resources that they need to do the work to accomplish the objectives, and the principal resource of the people is you, the leader. You have to serve the people and to think of yourself as a resource, as a servant to them. That's almost exactly the language I use when I'm talking to them.

So I never stand up and say, "I'm going to speak now about servant-leadership." For one, I find that people who are Biblically literate immediately think of the Bible, which is okay. Some, who are more literate than Biblically literal, tend to think of it in ways that I don't think are particularly helpful. And others who connect it to the Bible begin to think, "Oh, it's going to be about religion." So I don't say I'm going to talk about servant-leadership. Instead I talk about leadership, and then I use what I think are the precepts of being a servant-leader.

The number one precept is, "I am here to serve, to create the community in which you can do the work that you do in order to achieve the objectives and results we are all trying to achieve together. My principal job is to serve you." What does that mean? That means, in my view, to be the kind of leader who does the five things I said before. Project authenticity and vulnerability, be present, be accepting, and see your role as being useful, as being the servant. I think it's all the techniques we talk about; it's always operating, making every decision from a basis of values, what's the right thing to do, not what's the expedient thing to do. Perhaps not even what's the most profitable thing to do, but what's the right thing to do. To me, it is a confluence of morality, which derives for the most part from my faith. Incidentally, I often find that atheists respond to the word *spirituality.* So it's a confluence of spirituality and work.

I don't usually try to go beyond that. For one, I wouldn't know how, and two, the imperative of my work is always making myself useful to the people I'm presenting to. I don't think of myself as there to entertain them or tell them what to do, but to be helpful and useful. When people hire me, what I say to them is, "Look, I want to be useful, so I want to know what your objectives for me are.: And I always say—and this is not bravado—"If at the end of it all I haven't been useful, don't pay me!" Everything I write about, everything I talk about in these books is servant-leadership, but I don't know if I can come up with a nifty, clean definition of it. But that's the general realm of vocabulary that I work in when I'm talking on these subjects. And I always recommend your books.

JN: I wanted to ask you something about your poetry, and the process of writing your poems. How much is inspiration and how much perspiration?

Do you have an idea that you write a poem about, or do the words form and you write the poem?

JA: The answer is D: all of the above! Sometimes I get a good line and it just comes to me. Other times it's an idea, and other times it's a theme that I want to do something about that kind of percolates, percolates, percolates. It always emerges as an idea or a line. That's the inspiration part.

The greatest discovery that I made about poetry, back in the 1970s when I first started writing it, is that it yields to good craftsmanship, it yields to editing and to all the mechanics I learned as a journalist and a writer. For years I thought it just came, that it's very mystical, you get it down on paper, and you don't mess with it very much. But you do. You sometimes turn it upside down and write it in five or six different ways. I've thrown out whole sections of a poem. One of the things you learn about poetry is, the least said the better. It's not about how many words you can use; it's about how few words you can use, how can you get the message, evoke the idea, the imagery, the emotion in as few words as possible.

William Faulkner once said that the most difficult thing to write is poetry, and the next most difficult is short stories. The easiest is the novel. I've never written a novel, so I've not found that to be true. I sometimes carry slips of paper around in my pocket, and I'll write lines of poetry on them and carry them around. I work on a poem and carry it in my pocket. I write my prose on a word processor, but I always write poetry by hand. There's something about the click, click, click that destroys the rhythm of the poetry, the words. I lose the rhythm of the words. So I write poetry by hand.

JN: What do you think are the poems that you've written that folk will remember you by?

JA: Well, I guess I have to choose several. The poem I'm going to be most remembered by in business is "On Firing a Salesman." It's been anthologized in more books in more different languages, appeared in more settings than any poem I've ever written, and I always read it because it seems to grab people. Second in the business world would be "Threads." The one I'll be most remembered for in the South comes from my first book, *Nights Under a Tin Roof*, and it's called "Death in the Family." I think in the disability community, where I've written a lot of poetry, the one I'll be most remembered for is "Leo."

JN: At the beginning of *Love and Profit* you quote Rabindranath Tagore. Has he been an influence in your work?

JA: I wouldn't say he's been an influence. It's hard to say who is and who isn't, because almost everything I read has some influence, down deep somewhere. But Tagore I admire—his work and philosophy and a lot of what he's written and said. I love the mystical poetry. I love Rumi's work very much, I'm very taken with it. His work is both love poetry and mystical spiritual poetry, and he talks about the beloved. He's often talking about God, the mystery, and the ineffable, and he mentions Jesus by name in a lot of his poetry, even though he's a Sufi poet. He writes a good deal about religion. I love Rumi's work; it is so spare.

I continue to write poetry. I've gotten back into it a lot more lately, and I've written quite a bit about my son and his autism, as well as other matters. But my work seems to be moving very much more toward the spiritual relationship with God. It's not direct. I've written a new poem called "Death Bed Meditation." My beloved sister-in-law died this year very suddenly from cancer, and that poem is all I really know about life that I can say in a few words.

Death Bed Meditation

All I really know about life I can say
in a few lines:
In April the small green things
will rise through the black Iowa soil
whether we're ready or not.
The Carolina wren will make her nest
in the little redwood house
my son built from a kit.
Daffodils, tulips, irises will get the attention as usual
while purslane, pigweed, and lamb's quarters
will quietly take over a place
while no one is watching.
In June the corn shoots
will etch long green lines
across the dark loamy fields
and the greenest of all green grasses
will crowd into the ditches and line the roads.
In August the early bloomers
begin to burn themselves out,

but in September the late yellows appear,
luring the bumblebees and yellow jackets
into a frenzy of pollination.

You already know about October,
the color, the last burst of extravagant life.
And then all at once it seems
everything retreats, pulls into itself, rests,
and prepares for the inevitable resurrection.

JN: Is there a song or a poem, or even a line that someone else wrote, that you wished you had written?

JA: Oh, gosh. You know, it's popular to say, "I wish I'd written that" or "I wish I'd said that," but it gets a little close to envy. What I'm more likely to say is I wish I could write *like* that, I wish I could achieve that sense of excellence and the ability to polish my words, find the right word, put them together in such a way to evoke the emotional response in other people that that person has evoked in me. But sure, I've said, "Gosh, I wish I'd written that sentence" about Rumi's work, the work of Yeats, and my current favorite contemporary American poet, Mary Oliver. "The Summer Day"—now there's a poem I wish I'd had the talent to write. Genius stuff. So, yes, there are poets whose work and talent I immensely admire and I hope that I can achieve work that is of this quality.

LS: Do you have a different approach in writing poetry rather than prose? And do you have greater satisfaction in doing one or the other?

JA: I really don't. I get a great deal of satisfaction out of doing either one well. If I've crafted an essay that I think is particularly satisfying and good, I get as much satisfaction from that as I do from poetry. So I don't have a preference. Sometimes the message determines the form. I was going to write an essay about the experience of taking Communion to the shut-ins for the church. One of our jobs as elders was to take it out to the shut-ins, these elderly people, and I was going to write an essay about it, but it turned into a poem almost on its own.

LS: You spent the better part of a lifetime as an editor. Did you have any kind of philosophical approach to the art of editing in a general sense that you have followed?

JA: There are certain parallels with being a manager and being an editor, in that the fundamental objective is to bring out the best of people's own work, not to impose your own work on it. That goes right back to asking the question What would you do? So, there's that parallel.

But I think my philosophical approach as an editor was to do no harm, to try to find the essence of the good work there, and to help lead people to making their work the best it could be without my rewriting it. Sometimes I've had to just go in and rewrite something because the writer was blocked, or tunnel-visioned about it, or something, but my philosophy generally was to try to see the essence of what the work was and to bring this out. Sometimes it took a little bit of fiddling, or sometimes going back and conferring with the writer, and sitting down and discussing it and having the writer redo it. But always my objective was to have the writer himself or herself bring out the best that was in there. A good editor—and I think I was a competent editor, I certainly don't think I was a great editor; on the other hand, the kind of editing I was doing was not heavy literature—I think a good editor has the ability to see into that work, has to get through the words and see what's there, and then determine whether the words are adequately bringing out what is there.

Words are filters, really. Once you put a word on something, you fix it. If I say something is superb or something is good, that may mean it's superb or good, but it also means it is only that. What else is it? Put more words on it, and pretty soon you put new words on it, and then it doesn't mean anything anymore. It's nothing because it's everything, and you can't be everything. It is a constant frustration for writers to realize that words are filters. Yet we don't have another way to get the emotions of my heart into your heart, except through words. So I've got to use words, realizing that they're always going to be inadequate for what I really want to achieve, but I'm trying to make them the best they can be. Oftentimes a writer falls so in love with his or her filters that the essence of what the writer is trying to accomplish gets mangled or camouflaged or overfiltered. The good editor will see through these filters, see what's really there, and help the writer bring it out. So my philosophy is that editing is very much like management: helping people do their best work. It's in there, look for it, give them the tools, help them, and on the rare occasions, do it for them. Sometimes I had to rewrite something. Most often it wasn't because of a writer's lack of talent; it was frustration or blockage. Who knows? Writers are like everybody else—funny creatures!

LS: What's your sense of how a leader gets better at developing a servant's heart, and how to view oneself as a servant to others?

JA: To me, the road to servanthood has to be, almost by definition, a road away from ego. I think developing the servant's heart—you know if we want to, we could shift this over to Buddhism and say *path* of heart—that path of heart, that move to the servant's heart is a move away from ego. I think it has to be done in the context of one's own spiritual development, spiritual growth, the spiritual disciplines I mentioned before, and by reading other spiritual disciplines and picking heroes, picking people you think are the spiritual heroes, those who emulate how you would like to be, and following these models, letting them be mentors, even though they may have lived hundreds of years ago.

I think Jesus is a terrific model, but I think a lot of the interpretations of Christianity distort that model of servant-leadership. We see it manifest as judgment, manifest as trying to control people's lives, how they live, and what they believe. Here's what Jesus says to me as a role model: the strictures and structures of orthodoxy and hierarchy work against the human spirit, they work against the relationship with God, with the ultimate, with the mystery, the ineffable. And I think he said that, and lived that, over and over again, and he died for that. I like to tell the story of the Good Samaritan to people who want to listen because I want to tell it the way I really think it is, in a way I don't think Biblical scholars might say it.

This person lying by the side of the road is ignored by the high priests and the church people, not because they're not compassionate people, but because the purity code prohibited even being in the same room as a dead person or touching a dead person, and you were unclean if you touched a dead person under the Hebrew purity code. Jesus was saying, "Look, you take the code so far, you lose all your compassion and connection. For fear of breaking the rule, you won't even save a person's life." Along comes the Samaritan—and you know who the Samaritan would be today? The good Samaritan could be the good Communist, the good Nazi, the good Ku Klux Klan member, the good whore: whoever you perceive to be the very opposite of you. The Samaritan was the very opposite of the people Jesus was telling the story to. This is a powerful message to me about not letting the rules keep you from doing the compassionate thing, the right thing, the thing from your heart.

I think there are lots of other examples of the beatitudes being a wonderful message for us all. I think Jesus is a wonderful role model for servant-leadership, and he was a teacher. That's another thing I've left out of being a servant-leader. You don't hand down the policies; you are a good teacher and a good mentor. Jesus was a teacher. He wasn't anybody's boss. He got angry a couple of times, said some sharp things, and I think that's proof of his humanity. You could also look to the Buddha, to the prophet Mohammed, or to Moses; there are leaders and role models in all these faith traditions. My point is, whatever your faith, whatever your spiritual orientation, whatever your interest in wisdom literature, there are heroes there, there are lessons there, there are teachings there. I think you have to be active and intentional about exploring them—in the right way—not to become indoctrinated, but to become educated. It's not about trying to find something to help you be a more effective leader. It's about trying to be a better person. The other will follow.

Anytime people want to focus on my work, servant-leadership, or other values as a way to get better results, it's critical to start from the right place. You sincerely have to start with what *you yourself are wanting to become*, the being and becoming of you. To me that's what the servant's heart is about. I think it's like every other spiritual discipline or interest—I think it's all a matter of becoming. I like the scholars who say that if we really translated the first verse of the Bible, grammatically in English—it can't be done; there's no grammatical parallel. It's written in the present continuing tense, not the past tense. It's not "In the beginning God created the Heavens and the Earth," it's "In the beginning God is creating the Heavens and the Earth." It changes the whole context when you think about it that way. So I think that the path to the servant's heart is a never-ending path. You don't ever get there, but the journey is the objective.

Chapter Two

Michael R. Carey

Interviewed by Mary McFarland

Before coming to Gonzaga University, Michael R. Carey served as a teacher, campus minister, and vice principal at Catholic secondary schools in Los Angeles and Spokane. He received his BA degree from Loyola Marymount University in 1974, and both his MA and PhD degrees in educational leadership from Gonzaga University in 1983 and 1987, respectively. In 1987, he was hired to teach leadership studies at Gonzaga University. Carey has served in a variety of formal administrative roles during his twenty-five-year tenure at Gonzaga: six years as the first director of the Organizational Leadership program; four years as the first coordinator of the Council for Partnership in Mission; two years as executive assistant to the president; two years as the first director of Distributive Learning for the School of Professional Studies; four years as chair of the Department of Organizational Leadership; one year as the chair of the ad hoc Committee on Racial Equality and Cultural Understanding, which responded to specific incidents of racial harassment at the university; three years as vice president and then president of the Faculty Assembly; and one year as the chair of the Mission and Community Committee of the Faculty Senate. Currently, Carey serves as dean of Gonzaga's Virtual Campus, which supports learning and technology, especially for online graduate programs at Gonzaga.

Mary McFarland: Please tell us about the role of servant-leadership in your own life in the context of the study you've done about the interior life of the leader and the interior sense of servant-leadership?

Michael R. Carey: Most of my work in leadership has really been to focus on how a leader thinks and how a leader looks at the world. A lot of my thinking has to do with being able to see clearly, being able to have insight into what is actually going on in any situation, however complicated, or complex, or odd it is. One of the things I'm most drawn to in servant-leadership is that we look outside of ourselves to the other, whether the other is individual or to the community. Servant-leadership is connected to how I understand the authentic, interior life of a leader. The more the leader is focused on himself or herself, the more the leader is wrapped up in their own ego, their own agenda, their own biases, even their own hopes and dreams.

I think of Greenleaf's measurement of the true servant-leader: Do the people the servant works with become healthier, and wiser, and freer? The criteria of successful servant-leadership are the fruit of leaders who have transcended their own issues, their own agendas, their own issues of control, of trying to prescribe for other people what should and shouldn't be done. The success of servant leadership absolutely depends on the quality of the interior life of the servant-leader.

MM: You've examined for sometime the transformation, and the transforming leader in action. What connection do you see between servant-leadership and transforming leadership?

MC: When I first read and thought about servant-leadership, it was probably when I was studying leadership as a graduate student in the early 1980s. It was an impressive concept but it didn't really attach to my consciousness as much as it has lately. When I was doing my graduate work in leadership studies I was much more focused on what was called transforming leadership, a concept initially developed by James McGregor Burns in his book *Leadership*. I was taken by his concept because it seemed to capture human development and that there are good and bad leaders based on the type of approach they take to the relationship with what Burns called the followers, which we might just call the people that are a part of that relationship.

One of the most interesting parts of Burns's notion of transforming leadership, and one which I think has very clear application to servant-leadership, is the idea of power viewed as a relationship. Burns distinguishes between an old notion of power as commodity. People think of power often as who has more of it and who has less. So for example, in an organization someone with more power has greater ability than another person to get their will accomplished in a situation. And in fact, in the classic model of power we look at power sources and power types, and what we're really looking at is how does someone gain power? How does someone use that power to influence other people to do something?

But power as commodity means power is a zero-sum game. There isn't enough power to go around. Like all commodities, people are scrambling to get as much of it as they can to the exclusion of other people; other people lose when we win. So power as commodity is certainly one way to understand what happens in a leadership relationship. But for Burns that wasn't the most powerful leadership, and so he began to talk about power as relationship. I really think for the most part Burns is one of the first people in the mainstream leadership theorists to talk about power as relationship. But Greenleaf's notion of servant-leadership, which was written before Burns, is grounded in this concept of power as relationship as well. So I see a real clear connection between the two.

What's the difference in terms of what happens when a leader draws on power as relationship as opposed to power as commodity? As I said, power as commodity is a zero-sum game, there's not enough to go around; one person has a certain amount and therefore another person has less. Power as relationship is power that keeps producing; there isn't a limited amount of power available, relationship actually produces new power. The best way for me to illustrate that is when I think about people who have been mentors in my life through my education, through my work, and my teaching career. Those people who have been mentors have been people that made me grow more powerful in my abilities, in my sense of who I am. But never did that power, that development of my own sense of self come at the cost of their power. They didn't grow less powerful as a result, in fact in many ways these mentors became more powerful as well, as a result of the relationship. So the tremendous wisdom of Burns's concept of transforming leadership intrigued me as a graduate student in leadership and was my focus as I began to teach leadership studies.

The key connection I see between transforming leadership and servant-leadership is this notion of power as relationship. All of the characteristics that Larry Spears identified from the writings of Greenleaf really come back to the idea of aspects of relationship, aspects of why someone understands very clearly that they are not standing alone in the world, that they need other people, that they are responsible for other people. And so, in many ways, servant-leadership became for me an underscoring of Burns's notion of transforming leadership.

When I was first teaching in the late 1980s, and teaching transforming leadership, there was also a lot of literature that was coming out that struggled with how to deal with the concept of good or bad leaders. In other words, in the early days there was literature that looked at the leadership of, for example, historical leaders like Gandhi and Hitler and saw both of them as having transforming leadership qualities that they were able to transform other individuals or societies. It always bothered me that Hitler and Gandhi could both be viewed as kind of the icons for transforming leadership. So, as I struggled to understand how one could really grasp the essential difference between the two, I think Greenleaf's work on servant-leadership was very helpful to me because of what Greenleaf allowed in his definition of the measure of servant-leadership. Do people become healthier, wiser, freer, more autonomous, more likely themselves to become servant-leaders? I immediately saw what was missing in some of the literature of transforming leadership. I recognized that affecting people by transforming them into a different place wasn't necessarily the goal of leadership. I don't think it was the goal of Burns's notion of leadership either; rather, it was affecting people for the good, making them better people, raising them on a kind of developmental scale.

Burns used a tremendous amount of Maslow and Kohlberg. Even if you extend that past Maslow and Kohlberg to some of the more recent writings of developmental theory, Gilligan, Fowler, and others, what you end up with is a sense that authentic leadership, authentic transforming leadership is involved in the growth and development of the person, the transcending of the individual ego of the person. The transforming leader in a sense calls forth from other people the desire to grow, and develop, and become more than they have been. I think that's exactly what Greenleaf was getting at with his understanding of servant-leadership.

In many ways, I think transforming leadership is servant-leadership, servant-leadership is transforming leadership. As a teacher of leadership studies, I like to use servant-leadership because it focuses the need for transforming leadership to be working with people to help them transcend their own limited points of view, their own ego, and in many ways their own self-interests. Often the literature in transforming leadership has difficulty trying to figure out how to grapple with the questions of that form of ethical behavior.

MM: You talked about mentors. Tell me who your mentors are, and maybe give me a story?

MC: I've had many mentors during my life. The one who's been most consistently a mentor for me is my wife Marianne. Besides Marianne, I've had many people in very professional settings; but like Marianne the people that have been mentors for me have been very focused on relationship. I've always felt they had a kind of unconditional care or love for me. Certainly Marianne has had that for me as a friend and a husband. I've felt unconditionally loved by her and that's affected my ability to grow and develop and feel I can be all I can be.

In a professional sense the mentors I've had in university work, in high school teaching, even as a student in college, have had the consistent dynamic that there wasn't anything I could do that would have them turn away from me. That's a very powerful dynamic, a dynamic that is very connected to servant leadership is this sense of caring, of unconditional regard that challenges the person to be all they can be but also accepts when they fail, accepts when they fall short. So I think of people throughout my life, and in my most recent career at the university I've been very fortunate. The dean who hired me and the dean I worked under after him both treated me as a peer and as somebody they expected much from and supported me.

I've had other people, not mentors, also in one particular case a dean as well, in which when I failed, the relationship made me kind of withdraw. I thought, I don't want to step out, I don't want to put myself in any vulnerable situation, I don't want to make waves, I don't want to be noticed. And so I've had three deans in my time at the university here and both the first and the last were very supportive and nurturing and developing. The middle one, when I think about it, it's like a completely different life. I can see clearly the effect of that lack of care, lack of love, on me. So from the standpoint of servant-leadership, when I try to become a mentor for other people I try to keep that in mind. I try to make sure the person feels challenged by me to be all they can be but that I never give them a sense that there's something they could do or a mistake they could make that would make me turn away from them and say, "Oh I must have made a mistake to see anything in you." Unfortunately, many of us experience that way too often in our professional and personal lives. Love and care are key dynamics of both mentoring and servant-leadership.

MM: Greenleaf measures the success of servant-leadership based on the impact that person has on others. What is it within the servant leader him- or herself that allows the relationship to happen? What is at the center of the relationship?

MC: I've thought a lot about what is it that motivates a servant-leader to be a servant-leader. Greenleaf talks about the desire to be a servant comes first and then the desire to become a leader and I think he was extremely insightful. What I think Greenleaf means is that the servant-leader has a desire to touch into the way things really are, the reality of the world, the reality of the person. For me that means to touch into a kind of God's-eye view of the world. Rather than seeing the world as disconnected; seeing the world as it's me, my ideas against other people; even seeing the world in which academically we're taught to see it kind of dialectically. I think what makes servant-leadership work is not a dialectic but a dialogue. It's not trying to separate things out and see how they work against each other or how they're different from each other; it's trying to draw things together and see how they're all the same.

There's something within the servant-leader, this idea of wanting to be a servant first, that has to do with seeing that we are instruments of God in everything we do; that we are not God, that we are not the center of the universe, to the extent that we can free ourselves of the illusion that we are that center, to the extent we can in a sense become instruments of God. By doing that, immediately our role becomes that of a servant, a servant of God, a servant of other people, a servant of the situation; or if you don't want to use God language, a servant of what is best. And so for me that's probably the heart of what makes a servant leader able to affect other people. It isn't about the dynamic of leadership. It isn't about figuring out how I work with other people that comes first. It's a kind of centeredness and groundedness in the way things really are. And the way things really are, I believe, has to be understood in that God's-eye view, a view from the standpoint of the universe rather than the individual.

MM: You have spent considerable time in monasteries. When you come back or are going to the Valyermo monastery, something happens there for you and for the students that appears to come out of servant-leadership and intersects with the environment. What is the role of environment that helps support authentic servant-leadership?

MC: For about the last five years, I've been taking graduate students down to a monastery in California. I actually have had a connection with this monastery for nearly forty years now. When we take the students to the monastery, it's for a class called Leadership in Community. They do work before they go to the monastery online, and then they do additional work after they return from the monastery online. But for the week that they're at the monastery, it typically is a tremendously transforming experience and I think it has a lot to do with servant-leadership. In fact, in the rule of Benedict, which is the kind of foundational document for this particular Benedictine Monastery, Benedict starts the rule by saying that the monastery is a school for the Lord's service. So we tell the students that it's in a sense also a school for servant-leadership, it's a way of understanding both servanthood and leadership.

And what is it about the monastery that I think affects the students so much, especially using the concept of servant-leadership? What they see there is a community of people who are very, very different people, different personality types, different ages, and different approaches to doing things, all that. And yet they see people who have come together and are consciously trying to live in relationship to each other, in the way that all true relationships mean caring, unconditional love, and challenge.

One of the students asked a younger monk, did he find that a lot of the monks in the monastery were people he would have as friends outside of the monastery? And the monk said, "Oh no, no not at all." And he (the monk) was almost shocked by the thought that he would be good friends with these monks outside the monastery.

The students were slightly scandalized I think. And he (the monk) says, "That's the whole point. We come together because we aren't friends but we are committed to understanding each other through relationships with each other, and we know we can't do that other than with each other; if we only have relationships with our friends there's no growth involved in that."

The students would constantly bring up the monk saying, "You know the monks here are like rocks dropped into a bag and the bag is shaken up and the rocks are bouncing off each other. And what happens is the rocks all get polished, but, it's a little messy."

And the students said, "Yes." And that describes perfectly, for the students, their experience of family and organizations and all sorts of community life; it's a great metaphor.

I think the reason the monastery has such an effect on students regarding servant-leadership is they begin to ask the monks and themselves, how do you do that? How do you engage with other people who you don't necessarily find a lot of connection with or similarity with or that might not be the kind of person you'd be friends with in general? How do you stay in relationships in a way that is caring and engaging and dynamic that, like Greenleaf indicates, will produce people who become healthier, wiser, freer, and more autonomous?

For the monks, what was very interesting to the students is that they (the monks) all take three vows as they enter the monastery. They take a vow of stability, a vow of obedience, and then a vow of what in Latin is called *conversatio* or ongoing constant conversion. And I think the take-away that many of the students have from the monastery regarding servant-leadership is that these three dynamics are not just things for monks but they actually are things that describe anybody in a relationship.

The idea of stability is that the monks vow not to ever leave the monastery that they join. The interesting part of that is, I mean in some ways, the first reaction of our students is, well that sounds really boring. They're much more used to traveling and for many people they'll be in maybe five, ten different organizations through their career, so the idea of stability is a kind of interesting concept to them.

But for the monks what stability means is that they don't leave the monastery because things get tough. In other words, if they're having conflict with other people, if what's being asked of them is difficult, that kind of thing, they fight the instinct, which is I think a natural human instinct, to flee. And what they say by stability to each other in community is, "I will not leave when things get rough just because they're getting rough."

Now actually, I've known a couple of monks who have left the monastery. But in many ways I think even they have taken their vow of stability seriously. They left the monastery after a number of years there. They did not leave because things got tough and then they just took off. They left after dealing with the toughness of conflict and then really processing it and making sense of it and deciding, really am I called to stay or am I called to leave?

So stability is this dynamic, and I think my wife and I would say that's been very important in our relationship, where you tell the other person when I have an instinct to leave, because this is just too much trouble, I will fight that instinct. And all the monks know that all their brother monks are committed to that so that makes a difference. My wife, Marianne, knows that when it becomes difficult I'll stay and that makes a difference. It means a difference in what she can say and do and how much she can challenge me because she's not afraid of me leaving.

The second vow or dynamic of the monks is obedience. Parker Palmer reminded us in one of his works that the root of the word *obedience* comes from the Latin root for *to hear, to listen*. That's a good way to understand what's going on in a monastery as well. The monks take a vow of obedience to an Abbott. I've, I suppose, taken a vow of obedience to my wife Marianne. I'm sure that my superiors at the university hope I view that my allegiance to them is a vow of obedience to them.

What I would see in that, is obedience means that I'm committed to always be listening for what I'm called to do here. So it's a deep listening, it's not just simply say jump and I ask how high? It's when someone (and it doesn't necessarily have to be a superior; it can be a peer, it can be someone who is a direct report to me), asks me something, my stance is one of listening. What am I called to do in this conversation, in this relationship with this person? And that call to obedience really has to do with me letting go of my own bias, and my own agenda, and saying I'm being called to respond.

In a monastery, the fact is, the Abbott can tell you you're going to work in the kitchen as opposed to working in the garden, and you've got to do what he says. But a deeper way, a deeper sense of that is when the Abbott tells a monk that he's trying to train him for a larger sense of obedience. Rather than think that somehow it'll be better if he works in the kitchen as opposed to the garden, what the Abbott wants the monk to understand is, you'll work well wherever you are; it doesn't matter regarding your preferences, you might prefer the kitchen over the garden but that's a preference.

In the same way, if my wife does something and I think, wow that's really not something I like. I have to think to myself, is it that I don't like her behavior because it's against my preferences or because it's essentially a bad thing? I have to say in the thirty-six years of married life with my wife, I don't think she's ever asked me for a bad thing. She's asked me for a lot of things that are against my preferences, but part of my growth as a person has been understanding and being able to let go of my preferences to do what I'm being called to do by my wife, by my organization, by my children, or whomever.

The last vow that the monks take is this *conversatio*, constant conversion, and that's where they commit to taking the vows of stability and obedience and making them more than just individual discrete actions. For example, in my relationship with my wife Marianne, in the early days of my marriage with her there were times when I had to remind myself, "must remain stable, must remain stable."

We would have conflicts and I'd think, why did I ever get married? and I'm sure she's thought the same thing. But we had this sense of stability where we weren't going to run away from each other and so we stayed in it. And by staying in it we could listen and hear, are we called to be married or are we called not to be married? What is really going on here? What we heard was we were called to be in relationship, so we worked through things and that was a learning experience.

Conversatio means that if thirty-six years into my marriage with Marianne, if every time we have any kind of a conflict I say, "must remain stable, must remain stable," I haven't really grown very much. I would hope, and that's I think what the monks understand by the vow of *conversatio*, that rather than stability being something that's just a discrete action, a behavior that I have to choose to do, eventually I simply become a very stable person; that my stance toward the world is stability. The same with obedience, that rather than having to say I need to force myself to listen, I need to force myself to know what I'm being called to do here, *conversatio* says make your stance toward the whole world one of obedience, one of listening, one of wanting to know what I should do.

I think the vows of stability, obedience, and *conversatio* really make the monks able to live with each other in relationships, even though they aren't necessarily compatible in a variety of other ways, and I think the graduate students that go to the monastery see that and they realize that those dynamics really do make a difference. I think they take stability, obedience, and continual conversion away in their sense of what it means to be a servant-leader. The servant-leader has at the heart of the self an acceptance of the dynamics of stability, obedience, and *conversatio*, constant conversion.

MM: Is there anything else you'd want to share from your own personal journey around servant-leadership?

MC: As I struggle with myself to be open to others, to try to be a servant-leader in my career, over the years I've noticed how easy it is for me to fall into a state of fooling myself as to what my real motivations are. What I mean is that often I think I am interested in what is best for other people at work or in personal relationships, when really it's a more subtle issue of me wanting other people to be more like me.

One of the people that I've been very influenced by in terms of my reading both applied to transforming and to servant-leadership is Paolo Freire, who is a Brazilian educator. One of his key books is *Pedagogy of the Oppressed*. What he was writing about was how people can be liberated in their learning experience. Liberation has been important to me even as a teacher in the United States, not necessarily dealing with the kind of oppression that the Brazilians were facing at the time of Freire's writing, but just realizing how learning can become very oppressive. The teacher can become an "expert" who hands on to the students a prescribed set of notions or concepts that he or she expects the students to be able to give back on a test of some kind.

What Freire was really talking about in *Pedagogy of the Oppressed*, and a lot of his other writings, was the sense that if we really are going to be servants to the students' learning experience we have to let go of our own way of thinking about the world and empower or assist the students in gaining empowerment for themselves regarding their own way of naming the world. In my opinion, such liberation is incredibly essential to Greenleaf's notion of servant-leadership. If we really take seriously this idea that the people being served grow healthier, and wiser, and freer, and more autonomous, all of those very robust notions of what it means to be effective as a servant-leader start with the servant-leader not trying to control what is going on with the people he or she is in a relationship with.

Freire talks about the idea of prescription where the leader or the teacher prescribes for the student the best solution based on the teacher's experience, and the teacher's history, and the teacher's way of looking at things. This does not necessarily allow the student to understand what's best given their circumstances, given their history, given their way of naming the world. If I'm not vigilant, I can fall into a kind of prescription that makes me try to control others and try to control the situation all the while explaining how dialogic and liberating my work is. I see this as a caution for every servant-leader.

MM: Tell me your thoughts about Spears's ten characteristics of servant-leadership, especially with your work in the spiritual context of the interior of the leader?

MC: The ten characteristics of servant-leadership were developed by Larry Spears in some of his writing, based on his understanding and reading of Greenleaf's works: listening, empathy, healing, awareness, persuasion, conceptualization, foresight, stewardship, commitment to the growth of people, and building community. The ten have been very influential in my processing of servant-leadership and remain the key characteristics that describe the dynamic of servant-leadership for me. As I look over the different characteristics, I think everything they speak to is an aspect of what it means to be on a serious journey of self-awareness and enlightenment. If you're doing your work to become a better person, if you're doing your work to transcend the limitations of your own ego, your own agendas, your own biases, your own preferences, the ten characteristics either assist you in doing good work or are the fruit of you doing good work.

One of the things that Greenleaf mentioned in some of his writings and Larry Spears underscores is foresight, the ability practically see how things are working out. Greenleaf thought foresight was one of the most difficult aspects of servant-leadership to develop. For me, foresight is the fruit of many of the other characteristics, including listening and empathy. When we really are focused on the other, when we are focused on what is outside of our own self-interest, I think we can't help but touch into a cosmic sense of unity and connectedness with everybody else. As a result of that, I think that the servant-leader has foresight; the servant-leader is able to see things that other people don't see because he or she touches into a place of ultimate commonality with everybody else and every other thing in the world.

Larry Spears once mentioned to me that servant-leadership is like the new ecumenical language meaning that even in the midst of very different faith traditions and spiritualities people seem to understand that servant-leadership is a common connection. That's an insight into the commonness of spirituality; the further along we get on our own journey spiritually, the closer we get to everyone else who is on that journey spiritually. Whether you're a Muslim, or a Jew, or Christian, any one of a variety of faith traditions throughout the history of the world, the more you begin to see things from God's point of view, the less distinctiveness there is between these different paths. When you look at the characteristics of the servant-leader every one of those characteristics speaks to rich, deep connectedness with other people. That's why for me the ten characteristics are exactly the correct dynamics for the servant-leader, but I would say they're also the dynamics for the person who is searching and wanting to be authentic and live his or her life radically. The characteristics that are going to be the things that will both describe what they're doing and assist them in doing it.

MM: Mike, to take another step further into this area of foresight and thinking about American society from the interior, the spiritual, to a very exterior, global sense, foresight in society or in the world, what should we be tending to in a deeper way through the exercise of foresight?

MC: I think Robert Greenleaf, as he developed the notion of servant-leadership, was focused on trying to develop the ability for our society to work together in a way that at the time was not necessarily common throughout any society American or otherwise. The first center that he created was called the Center for Applied Ethics; there's some real importance there, the idea of ethics was important to him, but it was also applied ethics, ethics that actually makes a difference in the way people behave. His concept of foresight related to servant-leadership is very much connected to this as well.

Our current society, in many ways similar to his, struggles with how to go beyond our individual bias, and agenda, and opinion, and political viewpoint, to work together as a community. What foresight does is begin to see a world that doesn't necessarily exist right now but be able to see it and know that that is the more authentic reality. For Greenleaf, the foresight he had was to picture what this could look like in organizations that didn't yet have an authentic reality. In many ways his first writing about boards and board membership, trustees and trusteeship, was not saying, Well look at all of the boards that are doing this, and I'm just going to point it out, it was like this is what should be happening on a board. He had a vision of what was possible, of what the reality is and should be. I think in our contemporary society the servant-leader has to do the same thing. He or she has to be able to have a picture of the world, a world that works together, a world that cares about everyone in it, a world that is not only trying to facilitate growth everywhere but is also trying to create a real community among people from very different backgrounds, and ideas, and opinions. For a servant-leader, foresight is to see the strong true future as though it exists right now, and by seeing it in that deep way, be able to find new and creative ways to bring it about, to make it actually happen. I think that's the real need for our society, to be able to see a place where rather than fighting, people come together to make a better world for everyone.

MM: What would you like to ask Greenleaf if you could ask questions today?

MC: If I had the opportunity to talk to Robert Greenleaf today, given that he worked at AT&T when he was doing his initial writing, and a lot of his ideas came out of that, and then he was working in a very grassroots way creating pamphlets and getting the word out, I would like to know from him what sustained him? I mean it just seems like he was really at the front end of a movement that now has people all over the world saying, "That's important." But when he first started he was in many ways a lone voice crying in the wilderness. I'm impressed by anybody that can keep that up, even when maybe they're kind of the only people sometimes supporting themselves. What did he do, what made him able to keep holding onto this notion of how the world could work together despite the fact that when he looked around, it wasn't that way?

MM: How can the servant-leader best deal with conflict? Would you want to tackle that? It's an important area.

MC: Yes, thank you. Conflict is one of those things that's just inevitable. I remember when I was younger thinking it would be nice if I could eliminate conflict, but now I'm aware that eliminating conflict maybe isn't necessarily even a good thing because I think it's through conflict that we grow, and we develop, and we come up with better ideas; we come up with better solutions to things. I think the problem really is when the conflict becomes violent. So in that sense I look to Mahatma Gandhi and his work both in South Africa and in India as a way of understanding how the servant-leader needs to deal with conflict.

The servant-leader, like Gandhi, needs to, in many ways, provoke conflict to make people think, make people feel like something has to take place here, something has to change. But, like Gandhi as well, the servant-leader needs to do it nonviolently. In other words, conflict can never lead to the servant thinking that the other is less than he or she, that the person that they're in this conflict with is completely wrong, black and white. The servant-leader has to view conflict as something that can be very healthy; therefore, what the servant-leader needs to find is the way to create this conflict into something that will be life giving. Like Gandhi, the servant-leader at his or her very core must be nonviolent, must in a sense subscribe to the principles of nonviolence. I think certainly Robert Greenleaf, given his background in the American Friends Movement, the Quaker Movement, understood this, and nonviolence was just part of his very way of looking at the world. It's important for us, people who've not necessarily been raised in that tradition, to realize nonviolence is a very essential part of the dynamics of leadership.

Chapter Three

John Carver

Interviewed by Larry C. Spears

Nationally and internationally known for his exceptional work regarding servant-leadership and boards, John Carver is the creator of the Policy Governance® model and has authored or coauthored five books and over 200 published articles on nonprofit, nongovernmental organization (NGO), equity corporate, and governmental boards—thought to be the most extensive such oeuvre worldwide. His consulting experience has been in nineteen countries, on all continents except Antarctica. Carver earned the BS degree in business and economics and the MEd degree in educational psychology at the University of Tennessee at Chattanooga. His PhD was earned at Emory University (Atlanta) in clinical and research psychology in 1968. He has worked as the business officer in small manufacturing, then as CEO for a number of public service organizations. He has testified before state legislatures and the U.S. Congress. Dr. Carver has been an editorial review board member of Corporate Governance: An International Review, *and adjunct professor in the University of Georgia Institute for Nonprofit Organizations and the Schulich School of Business at York University, Toronto.*

Larry Spears: I recall you saying that you had not discovered or read Greenleaf's essay, "Trustees as Servants," prior to your writing *Boards That Make a Difference*. When you did read it, what ideas came to you? Are there questions that you would like to have asked Greenleaf?

John Carver: You are right. I did not even know the name *Greenleaf* until maybe 1991. Two reactions come to mind. One is the general idea of how much the philosophies of the two disciplines matched. If I had known that at the time, it might have enriched something that I had to say. I am sure that would have happened. But the other thing is that I would have had the chance to talk with him about the things he said about CEOs. In my opinion, the chief executive officer role, as Bob Greenleaf spoke of it, compromised the spirit of the primus kind of role that he outlined in *Institution as Servant.* I think that he would have seen it a different way had he known a method by which the CEO role could be made more palatable to his philosophy of servant-leadership.

LS: Your educational background includes a BS degree in business and economics, a master's of educational psychology, and a PhD in clinical psychology. I am curious to know if there are ways that you see your background in psychology has informed your thinking around the development of the Policy Governance model.

JC: If it informed my thinking, I am unable to trace it, except in the way that no matter what you learn in life has something to do with what you are able to do later. So in that sense, it must have had an effect. The effect that it might have had is not the content of psychology or education or business, but the effect it had on me about scientific modeling: what I wanted to find in governance was conceptual coherence. I wanted to find something that could be called a model in a scientific sense, not just a structural sense. That drove me to say, "I've got to produce something here that makes sense as a total wherein all the parts fit together, that, really a system." I think that's the greatest effect of my education.

LS: John, would you describe the evolution of your thinking around board practices that led you to create the Policy Governance model and to write your first book, *Boards that Make a Difference*?

JC: That was a time of turmoil. I had learned management by finding out how little I knew about it and then trying to get better. After going through a PhD program in clinical and research psychology, I wasn't ready for management. After I started getting a feeling for management I found out that I was woefully uninformed about governance. I worked for boards at that time, in fact I was on several boards myself—I had chaired a national board during that period—and I *still* did not understand governance. It didn't make sense to me. So what drove me was, frankly, a feeling of profound stupidity. I was driven to make sense out of the board role. And the more I read, the more I studied, of what had been written at that time, the more I became convinced that the reason I couldn't make sense out of it was that it simply didn't make sense; it became that obvious.

So, being unable to make sense out of it the way it was, I thought I could think it through in a way that would make sense. And I set out to do that. I think—serendipitously, as a matter of fact—I did it by stripping away all the common governance functions and roles, like the sculptor who strips away all the stone that isn't David. I started asking myself questions about what truths can be named about the governing body role which would be true in any circumstance. So if I said, "Would an executive committee be like this or this?" I would have to throw that away because not all boards have to have an executive committee. Or, "Should a committee be like this or this? Wait a minute, not all boards need committees." Those aren't universal. So I kept throwing out things that were not universal. It sounds simple now, but at the time, people were saying that boards are so different, one from another, that in fact you cannot find things that are true of all of them. "They're all different!" Well of course, they are all different, but the job of finding out what is true of all of them will in fact get to the foundation upon which all that other variety is built.

So that's what I was doing. I would get to the point of saying, "Can I find anything, *anything* that is or should be true of all governing boards?" I started with the extremely simple: They should all know what their job is. Well, that's kind of silly, but it is hard to argue that it isn't universal. Finding it just means I know that it's not impossible to find a universal truth. So now, after that, what's next? That's what led to the Policy Governance model, going through and reducing—right down to the point where I could not reduce it further—and I came up with just a few basic principles with some concepts to hold them in place. I cannot tell you how hard I was on myself during that period—brutally rough on any errors in logic. And that's how I got the Policy Governance model.

LS: Would you describe those essential ideas that make up the Policy Governance model?

JC: The essential ideas of the Policy Governance model are several. I can give you a quick rundown on some of them. One idea is that the board holds its authority and must express its authority as a group, never as parts. For example, the committee has no power over the staff; the board does. The chair has no power over staff; the board does. It is a unitary body in expressing and holding its authority and accountability.

Another is that boards are representative bodies of an ownership of some sort. The ownership might be as clear as shareholders in an equity corporation or as clear as members in a membership association. In any event, it is some group of human beings that we can look at as morally or legally owning the organization. For some organizations, it is very easy, like the ones I just mentioned. For other ones, it is harder, like a public television station. Who is the ownership? Well, you have to play with that idea for a while. But, no matter what the ownership is, the board is speaking on its behalf.

Another of the essential elements is that the board, when it expresses what it needs to say to a management system, must do so in such a way as to find the optimal balance between empowerment and rigorous accountability. In other words, the board must take delegation seriously, but it also wants to give as much freedom as possible for people to use their own creativity and their own thinking.

Another is that board members should deal with the largest questions very carefully—not voluminously, just carefully. Then, having decided the broadest possible issue about for example, what we exist for or what ethics and prudence values we want observed—are we willing to let somebody else use any reasonable interpretation of those words in the making of subsequent, smaller decisions about every topic our statement addressed? And if we're not willing to give somebody that right, then we must say some more, that is, go into a little more detail. What constitutes "a little more detail" is the concept of rigidly descending into more detail step by step, never jumping several steps into great detail. So the board steps through the descending breadths of decision making, until at some point the board is able to say, "We've nailed that issue down far enough that we *are* willing to accept any reasonable interpretation of what we said. We can now let go of it." And at that point, it's turned over to a chief executive officer who then takes the decision making further into as much detail as is needed for the job to get done. The CEO, of course, can delegate whatever authority the board will have thus given him or her to subordinates, but remains accountable to the board for the total.

This rigid level-by-level specificity does not exist in other approaches to governance. That framework is a basic principle, though the content inside each level is up to each board. Construing decision making in this level-by-level configuration makes many otherwise confusing things clear. For example, when dealing with the historically difficult question of drawing the line between what are board decisions versus staff decisions, in Policy Governance it is easily done and tailored to each board because the line is where the board stops needing to further define its values about whatever is being addressed. Take budget for example. Who decides upon any specific budget? In Policy Governance, the staff does, not the board. But it does so under larger decisions/values about budgeting and financial planning that the board has set so that as long as the staff sticks with those values, any set of numbers will be okay. That kind of thinking in which the board starts from the outside and works in gives the board a way of having its arms around the organization and never having its fingers in it. It enables the board to say, "We as a group set out our values at the front end, not later." In fact, everything is proactive this way. The board starts the ball rolling. It is not the final decision-maker, as we often say, it's the initial decision-maker. By doing that, it keeps the board closer to the values of the ownership. So instead of seeing the board as we usually do, as "management one step up," we see it as "ownership one step down." It changes the whole perspective, absolutely changes the whole way a board sees its job.

So the model does that. It also clarifies ways in which we can know what information a board needs and which information it only gets bedazzled by, the "fancy-footwork, show-us-a-lot-of-PowerPoint-presentations" approach to governing knowledge. It's much more specific about what information boards need. It is much more specific about how the board does CEO evaluation: relatively painlessly.

So the model has a number of essential characteristics. I have not mentioned all of them, but these probably give you a flavor of the mentality of the model. It is a consistent, conceptually coherent system, not just a set of tips.

LS: How many organizations do you believe have worked with this model, have adopted it?

JC: I have been working with Policy Governance for thirty-five years, further back than the first edition of *Boards That Make a Difference* in 1995. Over that time, the model has been applied in an unbelievable range of settings: in the United States and Canada, but also in Australia and New Zealand, in a number of places in Europe, especially the U.K. and the Netherlands, and in parts of Africa and Asia. So the model has had worldwide distribution. Some of that I have done personally, or Miriam, my wife, has done personally. But a lot of it has been done by the people we have trained in the advanced consultant training that we do. It is like a small army. However, they do not report to us or pay any royalties to us; they are independent consultants.

More important, I think, is the range of types of organizations in which Policy Governance has been applied: equity, for-profit corporations; nonprofits, the NGOs; government organizations like city councils, school boards, and airport authorities. We have covered all kinds of organizations like that, and found that they are strikingly similar if you go all the way to the basics of governance rather than the superficial surface characteristics. A city council will obviously have a different set of decisions to make than a third-world relief organization or the board of a nuclear power plant. But the basics of governance are the same.

One of the problems, though, with Policy Governance—I think it is the biggest problem—is that it requires discipline. It requires board members to be as disciplined in the board process as their staffs already are in the management process, or as the board members are in their other jobs. Boards are not accustomed to being that disciplined. They are accustomed to being sort of freewheeling or, at least, satisfied with less precise practices. Like, for example, being "managers one-step-removed." The history, then, of what has happened with organizations that started with Policy Governance is a mixed history. Those that stuck with the model very carefully have found that it has saved them huge amounts of problems that have come up when their organizations hit bumps in the road. We have had many organizations tell us that that Policy Governance has gotten them through unexpected crises. We have also had many that let their newly acquired discipline fall apart. Governance does not stay fixed any more than the dishes stay washed or the bed stays made. It takes constant work, just like management does.

So the model asks a lot of boards. It produces a lot, too, but it does ask a lot, and that the continued discipline isn't always met.

LS: In 2001, you asked the question, "Is translation of the wishes of owners into organizational performance not the heart of servant-leadership?" What do you see as the essential heart, or core, of servant-leadership?

JC: That is a question that Bob Greenleaf ought to answer, not me. I do not claim to be an expert in servant-leadership. But if I try to pin down what I think is the central core, to me servant-leadership is a fine-tuning of the Golden Rule. It is fine-tuned in terms of certain aspects of relationships. It translates into Policy Governance largely in the ways boards look at their roles as servants of an ownership. So let me bring the ownership concept in Policy Governance back into this. A board is servant of the ownership, but the servanthood that they're being asked to display is the servanthood of leading that which the ownership owns, of leading that school system, leading that city government, leading that petroleum company, and so forth. The central core simply goes back to the Golden Rule. It is trusteeship.

LS: Are there other ways in which you see servant-leadership and Policy Governance either intersecting or ways in which they may reinforce one another?

JC: There's another way in which servant-leadership and Policy Governance intersect, and that has to do with the way the board deals with those who report to the board, that is, how boards deal with management staff—and I'm using management to mean all the staff—and specifically how the board deals with a CEO. The intention in Policy Governance is to balance the need for rigorous accountability and the need to give people as much room as possible to be able to move, to stand behind the exercise of human creativity and individuality, and still get the right production out of the whole system. That's hard to balance. Boards typically have a tremendously hard time walking on that fence. In trying, they will frequently fall off it in the direction of getting involved with the staff in a micromanagement way; that is, the meddling board. Or they will fall off it in the other direction by just letting things go; that is the rubber-stamping board. To me, the board should set up a situation in which people can be all they can be without forgetting that they are not there just to do their own thing. They are there to serve something and someone else. So in that sense I see another way in which servant-leadership gets itself expressed in the delegation system. As Miriam, my wife and peerless Policy Governance teacher put it, the guiding principle is "Control all you must, not all you can."

LS: How can servant-leadership help boards and board members to encounter their weaknesses and then help to heal and perhaps to overcome them? Is this something that you see as being relevant to the Policy Governance model?

JC: Are you asking whether servant-leadership plays a role in helping heal whatever is going on within a board? I have never thought about it in quite that way. But when I stop to think about it, perhaps there are ways. For example, the model focuses people on the conflict of issues as opposed to the conflict of people. Perhaps that sounds a little strange. Let me explain this way: Policy Governance counsels boards to see themselves as present at the board table to disagree, not present to agree. If they are there to agree, we only need one person. We can pass the board job around: George is the board in February and Sally is the board in March. The purpose in having them together is to disagree, and not even to disagree just to the extent of the board members' personal disagreements. They come together to bring the disagreement and the variety of opinions of an ownership, that is, of the organization's legitimacy base. So if an ownership point-of-view is not actually held by any of the board members, it should still find expression in the board process. For the board to really do its job in being a servant to the ownership and then let that turn into the leadership of that which the ownership owns—the organization—it must incorporate things that go beyond the small-mindedness, if I might say it that way, of George and Sally disagreeing, or Mary and Harry, and so forth. The job is something bigger than that, and that bigness helps get out of the person-to-person kind of confrontation. It is more a confrontation of ideas; so since that is what we are here to do, let's be about it.

LS: Robert Greenleaf talked a lot about some characteristics of servant-leadership. One of them was foresight. What is your own sense of the use of foresight within a board context? What can boards or board chairs, in particular, do in terms of exercising some heightened sense of foresight to help organizations?

JC: Foresight is not just one of the characteristics of a board; it is almost the total engagement of a board. The board should be dealing with the future, a future that is as far out as makes sense. For example, the board of a nuclear power plant should not be dealing with just a five-year future, but the board of a small counseling agency might be dealing with a five-year future, or ten years. So foresight is really what the game is about for the board. The board is there to envision and create a future, not to go over last month's financial statements—there are ways of handling that another way—but to create a future, which means foresight is that which plays the "what if" game over and over and over. "What if this happened? What if that happened?" or, "Is the nature of the world around us changing? Maybe we haven't changed yet, but is the world around us changing such that what was not a risk before is now a risk?" The board should live with vision and grasping the bigness and instability of the world that the organization is moving into. For example, our petroleum companies should have boards which deal with the fact that, certain kinds of their operations, should they go wrong, can cause untold damage, damage which might in fact be as great as the total capitalization of the company. Maybe that wasn't true even twenty years ago, but now it is true. So what are we going to do with that? How will we look at that? What should the board require of its organization, not only on behalf of the owners—which it must do—but with an ethical obligation to the rest of the world?

Now that obligation strains our imagination that there could even *be* that much foresight. That is exactly what is called for. That's what's called for in the public schools, what's called for in relief agencies. And it certainly is called for city governments who don't usually have the foresight to talk about the fact that their infrastructure falls apart a little bit more every year. We don't even use an accounting system in such a way that we take account of the deterioration; we wait until it all falls apart later. Foresight is so important that I would say it is the main mentality of the board.

LS: Another characteristic, and the one that Greenleaf talked about as being of greatest importance, is listening. I have seen a wide degree of listening take place within boards, as I am sure you have as well. The question here is what aspects of Policy Governance model help to encourage greater fealty to listening? What are some things that board members, board chairs, might be able to do to help their organizations around listening?

JC: I would think that it is impossible to govern with excellence without having a huge investment in listening. First of all, listening to the ownership. That is where the listening begins, listening to the ownership. We have in Policy Governance a term we often use called *ownership linkage*, which simply speaks to the obligation of a board to connect itself to the ownership in some way. Sometimes, if you have a small ownership, you can actually connect to the individual people: you can survey them; you can have them all in the same room. If you have thousands or hundreds of thousands or millions of owners—as many organizations do, even some massive nonprofits, and certainly equity corporations—then the listening has to be done another way. It has to be done in a way that has statistical validity so you're not just listening to the loud voices or the voices that your board members connect with best, but broader and representative listening. Therefore, listening frequently has to be taken to a technological level. How do you find out what the values are of a hundred thousand people about public education if you are a school board? Well, that is your job. Figure it out. And the listening must be done in a very careful, statistically accurate way in order to have the confidence that you have actually heard. The kinds of public meetings school boards have is a stark counterfeit of listening to the ownership—their participation is mostly staff, vendors, and disgruntled "customers."

The other kind of listening is that boards have to listen to their staffs. I don't mean listen to their staffs in the sense of being pushed around by them or even representing them the way representation is owed to owners. So I don't mean giving up the obligation boards have to make decisions on behalf of the owners. I don't mean letting the staff make decisions on behalf of the owners, but to listen to the wisdom that resides in staff because staff have a tremendous amount of wisdom that the board can draw on. Listening to staff is not to give up the board's governing role, but to enhance that role.

So listening plays a big part in governance. It has to . . . it has to. The board should spend more time listening than it does talking, by a long shot.

LS: You spoke some years ago about the Policy Governance model as a kind of technology of servant-leadership. Would you share some insights about that idea?

JC: I see servant-leadership as a way of being, not a set of behaviors necessarily, but a way of being. It is translated into behavior, but that behavior will look different in the classroom by a teacher, versus in a boardroom by a board, versus in the accounting office by a clerk. It looks different; you are carrying out very different tasks out of that "way of being." Policy Governance is a technology of servant-leadership in a specific location: the governing board. I didn't start with servant-leadership to do it, but you could easily see Policy Governance as being a technology, technique, or concretization of servant-leadership in this one very specific setting.

LS: The Policy Governance model has been around for more than thirty years. Have you adjusted the model in some way over the years? In addition, if so, how?

JC: The model has had a history of development over the last thirty-five years, but I would have to break it into two parts. The model basically consists of a few—very few—principles. They're unfamiliar and so different that people think of them as complicated, even though most sports have more rules than Policy Governance. These principles themselves have stayed pretty much unchanged during that period of time. It turns out that they held water well enough that there have not been new principles added nor some tossed out. That just has not happened. What *has* happened, however, has been the ability to translate that into action, the ability to design a way of, for example, getting monitoring information so that a board can feel reasonably secure that what it has set forth as what it wanted done or what it wanted avoided has been achieved. So we have gotten much tighter, more exacting, about the monitoring process. The Policy Governance principle that boards should only do performance monitoring of what they've given criteria about ahead of time, that is, that you only make judgments when people have had the chance to know upon what the judgment will be made—those principles have stayed the same. So I'd have to say that the model itself, *qua* model, has gone virtually unchanged and has stood the test of time, but the implementation techniques have gotten better over time

LS: Have you found any resistance to the Policy Governance Model, either among individuals or organizations?

JC: Far more than I first expected. Resistance to Policy Governance comes in many flavors. I think I could break it down this way. First, let me preface that by saying that most groups who hear a full explication of the model—that takes about five hours without great detail, but it does cover the total—most of them find it is highly logical, highly reasonable, and ideal. Not everybody, but most in any given group. So it starts off with very little resistance. However, after that point, one type of resistance is the resistance to the conceptually coherent idea of "model" at all, a resistance to having a firm set of principles to follow precisely. Basic principles as a rigid foundation upon which can be built a great variety of personalized "superstructure" is resisted in a social construct like governance. That is true even though we have no trouble understanding that you can build many kinds of bridges, though engineering principles are the same.

Maybe the resistance comes about because of wanting to "fly by the seat of your pants" sometimes, or board members wanting to bring the experience of what worked at some other place and apply it, even though they're now using Policy Governance and the whole game just changed because things that you bring that are useful in some other setting can be exactly the wrong things to do under a new set of principles, like Policy Governance—like trying to apply good baseball practices in football.

The other resistance is because almost any real change involves a shift in power relations. Staffs who like to wind the board around their fingers don't like it, because the board actually assumes its responsibility to be in charge. Or boards who like to interfere and get in the middle of staff operations don't like it because it takes away one of the things that they get a kick out of, or that particular board members get a kick out of. Boards who have leaned more toward rubber-stamping find that there's a lot of work to be done in governing. Governing is not just showing up for the meeting, keeping the seat warm for an hour and a half, and going home after listening to some nice presentation with the staff. That is not what governing is all about.

So there are a number of things that drive resistance to a rigidly applied model. It is definitely rigid at the principles level. It is not rigid in terms of all the different varieties of governance that can be built on top of those principles. But a board has to be able to distinguish the rigid, rigorous, theory-based principles from all other decisions that are based on personality and on what people like to do. Those things, that great range of organizational uniqueness, is fine as long as you hold the foundational principles in place. So being able to tell those two things apart distinctly is absolutely important. If boards let those run together, then the principles will be weakened and their ability to maintain the model falls apart.

LS: When did you first encounter Robert Greenleaf's writings, and what book or essay did you first read?

JC: My first taste of Bob Greenleaf was, as I remember it, *Trustees as Servants*. I mean, obviously, that is what I would gravitate to, isn't it. But there are two others of his writings that I also really took to. One was *Institution as Servant*. In fact, I would rate that second for my own utility. And the other was the curiously titled *Advices to Servants* because, in that order, they have a lot to say specifically about boards of directors. I have just finished rereading those. I have a tendency to write in books, so I am writing and arguing with him and agreeing with him in the margin. I have found that those three booklets, short as they are, have a great deal of material, so much philosophy, condensed into them.

LS: In *The Servant as Leader*, he wrote his definition of servant-leadership: "It begins with the natural feeling that one wants to serve, to serve first, then conscious choice brings one to aspire to lead. The difference manifests itself in the care taken by the servant, first to make sure that people's highest priority needs are being served." And then he said his best test of servant-leadership: "Do those served grow as persons? Do they, while being served, become healthier, wiser, freer, more autonomous, more likely themselves to become servants? And what is the effect on the least privileged in society? Will they benefit, or at least, not be further deprived?" Are there differences between that understanding and your own, that you think are worth mentioning?

JC: I don't know whether there is a substantive difference between the way Greenleaf defined servant-leadership and the kind of definition I would try to give it. I don't know that there is a difference.

LS: You named *The Institution as Servant* as a close second in terms of Greenleaf's writings and their influence. What is it in *The Institution as Servant* that you find most interesting or striking as concepts?

JC: Well, *The Institution as Servant* obviously has many concepts that one can latch on to but the part that I enjoyed the most was probably the part that I disagree with him the most about: what he had to say about chief executive officers. Robert Greenleaf sees the board as a group of equals that has asked one person to be servant in the sense of keeping order and keeping them on track and reminding them of what they said they were obligated to, things like that. That role is normally called chair or chairperson. Because I've given that role more meat, if you will, in Policy Governance, I've changed the name of the function to "Chief Governance Officer," CGO. The name of the function makes it parallel in form with CEO and CIO and CFO and all the other "*C* dash *O*'s," but it also gets rid of the awkwardness of *chairman, chairwoman, chairperson*, along with the social and verbal awkwardness they entail. Greenleaf saw the chair as being a primus in that group, not the boss of the group. I totally agree, and I was blown away when I read his account. I loved it. But then I encountered the disagreement between us.

He carries the same thought into the managerial area, so that what would have been a CEO, for example, becomes the first among equals in an executive team. Not the entire staff, just the executive team, so he was not talking about everybody, just one level of everybody. The reason he gives for not wanting to have a single-person CEO is that he had reasonable fears of what happens when somebody as a single individual has "unchecked authority," if I remember his wording right. However, I strongly believe that if Robert Greenleaf had been privy to the kinds of safeguards and ways of delegating that are built into Policy Governance—which are very different from more traditional ways of looking at board-to-CEO delegation—he would have softened that point of view considerably.

LS: That is a great example of ideas that Greenleaf wrote about that are disagreed with. Another area of controversy has to do with his brief writings about the distinction between "conceptualizers" and "operationalizers." Could you speak to that and whatever viewpoint you might have about that?

JC: Greenleaf's division of the world into conceptualizers and operationalizers, I am sure he didn't mean it as a rigid, "All *A* or all *B*, but never *AB*." I am sure he didn't mean it that strongly, that rigidly. But he did talk about two separate kinds of ways of looking at things, and the board absolutely has to be conceptualizer, he makes that very clear. And, of course, the staff has to be operationalizers. Now—and I don't disagree with that point of view, I really don't—but what I would amend it with is that there is a continuum where the one fades into the other. At the board level, let's say—I'm making this up for purposes of argument—the people are being 90 percent conceptualizers and 10 percent operationalizers, because they also have to operationalize the board's own specific operation, for example, how they keep policies in place, what model do they use for governance, and things like that. And then at the very lowest rung of some organization, that person might be 90 percent operationalizer, and 10 percent conceptualizer. I don't think we can say the janitor or the accounting clerk does no conceptualizing at all. But the percentage probably changes from high-percentage conceptualizer to high-percentage operationalizer, with some sort of continuum in between as one fades into the other.

LS: The third title that you named was *Advices to Servants.* What drew you to it?

JC: Its commentary on trusteeship.

LS: Greenleaf identified a number of characteristics that he said you were likely to find in servant-leaders, not that everyone has all of them, but that these are characteristics that he thought were important to servant-leadership. They included listening, empathy, healing, awareness, persuasion, conceptualization, foresight, stewardship, commitment to the growth of people, and building community. Which, if any, of these characteristics do you see as being particularly helpful in the effective practice of the Policy Governance model, and why?

JC: The characteristics of stewardship, of building community, are definitely part of what Policy Governance connects to. Stewardship for the ownership is definitely a critical "agency" relationship. The conceptualizer role is important, mainly because at the board level there is much that is not hands-on, but abstract, such as dealing with what should be in ten years, or dealing with what are the values that underlie what we're all about. That is pretty abstract work, which takes thoughtful conceptualizing.

The idea of building community, which I kind of skipped past there, is important in that the board in speaking for the owners is having to consider a group of people to whom it owes not only a legal but a moral accountability, a group of people as a repository of a huge range of diversity of ideas. The question for a board is not What does the ownership think? It thinks many things, so it is harder than that. It's like this: among all the different points of view and opinions, sometimes vehemently held points of view, the board's job is to find a way to grapple with that booming, buzzing confusion, to misquote William James, and bring it into the board room and let all that diversity live right there. The board's job consists in large part of somehow picking through this complexity, and with as much foresight as possible building whatever community out of that that can be built.

LS: Using Greenleaf's definition of a servant-leader as being one who serves first and then leads as a means of helping others, I am curious to ask whether there are people in your life who were servant-leaders for you.

JC: Oh yes, oh yes! My sixth-grade teacher, Ira Douthitt in Chattanooga. I think the school system named an elementary school after him later. "Mr. Douthitt" just had to be a servant-leader though at the time I wouldn't have known what the term meant. There was Dr. Walter Ruby, who taught at the University of Chattanooga, my major professor during that period of time. He was an educational psychologist, who simply would not abide my taking what appeared to be a great job at the time, but one that would have kept me from following a brighter star. There have been more, but those two come to mind so quickly that their leadership must have particular meaning for me.

LS: Are there places where you see servant-leadership being something you talk about to groups that are not servant-leadership focused per se?

JC: In presenting Policy Governance and trying to teach people what it's about—whether it's just a short three-to-five hour time or whether it's a much longer engagement like advanced training for consultants, I don't think I ever fail to mention servant-leadership, because the concept is so useful in explaining Policy Governance. I cannot imagine talking about Policy Governance very long without mentioning servant-leadership, because it so adequately captures the relationship of, well, anybody to anybody else; but specifically in Policy Governance, it captures the relationship of board to owners, it captures the relationship of board to chair. As I've had the opportunity to say in Greenleaf Center presentations I've made, the chair is the most beautifully simple picture of a servant-leader. A board says, "You, our chairperson, begin with no more power than anyone else. We each have the same power as board members, but we're going to take some the authority we have as a group and give it to you, we're going to give it to you for specified purposes, with specified limitations." In carrying that out, it is very clear the chair works for the board, not the other way around. The chair works for the board, and is given authority to act as an individual in the way the CEO is, but about different things. That is, the domains in which each is assigned authority are clearly differentiated. Because they don't overlap, they don't conflict. Servant-leadership captures the resulting relationship between the board and its chair so perfectly that it helps explain it, faster than we could otherwise.

LS: What advice would you have for a board in selecting a board chair, or *CGO* as you use the term? Particular qualities or things to look for that are likely to be most helpful.

JC: When boards choose a chief governance officer, by whatever title it may use—chair, president, moderator, mayor, it is best to choose a person who is comfortable confronting a group with itself. Not bossing the group, but saying, "Look, this board decided not to dictate this kind of thing to the staff, but to leave them the freedom to make the choice. Yet our discussion right now is as if we're doing that. Do you want to change the rule, or do you want to get back in line about what we said we'd do?" It is as if you are confronting the board with its own decisions. It's not that the board is obligated to be the board the chair says the board should be, the board should be the board the board says the board should be. But the ongoing relationship is one in which it needs somebody to say, "Hey, wait a minute, we are violating our own code of discipline!"

Now the way I said that has some danger, for it could be understood as taking other board members off the hook for discipline. But it should not take them off the hook. Every board member has equal authority and equal accountability for the total—every board member has accountability that the board is what it should be. Every one. Which means if the board is off topic or doing things it said it would not get in to, every hand that does not go in the air to say, "Hey, wait a minute! We're off track" is culpable. Every single board member whose hand does not go in the air is culpable, not just the CGO.

Of course, the chair has one more little dollop of authority that others do not have; the chair does not have to put a hand in the air. The chair has a gavel. The chair can say, "Stop. Right now." And the chair is saying stop not out of his or her own authority, but out of authority the board as a body assigned to the chair, a very specific statement of that authority. So the board needs a chair who can play that role well without slipping either into Mr. or Ms. Dictator or slipping into Mr. or Ms. Milquetoast. The board needs somebody smart enough, strong enough, and assertive enough to do it, and someone who sees the board as very clearly his or her boss. And for boards that choose their own chair, if the chair doesn't do these things well, the board is accountabile for changing chairs or changing chair behaviors. In other words, the board cannot blame its chair if the board doesn't get its job done.

LS: A number of people over the years, me included, have referred to the Policy Governance model as offering a revolutionary approach to board governance. Do you personally describe the Policy Governance model as a revolutionary approach to board governance?

JC: I typically do not use the word *revolutionary* when I'm talking about Policy Governance, although I probably do imply the same thing. I tend to use what has become a rather tired word, *paradigm shift*, in that it certainly shifts the paradigm. What I would typically do is to say that the Policy Governance model is not just a tightening up of our other governance ideas. It is not just a set of tips about how to make it better. It reorders the whole ball game. In fact, it is like moving from baseball to football. What makes sense in one does not make sense in the other, so you cannot bring the same hard-won wisdom that you had in one to the other. Maybe that is what is *revolutionary.* If a board tries to use part Policy Governance and part of what they had before, it will fail. It does not necessarily fail any worse than how they were already failing, but it will fail in that the promise of Policy Governance will be foregone.

So, is it revolutionary? Yes.

A corollary to that all-or-nothing point is that trying to install Policy Governance into place one piece at a time does not work. It just does not work. The transition is more like saying "Okay folks, put down that funny-shaped ball, we're going to stop kicking it and throwing passes with it, and we're going to use this other ball. And our foul lines aren't going to be parallel anymore; they're going to be at a 90-degree angle." So we move from football to baseball. We do not get there by slowly changing one game to the other. The same thing applies for a transition to Policy Governance—that is its blessing and its curse.

LS: What is the reaction that you get now, compared to twenty years ago?

JC: I can give you a bifurcated kind of answer to this. In one way, there is greater reception in that the model has been spread a lot more. Even when people do not know much about Policy Governance, some of the ideas have seeped into the general discourse, so people talk about ends and means, or they talk about some of the other things that Policy Governance brought to the party. There are a number of ways in which people are more ready for it, since so much has been written, even books published on it. It is true, though obviously unjustified, that authors in public perception become much smarter after having a book published.

Now that is one reaction to Policy Governance. The other direction is the time since inception gives more time for resistance. There is more time for people to say, "Well, gosh, this has been around for thirty years; maybe it's time for something new." In my opinion, people saying that never understood the model to start with, because even now there isn't anything that outpaces it. I am unaware, though, of any point-by-point refutation of Policy Governance by someone who actually understands all its facets.

LS: I have noticed that over the years you have made a point in your books of thanking people who have made their homes available to you for "get-away" writing. How do you approach the task of writing?

JC: I tend to write anywhere and everywhere. It has to do more with whether the mood strikes me or a deadline is haunting me. Those two motivations can certainly cause me to write. I started writing in my twenties. It was a way of figuring something out. In other words, I might not know what I really think about something until I start trying to write it. And it is not like I usually would have a totally different idea than I started out with—although that has happened—but that the writing becomes a mechanism for driving and refining the thinking. Many things have happened over the years that are just like that: "I'm going to try to write what I think about this. I have no idea what I think about this but let me see if I can write about it anyway," and it starts coming out. I have absolutely surprised myself many times. I guess people see me as very business-like, somber in some ways, but I am really kind of childlike about writing. I mean, I get gleeful when I have finally said something the way I wanted to say it and it comes across well. I get positively gleeful.

So writing, for me, is something I love and hate, depending on which time you catch me. Sometimes I'm trying to get something out and it's just killing me because I can't quite get it right. The subject may be complex and that makes it hard, but then, that's the job—finding a way to say explain something complex so that it makes sense is stimulating and exciting and deadly all at the same time. Writing, for me, is an adventure. It always is, and I'd love doing it, on, some that never get published.

I love writing in strange places. I remember sitting out on a big rock—one of those huge boulders—in one of the streams that come down near Boulder, Colorado, carrying a portable typewriter with flowing water all around and writing something with my little typewriter out there. Or sitting where a cannon was positioned in a castle parapet in Puerto Rico. That was out on a tip where you look down for maybe seventy-five feet to crashing waves. I sat out there with a typewriter on my lap writing. I love things like that. It is just wonderful. I have written in people's homes when they take off and leave their home to me. And I should not leave out airplane composition on almost every flight. Writing can be done almost any place.

LS: I have had the unusual experience of having three separate occasions in my life where I was part of discovering previously unknown writings by people, and then going through them, editing them, and publishing them as books, posthumously published books. The first time was in 1990; after Greenleaf died his children sent me his personal papers and I began to go through them and was astonished to discover, ultimately, almost one hundred pieces of writing that he had done for exactly the same reason that you described just now, as a means of working through his thinking on a whole host of topics. And it was those pieces that I discovered that in 1996 were published by Jossey-Bass as *On Becoming a Servant Leader* and *Seeker and Servant*. The second was years later when a friend, Bill Bottum, passed away. I asked his family if I could go down into his basement and go through his boxes of materials and, lo and behold, we found about 1,100 manuscript pages that he had written over about a forty-year period. That resulted in the book, *Within Your Reach*. Finally, I helped Paul Davis, a friend and colleague, to produce a book called *The Human Treatment of Human Beings*, which came about as result of a last-minute rescue of papers of a Michigan executive named John Donnelly, who had passed away several decades earlier.

With that as a background, my question is this: Have you published pretty much everything you have written and wanted to publish, or are there writings that you have done over the years that may be sitting in your files?

JC: I don't have a repository of writings to be discovered posthumously at all, as Robert Greenleaf did, and others. They've either been thrown away and replaced by something that did get published or they've been published. In addition to usual places to publish, I have something they didn't have at the time, I think, and that is a bimonthly that Jossey-Bass/Wiley Company publishes. It is called *Board Leadership: Policy Governance in Action*. Miriam Carver—my wife and colleague, also authoritative source about Policy Governance—and I write and edit that. So we have, if you will, a captured publication. Many things we really think is worth publishing we will publish in that. So we have an outlet. There is a downside to having that outlet. Because it is so available and certainly gets more material published, I will write for that when otherwise I might publish more in a wider variety of publications. The closest to a repository I have would be not on Policy Governance at all, but on philosophy with friends, much now in e-mail exchanges, some of which became rather voluminous.

LS: Which is your favorite book that you have written?

JC: I have two daughters, and if I were asked which one was my favorite, I would have a bit of a hard time with that. [*Laughs*] As to what is my favorite book, I really don't know. I think *Boards That Make a Difference* in its third edition is probably the one I would have to pick as a favorite, only because it is the one that most thoroughly covers, in a sequential, rational line, the building of the idea of Policy Governance. I love all of them. I love the one that Miriam wrote with a gentleman named Bill Charney called *The Board Member's Playbook*, in which it actually takes a board through a variety of "what if" situations. In that book, an event—usually a bad one—is presented as just having happened and the board is taken through how to use its Policy Governance policies to deal with it. Policies as designed in Policy Governance will either solve the problem or point toward the solution. With the book, a board would use its own policies to practice dealing with a crisis or other unfortunate event.

You know, we have a strange approach to practice. Armies, rock groups, symphony orchestras, sports teams—all practice more than they perform. It is obvious that they must in order to perform well. Boards do not practice, and their performance shows it. Of course, if they were to practice they would first have to figure out, "What do we practice at?" and there is the hang up. But a Policy Governance board can practice using the policies they've already developed. One drawback of Policy Governance is that it clears up so much silly stuff that a board can relax, except it may relax prematurely. Organized practice gives a board something to use every board meeting or every second or third board meeting to actually confront an imaginary crisis. Real crises that come along are, first, less likely and, second, more easily dealt with.

But I also like the book on corporate boards, *Corporate Boards that Create Value*, that I wrote in conjunction with Caroline Oliver, who's one of the persons who went through our advanced Policy Governance training like Bill Charney did. Caroline and I put the model as expressed in *Boards That Make a Difference* completely into equity corporate language, because people have a mistaken idea that Policy Governance applies only to nonprofits. No, it applies to nonprofits, governmental boards that have governing authority like school boards and city councils, and to equity corporations as well.

LS: In "A Theory of Governing the Public's Business" you wrote, "The owner-representative role of the board is a source of both board authority and board obligation for servant-leadership." Could you say more about that?

JC: Yes. That article was published in *The Public Management Review* in the United Kingdom, originally, and then it was repeated as one section in *John Carver on Board Leadership.* Yeah, if you drew an organizational chart the board sits directly between the owners and the operational organization. It sits right on the line between those two. It is therefore accountable for everything that happens below it in that chart and it is accountable to everything that is above it, i.e., the owners. The fact that it's in that spot sets up the obligation—not just the choice, but the obligation—to be a servant-leader

In that publication I was talking about city councils, county commissions, or similar political bodies. The relationship of the governing group with owners includes not only the job of listening to them and condensing their various points of view—which are so discrepant one from another—but also of helping them to be better owners. You can hear a little reverberation of Greenleaf in that, can't you? Helping them be better owners. For example, can a school board or a city council help people understand how to be better citizens who recognize that they own those school systems and city governments? There are some tremendous ways in which they could do that. They do not, but they could.

What they do, by the way, is almost laughingly misguided. Have you ever watched a school board having public meetings? Ten minutes for public statements is virtually useless. First, they are not hearing from "the public." They are hearing from a few disgruntled customers most of the time, or a few would-be vendors. But they are not hearing from the public, because if they were to hear from the public they would have to say to themselves, "We've got a public of one hundred thousand (or a million). How can we see what this one hundred thousand public feels or values? We'll have to design something. If we wait for them to come to us, we cannot help but get a biased input." So the public meeting, which is good for being transparent about what is going on, is fine. But it is not good for public input. It is a counterfeit of public input. We have to start looking at things like that in order to transform political linkage from the fantasy and from the pretense it now is.

LS: That's helpful. In *The Institution as Servant*, Greenleaf said, "A new condition of these times is the need for a high level of trust in institutions. Without it, they cannot serve and may even lose much of their present autonomy." What is your reaction to that statement?

JC: [*Laughs*] The first thing I thought of was petroleum companies and banks. Bigness absolutely characterizes our new world. Greenleaf said there is nothing wrong with the bigness itself, he made that point parenthetically in one of his books, but it's like we're dealing with bigness and therefore the ability to hurt as well as help a lot of people, and even people they weren't there to either hurt or help.

It seems to me that bigness brings problems of trustworthiness no matter how well intended the corporate leaders and those who carry out corporate business. Companies consider risk in many ways. But one risk that is low on their priority is what would happen if the company fails. What would it cost to clean up the mess? If an organization creates an environmental disaster of monumental proportions despite whatever care was taken, how do we look at that? If the company is not able or is not around to right the wrong, how should it and how should we look at the risk involved? And the problem is that boards—in this case, corporate boards—don't deal with that. I suppose public policy could see to it that they do. But government itself has a terrible record with regard to low probability high damage events. Our cities don't even take care of the *high* probability high damage events, like infrastructure deterioration. I'd rather corporations get it right to start with rather than leave it to government and lose the autonomy they might have had. But, if boards are irresponsible enough, they are just inviting government to come in even though it is no paragon of trustworthiness. I don't know whether issues of this sort are what Bob Greenleaf meant by his statements or not, but that's part of what I get out of them.

LS: In *A Few Tips for the Chairperson*, you said, "Your job as Chairperson comes as close to a pure instance of Robert Greenleaf's servant-leader as I can imagine. You are clearly the board's leader, and just as surely its servant as well. You might get a philosophical boost for that challenge by reading Greenleaf's thoughts on the matter. Understand servant-leadership. Understand governance. Understand your board. Then you'll be ready to help your board understand itself." Any elaboration you would care to make on that?

JC: I don't think so. I think I said exactly what I wanted to say.

LS: In *The Importance of Trust in the Board/CEO Relationship*, you wrote, "Under conditions of mistrust the human toll is high. The board's commitment to its word will have little effect in the short term unless the CEO has confidence that it means it. While CEOs should be prepared to deliver performance, they need not be tormented by board caprice or 'gotcha' games."

Could you address that statement and the nature of something else you have written about, I think that you have called it "the Rogue Board Member"?

JC: Trust is a big deal. It is a really big deal. But the organization should not run based on trust; it should run based on clarity about its expectations and commitment to live up to the discipline that it said it'd operate under. One implication is that it won't judge the CEO based on something it didn't set out ahead of time. That commitment should be written and lived with. Happily, under board conditions of clarity and sticking with what it said, trust blossoms. Trust blossoms. But if we rely just on trust, then the board is being irresponsible, because it is saying to an ownership, "We don't have many controls here because we think the CEO's going to get it done just fine." That is just not responsible. So trust by itself is a problem.

When I have run into trust problems in organizations they are usually phrased in terms of the board being worried that it cannot trust its staff. But trust in that direction needn't be a problem. There are ways of handling the ability of the board to trust the staff that are so easy. The difficult problem is the staff being able to trust the board! Just as boards are frequently incompetent groups of competent persons; they are very often untrustworthy groups of trustworthy persons. For example, it's not uncommon to see a board let its CEO hang out to dry by being castigated by one board member who doesn't like what he or she did. The board just stands by and lets it happen. It is as if the board is saying that abuse of authority by a board member is acceptable. In Policy Governance, it doesn't matter that the CEO please a board member, it matters that the CEO please the board. Any board member who castigates the staff for doing only what that board member thought shouldn't be done has to be reined in by the board immediately. That's a rogue board member who's abusing authority, because the issue isn't for the CEO to make that board member happy. That board member has a role to play, but the rogue's legitimate argument is not with the CEO, it's with the other board members, to have them adopt his or her point of view in terms of what's expected. This problem is widespread, but easily solved; it but requires a board to stick with very fair rules. Boards can be extremely untrustworthy and that causes staff members to do a whole lot of covering their rears. The staff perception that it is necessary to protect itself from the board is deadly. Yes, CEOs are survivors; they find out how to protect themselves, and they do it. But it is not to the benefit of the organization or the integrity of human relationships at all. The board as a body is obligated to protect the staff from the board as individuals. Obligated. That preserves both trust and the integrity of the governance process.

LS: Thank you very much for sharing your thought and your wisdom, and for a lifetime of work, writings, and teachings around the Policy Governance model. You have done great service for many people and many organizations. I appreciate it and I know many, many others who do, too.

JC: It was clearly my pleasure.

Chapter Four

Larry C. Spears

Interviewed by Shann Ray Ferch and Peter Tormey

Considered one of the foremost thought-leaders on servant-leadership, Larry C. Spears is president and CEO of the Larry C. Spears Center for Servant-Leadership, Inc., established in 2008 (www.spearscenter.org). From 1990 to 2007 he served as president and CEO of the Robert K. Greenleaf Center for Servant-Leadership. Spears previously served as director or staff member with the Greater Philadelphia Philosophy Consortium, the Great Lakes Colleges Association's Philadelphia Center, and with the Quaker magazine, Friends Journal. *Spears is also a writer and editor who has published hundreds of articles, essays, newsletters, books, and other publications on servant-leadership. Dozens of newspapers and journals have interviewed him, including* Fortune, the Indianapolis Business Journal, the Philadelphia Inquirer, the Washington Post, *and* Advancing Philanthropy. *A 2004 television broadcast interview of Spears by Stone Phillips on NBC's* Dateline *was seen by ten million viewers. Larry is the creator and editor of a dozen books on servant-leadership, including the best-selling* Insights on Leadership. *Larry serves as the senior advisory editor for* The International Journal of Servant Leadership *(2005–Present). In 2010, he was named the Gonzaga University Servant Leadership Scholar, a title granted in recognition of his role as one of the leading scholars in leadership world-wide, and since 2008 he has taught graduate courses in servant-leadership for Gonzaga University. Among several honors, Spears is the recipient of the 2004* Dare-to-Lead Award *given by the International Leadership Network, and the 2008 Community Leader Award given by DePauw University. Larry has thirty years of experience in organizational leadership, entrepreneurial development, nonprofit management, and grant writing, having envisioned and authored thirty successful grant projects. Special thanks to Peter Tormey, associate director of Community and Public Relations, Gonzaga University, for his involvement in this interview.*

Shann Ferch: When did you first encounter the term *servant-leader*?

Larry Spears: I first encountered the term *servant-leader* in the early 1980s. I was on the staff of *Friends Journal*, a Quaker magazine in Philadelphia, and a manuscript had come in which was actually a chapter from *Teacher as Servant*—written by Robert Greenleaf and published by Paulist Press. He had sent a chapter to *Friends Journal* to see if we might want to publish it, which we did. That was my first introduction to Robert Greenleaf's name, and to the term *servant-leader*. I recall that a kind of electricity of recognition went through me as I realized that Greenleaf had put a name to a feeling that I felt deep within me, but that I had not been able to articulate up to that point. In naming this, he had given voice to a personal yearning within me that I had not been able to clarify. It helped me to realize that I was not alone. Here was a concept, a philosophy of life, rich with meaning. It helped to set the trajectory of my life from that day forward.

SF: Do you have one or two stories of servant-leaders in your own life that you can share with us?

LS: I have come to see my grandfather, Lucian Spears, as the first servant-leader in my life. He was six feet two, 200 pounds, both physically and mentally strong. He was born in southwestern Virginia in 1898. For thirty years he worked in the coal mines during the day and then came home and worked some more in a garden, where he grew vegetables. Then in 1954, he was in a mine cave-in where he had his back broken. After many months, he eventually healed enough so that he could return to a normal life, but he never went back into the coal mines.

I was born in 1955, and I was blessed to grow up with my grandparents living nearby. Many of my earliest memories are of my grandfather as a strong man who also had a wonderful gentleness within him, and of someone who would do anything he could for others. As a child, I heard stories from other family members: It did not matter who you were, if you needed something and there was something he could do to serve you, he would. He epitomized the very idea of serving others, and leading when opportunities called for him to do so. I recall having wonderful conversations, sitting on the sofa together. He didn't talk a lot about his time in the coal mines, but occasionally if I asked a specific question, he would. In retrospect, it is clear that my grandfather had acted as a servant-leader for many people who worked in the coal mines and who lived in the mining camps, as well as with his family and friends.

Another person in my young life who was a servant-leader to me was Mrs. Erma Colding, my fourth- and fifth-grade science teacher. In the 1950s and '60s, my parents, grandparents, sisters, and I lived in Detroit, and I went to Harms Public School on Central Avenue. I think that they had administered IQ testing in the third or fourth grade. To this day, I have never known what my IQ score was. What I do know is that my mother was asked to meet with someone at school, and that shortly thereafter I found myself placed in some new learning situations, both during school and after school. I began to get some special attention that I had not had before—things like taking French lessons, violin lessons, and other things. By far, the most significant attention I had in fourth and fifth grades came from my science teacher, Mrs. Colding. She was a tall African-American woman, very deeply schooled in science. Mrs. Colding asked me if I would like to be her homeroom helper, and to spend time with her doing some extra reading and talking about science. I loved reading about astronomy and the space program, also about dinosaurs. Occasionally, Mrs. Colding would take me to the Cranbrook Museum, outside Detroit, and we would walk through various science exhibits and then see the planetarium show. I fell in love with planetariums at that time. The attention that she gave me, and the interest that she took in my education, was amazing. She served and led me very well.

There is something about proximity to a servant-leader that can be very important. I believe that our greatest influences are likely to be found among those people whom we see most often. For me, both my grandfather, and my science teacher, were two early examples of personal servant-leaders who made a big difference in my life.

There is an interesting coda to this story about Mrs. Colding. A few years back I decided to see what I could find out about her by doing an Internet search. I had not had any contact with her since 1966, when I was ten years old. I went online and discovered that, decades later, she had been recognized by the Detroit NAACP for her contributions to promoting good race relations, and that she had become a major force in helping to bring together the Arab-American and African-American communities in Detroit. I also found a reference to her in a book that suggested that Mrs. Colding had brokered opportunities for community representatives to come together and to learn from one another. Through my online search, I also discovered that she had passed away years before.

In hindsight, I realized that here was a woman whom I had known as my grade school science teacher, and who I now saw as a great personal servant-leader to me—but also someone who had served-and-led countless others in-and-around Detroit during times of great social unrest. We may never know what impact one person may have on another until years or decades later. You are likely to find that servant-leaders have had this kind of impact on more than one person—oftentimes many people. It wasn't just one person whom they influenced.

SF: What personal habits or practices have you found to be important in your own understanding and practice of servant-leadership?

LS: There are a couple of things that are important to me when it comes to understanding servant-leadership. While our personal encounters with servant-leaders always have the greatest impact on us, I do think that reading about servant-leadership can be helpful, too. I have always been a big reader and, unfortunately or not, I tend to be a slow reader. I have always envied people who read quickly and seem to have the comprehension that one would hope to have after reading something. Reading has always been a key to how I learn best. At its best, reading offers a deep introduction and reflective immersion into understanding ideas. I have certainly found that to be the case in my own reading of Robert Greenleaf's work.

As I read, I try to stop every so often and to make the time to think about what I have read—the inherent meaning—and I will make notes on what I have read. Robert Greenleaf was also someone who took many notes on things that he read. In fact, he often wrote as a means of better understanding ideas. That is how I learn best as well, taking notes on what I am reading and then going back through them and thinking about it.

My own understanding and practice of servant-leadership has also been enhanced through dialogue and conversation with others. I find that I can get so far with reading, and then a bit farther with my own self-reflection, but many times it is through dialogue with someone that I am led to see or hear questions that I hadn't heard before, and this takes my understanding of servant-leadership to a deeper level.

SF: Who is a servant-leader? Greenleaf said that the servant-leader is one who is a servant first. In *The Servant as Leader* he wrote, "It begins with the natural feeling that one wants to serve, to serve first. Then conscious choice brings one to aspire to lead. The difference manifests itself in the care taken by the servant, first to make sure that other people's highest priority needs are being served. The best test is, do those served grow as persons? Do they, while being served, become healthier, wiser, freer, more autonomous, and more likely themselves to become servants? And what is the effect on the least privileged in society? Will they benefit, or at least not be further deprived?"

How close does that come to your own definition of servant-leadership? Are there differences between your understanding and this one?

LS: Robert Greenleaf's description of servant-leadership, and his best test in particular, are very close to my own view of servant-leadership. There is not much difference between how I define servant-leadership and how Robert Greenleaf did in his writings.

While I think that I understand what Greenleaf had in mind with his emphasis on autonomy as a key part of the Best Test, I also believe that our understanding of the importance of interdependency has advanced in the decades since Greenleaf defined servant-leadership. Both autonomy and interdependence are key to the understanding and practice of servant-leadership.

Also, after reading Max DePree's *Leadership Is an Art*, where he talked about love, I began to view love for one another as being part of my own deepening understanding of servant-leadership. That isn't a word that Greenleaf addresses often in his writings. So, no disagreements with Greenleaf, just ongoing thinking.

SF: I think about the ten characteristics of servant-leadership that you brought forward. Can you speak to the list of the characteristics of servant-leadership that you put together by looking at Greenleaf's writings in 1991. These include: listening, empathy, healing, awareness, persuasion, conceptualization, foresight, stewardship, commitment to the growth of people, and building community. So maybe first, tell us, how did you exactly do that? I think a lot of students of leadership are fascinated with that, and the answer, I think, is fascinating, too. So, how did you do that, and then share any thoughts on one or two of these characteristics?

LS: Since 1990, my work in servant-leadership has included a focus around the identification of ten characteristics of servant-leadership. The story behind that is that when I was hired in 1990 to head up the Greenleaf Center, I read and then reread all of Greenleaf's published work. In so doing, I began to see the recurrence of certain words and phrases in different essays, on different pages, and in different books. My experience was a little like that scene from the movie, *A Beautiful Mind*, where the main character sees certain words highlighted in glowing letters within larger pages of print! That was the essential feeling that I recall having as the thought began to emerge of these ideas and themes running throughout Greenleaf's writings.

There was also another aspect to all of it: While I view Greenleaf's essay, "The Servant as Leader," as the single most important source of understanding his thinking about servant-leadership, it is also not an easy introduction. Greenleaf's writing can be seen as elliptical at times, and in my first year at the Greenleaf Center, I had heard from a number of people who were drawn to the idea of servant-leadership, but who had mentioned that they were challenged in their reading of his writings. I began to wonder whether there was something that could be done to make Greenleaf's ideas more accessible to a larger audience. One idea that emerged for me was that by extracting his ideas on key characteristics of the servant-leader, I might be able to offer another entry point that would enlarge the base of those who might wish to explore the meaning and practice of servant-leadership. I also decided that I could perhaps help by writing short introductions to servant-leadership in many, many different places. This is something that I have done consistently for nearly a quarter of a century now, and it is something that I hope and believe has helped to increase the numbers of people and organizations that are working with it today.

And so, around 1991, I became curious about what were the most frequently mentioned characteristics in Greenleaf's published writings. He never put together a list of them, but I kept seeing certain ideas repeated over and over again, and so I just began to go through with a yellow highlighter and every time I found a characteristic of servant-leadership—and I think there were ultimately maybe forty of them on my initial list, I would just make a little tic mark on a yellow pad where I had written down these words and phrases. While it wasn't rocket science, it did involve for me a mixture of intuition, awareness, and analysis that seems to be a part of how I see things.

These are all characteristics that Greenleaf, himself, identified as being important in servant-leadership—I simply extracted them from his various writings and brought them together in a list of ten, which I think has been helpful over the years. I think it has had the impact that I had hoped it might have, as another way for some people to begin their own exploration in servant-leadership. The more ways that we have for people to come into contact with servant-leadership, to get excited about wanting to learn more, and then to become living practitioners of it, the better. In some measure, this has helped to guide my own work over the past twenty-five years.

Having identified then these ten characteristics, there was only one of those ten that clearly had both many more tic marks next to it and that Greenleaf himself also referred to as being of greatest importance, and that was listening. Greenleaf is very clear that the process of evolving as a servant-leader is founded upon a desire to want to listen to others, to listen more than speak, and he sees it as a very strong foundation for growth as a servant-leader.

I've spent thirty-five years working in and around Quaker-related causes myself, and listening is a key aspect of the Religious Society of Friends. Something that is not very well known is that Robert Greenleaf and his wife, Esther, created a course on receptive listening that was offered at the Wainwright House in New York; and, for many years, the Greenleafs facilitated this course on receptive listening. Over the years, as more people got involved in the course, the written materials for it were worked on by many different hands, and at some point, Bob and Esther were no longer involved in it. But the receptive listening course continued to be offered for nearly forty years. In the late 1990s I made a point of tracking down information and people who had been involved with the Receptive Listening course, and I was eventually able to locate a copy of the manual for it. It wasn't the earliest version, but it was fairly early on. Here and there, I was able to identify Robert Greenleaf's writings within it. The point of this is that Greenleaf was clear that listening is much overlooked in relationships, in the workplace, and in our lives, and that we would all be better off if we listened more than we spoke. I am reminded of the line that God gave us two ears and one mouth, for good reasons.

The other characteristic that is of great interest for me—and they all are, of course—but coming out of Quaker tradition, is the use of persuasion. Of all these characteristics, it is probably the one that was most directly inspired through Greenleaf's experiences as a member of the Religious Society of Friends. What I take away from reading Greenleaf on decision making is what is our default position when it comes to how we choose to make decisions in organizations. Do we use persuasion first, or do we rely upon our positional leadership or even on coercion? Greenleaf suggests that servant-leaders will seek to use persuasion wherever possible, and that they will rarely, if ever, resort to using manipulation or coercion as a means of relating to others. Friends, in their Meetings for Business, go to extraordinary lengths to listen carefully to others, and to seek a sense of the meeting.

Part of what goes on today has to do with the pace of how decisions get made within our organizations. There also seems to me to be a higher degree of incivility in many places; one need only look at twenty-four-hour news channels to see that people aren't generally engaged in dialogue. It is mostly shouting at one another, and it strikes me as a damaging way of relating to one another. Servant-leadership can be a strong antidote to that. We've got a long way to go before it reaches the level of awareness that any of us would like to see, but I think that for many of us who are drawn to servant-leadership, it is in part a native desire to want to listen more, to use persuasion as much as possible.

Greenleaf talked about one of the most important things that he did having been his study of the history of the Religious Society of Friends, and that out of that came an understanding of the role that John Woolman had played as a Quaker in the early years of this country. Woolman spent decades traveling up and down the Eastern seaboard, visiting with those Quakers who, at that time, were slaveholders. Woolman's efforts to end slavery among Quakers involved his use of persuasion and listening. In particular, he adopted a Socratic method of asking open-ended questions of Quaker slaveholders that were designed to encourage thinking about the implications of what they were doing. It was a slow process in some ways, but over the course of thirty years Woolman managed to accomplish his goal through honest, friendly dialogue, through asking questions of Quaker slaveholders, and through the use of persuasion, so that by that point there were no longer any Quaker slaveholders in the colonies. It is an example of the power of persuasion and it is illustrative of the possibilities that are there if you are willing to take the time to listen and to use persuasion.

SF: What are your thoughts on the differences between knowing and doing, or understanding and practicing, when it comes to servant-leadership?

LS: I think sometimes there is a tendency to want to jump right into organizational practices of servant-leadership before the inner work has occurred. I have occasionally encountered people who are wonderfully excited about servant-leadership and who want to immediately attempt to bring servant-leadership into the organization. While, at one level, that is easily understood, it is important to consider both personal and organizational timing and readiness. Over the years, I've tried to emphasize the importance of laying the groundwork in right order: making sure the inner work has been started; identifying two or more people who have a shared passion and desire to introduce the idea of servant-leadership in an organization; bringing together folks in a voluntary and informal way for focused learning—basically tilling the soil, planting multiple seeds, and watering them in the hope of a kind of harvest at some point in time.

I love the example of Jack Lowe Sr., who, having battled tuberculosis, decided that he wanted to reshape TDIndustries, and to do so around servant-leadership. In 1970 or 1971, Jack had come across Robert Greenleaf's essay, *The Servant as Leader*. He bought hundreds of copies of that essay from the Greenleaf Center and began to share them with people in the company, inviting them to his home in groups of ten and having conversations. He asked many questions and invited even more questions from others. Through this process, which also reminds me of the John Woolman process in some ways, Jack Lowe Sr., was able to expand the idea of servant-leadership at TDIndustries. It is a great example of understanding and practicing servant-leadership personally before attempting to bring it into organizations in a formal sense.

In anything in life—and servant-leadership is no different in this way—there are differences between our understanding and practice. You can read a book and have a certain level of understanding of anything, but unless you are practicing it, or making repeated efforts to try to understand and practice it, the impact may not be too great. It is also important that we understand that there are no perfect servant-leaders. All servant-leaders are human and therefore fallible. With the best of intentions, at times, bad decisions can be made by anyone. And, there are sometimes those who look for a reason to dismiss any idea or person (in this instance, servant-leadership), who will point a finger and say, "See, I told you so."

We live in a very cynical time. I am not a historian, but it seems to me that the last fifty years has witnessed the emergence of the age of cynicism. There are many reasons why this is so. Yet to succumb to cynicism is, for me, something that I try hard not to do. I just don't see it as something that is good for anyone. The opportunities that come out of having an open heart and cautious optimism can be great. Greenleaf talked about being sort of a practical idealist, wanting to encourage change, both in ourselves and in the world, recognizing that it takes time and that rarely does substantive change occur overnight.

SF: Greenleaf wrote about servant-leadership in three distinct contexts: individuals, *The Servant as Leader* in 1970; organizations, *The Institution as Servant* in 1972; and organizational boards, *Trustee as Servant* in 1974. Would you share an insight or story concerning servant-leadership in one, two, or all three?

LS: There was a progression of Greenleaf's thinking around servant-leadership and it was in the context of his first three essays. In 1969, he wrote *The Servant as Leader* and published it in 1970. The first version of *The Servant as Leader* that Bob published was substantially different from the one that exists today and which has been in print since 1973. From 1970 to 1972, those first three years, there was a very different version of *The Servant as Leader* essay that he wrote. It differed from the revised version by about 50 percent, and it contained many more illustrations, examples, and insights into servant-leadership as it related to higher education. Greenleaf had written that first version for universities and colleges, faculty and trustees, presidents, and students. Interestingly he quoted a number of student leaders in that initial version of *The Servant as Leader*, which he later took out of the 1973 revision. One of the student leaders whom he quoted at that time was Hillary Rodham, now Hillary Rodham Clinton. Greenleaf had read a speech that she had given and was much impressed by her thoughtful expressions.

In 1973, Greenleaf published a substantial revision of *The Servant as Leader*. What seems clear is that his own thinking had evolved, and that he wanted to try to broaden out the potential for people to read that essay. He chose to do that by taking out much of the focus on higher education and replacing that content with other ideas and examples. Given the purpose that he had in mind, I think his instinct was right. Had he not done that, who knows where the servant-leader movement might be today? I think it had the intended outcome that he wanted.

Fast-forward from 1973 to 2003: Greenleaf's first version of *Servant as Leader* had not been available for thirty years, and I wanted to find a way to put it back into print. On several occasions throughout the 1990s, Jack Lowe Sr.'s wife, Harriet Lowe, had sent me notes urging me to find a way to bring the original 1970 version of that essay back into print. And so I ultimately took *Teacher as Servant*, plus the initial *Servant as Leader* essay, and a couple of other shorter pieces and brought them together in the book *The Servant-Leader Within* that was published by Paulist Press in 2003.

Robert Greenleaf's second essay, *The Institution as Servant*, was published in 1972. Historically it is the one that people wrestle with the most: How can a servant-led institution come to be? And, what does that mean for an organization to practice servant-leadership? Greenleaf's ideas are helpful guideposts for understanding what it means to bring servant-leadership into an organization and to try to live that out faithfully. One aspect of *The Institution as Servant* that has increasingly brought me into conversation with others has been the idea of *primus inter pares*, or, the first among equals. His thinking on the council of equals, the first among equals idea is powerful. He looks at the typical hierarchical model—the "Moses model," as he terms it—and talks about the problems with that approach. There has been a real flattening of organizations as a general trend over the last forty years, which has moved us in the direction of teams and councils.

So I have an interest in this idea of *primus inter pares*, particularly around this council idea: How can councils operate effectively as servant-led organizations? The U.S. Supreme Court is a great example of *primus inter pares* in the way in which it operates. I think we are closer to what Greenleaf was advocating in *The Institution as Servant*. My friend and colleague, George SanFacon, has pioneered this Council of Equals work, and he and I have collaborated on several writings and presentations on this in recent years.

In 1974, Greenleaf published the third essay in the Servant as Leader series, this one titled, *Trustees as Servants*. Greenleaf had looked at what would it take for institutions to be more likely to take on servant-leadership, and he came to realize that it was boards of directors, boards of trustees, where the ultimate leverage of power was to be found, and it was within boards where one might create the possibility of change. For Greenleaf, servant-leadership was very much at the heart of the true role of trustees. Yet, he also asked why is it that boards appeared unable to function in that way. One interesting piece that Greenleaf wrote about in *The Trustee as Servant* was the idea that perhaps boards of trustees should have their own advocate for the board, someone other than the CEO. Perhaps a kind of board ombudsman. He has some intriguing ideas. Greenleaf has had a profound—and I think often overlooked—impact on our understanding of boards, particularly for nonprofit boards, but also for-profit boards.

Two other comments: one is that Robert Greenleaf was a consultant to Lilly Endowment, one of the major grant-making foundations in the country, and through his consultancy with them throughout the 1970s, he began to have an influence on Lilly Endowment in terms of its own understanding of what it meant to transform institutions and society for the better through boards that could understand and practice servant-leadership in the ways that Greenleaf was talking about. And so it was that Lilly Endowment began to fund organizations and projects that were trying to create opportunities for boards to learn and practice as servant-led boards. Greenleaf's impact in the field of trustee education has been rather significant because of this relationship with Lilly Endowment and how seriously they took his thinking.

Also, John Carver's Policy Governance model has gained a great deal of understanding and practice over the past three decades. Carver, who has written and spoken on servant-leadership, has really gone out of his way to talk about how servant-leadership and Greenleaf's writings have helped to inspire his work. I find in Carver's work, and in Greenleaf's writings in *The Trustee as Servant*, some serious possibilities for improved ways of operating as a board and for lifting up both organizations and society in general. Everything takes longer, and progress seems always too slow, but when I look at trustee education I do see that we're moving ahead.

SF: You are well known for your work as a writer and editor in servant-leadership, going back to the early 1990s. During your years with the Greenleaf

Center (1990–2007), you cocreated a total of nine books, including five books of Bob Greenleaf's writings and four servant-leadership anthologies. I don't think many people are aware that 100 percent of all royalties on all the books you have worked on have gone to the organizations with whom you have worked, as yet another way of supporting the work of the organizations that you lead. In recent years, your work as a writer and editor has brought forth a series of wonderful new publications. Would you talk about that? What are some of these new publications, and what other ideas do you hope to work on in the future?

LS: Since 2007, I have intentionally given over as much of my time as I can to helping other servant-leader writers find audiences for their own ideas through various editing projects, as well as working collaboratively with a half-dozen writing partners on a widening range of essays and articles. I love editing and writing in equal measure; and, I have come to see my work as a servant-leader editor as a kind of personal calling by which I am able to serve both other authors and readers. The role of an editor is, by its nature, a collaborative one, and so I have always found great joy in the process of identifying potential authors, encouraging them to write, then working with many of them around the shaping of their ideas into the finished piece of work. I enjoy my relationships with publishers and have developed a number of friendships over the years. I have even enjoyed promoting sales and awareness of each new book over the years. I don't see it as "selling books"; rather, I view each publication as a new opportunity to further the awareness and practice of servant-leadership.

Let me try to list as succinctly as I can some of my recent publications work.

To start, I have cocreated the following books since 2007: *Scanlon Epic Leadership: Where the Best Ideas Come Together* [Paul Davis and Larry Spears, editors; 2008, Scanlon Foundation]; *The Human Treatment of Human Beings* [John F. Donnelly, author; Paul Davis and Larry Spears, editors; 2009, Scanlon Foundation]; *Within Your Reach: The Beatitudes in Business and Everyday Life* [Bill Bottum, author; Dorothy Lenz, George SanFacon, and Larry Spears, editors; 2010, Lulu]; *The Spirit of Servant-Leadership* [Shann Ferch and Larry Spears, editors; 2011, Paulist Press]; and, *Fortuitous Encounters: Wisdom Stories for Learning and Growth* [Paul Davis and Larry Spears, editors; 2013, Paulist Press]. Altogether, I have coproduced fourteen books since 1994.

As a writer, I have contributed one or more chapters to each of those books. Since 2007, I have also contributed chapters or Forewords to another half-dozen books edited by others, including the following titles: *The OnTarget Board Member: 8 Indisputable Behaviors* [Mike Condruff, Carol Gabanna, and

Catherine Raso, editors; 2007, Elim Group]; *Servant Leadership: Developments in Theory and Research* [Dirk van Dierendonck and Kathleen Patterson, editors; 2010, Palgrave Macmillan]; *The Jossey-Bass Reader on Nonprofit and Public Leadership* [James L. Perry, editor; 2010, Jossey-Bass]; *Leading Wisely in Difficult Times: Three Cases of Faith and Business* [Michael Naughton and David Specht, editors; 2011, Paulist Press]; *Setting the Agenda: Meditations for the Organization's Soul* [Edgar Stoesz and Rick M. Stiffney, editors; 2011, Herald Press]; and, *Forgiveness and Power in the Age of Atrocity: Servant Leadership as a Way of Life* [Shann Ray Ferch, author; 2012, Lexington Books]. All told, I think I have published essays and articles in twenty-seven books and a dozen journals since 1990.

Of course, Shann, since 2005, I have had the great joy of collaborating with you on the annual *International Journal of Servant-Leadership*. For readers who may not be familiar with it, *IJSL* is a wonderful publication that contains a wide range of both scholarly papers and essays by practitioners, as well as servant-leadership writings in the form of poetry, book and film reviews, and much more. It is a joint publication of Gonzaga University and the Spears Center. You serve as editor and I serve as senior advisory editor. Part of the excitement of this venture is the opportunity that gives to showcase the leading-edge writings of dozens and dozens of servant-leaders. I generally write one or two essays or articles for each issue of *IJSL*.

Many of my writings on servant-leadership can be found in each of these books and journals, and in pretty much all of the books that I have worked on since the early 1990s.

I started seriously writing when I was about ten years old. Writing and editing of all kinds has always been a focus of my work ever since. From the ages of ten to fifty, nearly all of the writing that I did involved essays and articles that I wrote on my own. However, starting in 2007, I began to experiment with cowriting with others. I quickly discovered that I enjoyed writing in collaboration even more than I had in writing hundreds of articles, essays, et cetera solo. Of my more recent articles, these are some of what I consider to be among my key writings:"The Seeker's Journey" [John Izzo and Larry Spears, 2007]; "Holistic Servant-Leadership: A Multi-Dimensional Approach" [George SanFacon and Larry Spears, 2008]; "Why Scanlon Matters: EPIC Leadership Principles" [Paul Davis and Larry Spears, 2008]; "Savoring Life Through Servant-Leadership" [Richard Leider and Larry Spears, 2009]; "Bill Bottum, Servant-Leader" [Larry Spears, 2009]; "Seeker's Anonymous: On Being a Seeker in the 21st Century" [Richard Leider and Larry Spears, 2010]; "Myers-Briggs and Servant-Leadership" [Ralph Lewis, Beth Lafferty, and Larry Spears, 2010]; "The Heart of Giving: Servant-Leadership and Purposeful Philanthropy" [Richard Leider and Larry Spears, 2011]; "The Promised Land: Robert Greenleaf, Bruce Springsteen, and Servant-Leadership" [Joe Albert and Larry Spears, 2012]; and "Understanding Fortuitous Encounters" [Paul Davis and Larry Spears, 2013]. I would guess that I have published some 300 articles or essays on servant-leadership since 1990.

While I have enjoyed doing many different things as an organizational leader and manager, going back thirty or forty years now, it is my belief that I have been able to make my greatest contributions as a writer, editor, and teacher.

Peter Tormey: I really liked what you talked about in your quote for the 2010 Gonzaga University news release in terms of what the servant-leader scholar role means to you in your affiliation with Gonzaga. I was wondering if you could talk a little bit about your feelings upon becoming the Gonzaga University Servant-Leader Scholar.

LS: It was in the late 1990s that I first had my initial contact with Mike Carey and Shann Ferch. I recall that Shann had sent me an essay that he had written. I was traveling and I had put it in my briefcase to read. I was in an airport in Memphis when I sat down and read it. I have worked with hundreds of contributing authors to books and newsletters and other sorts of publications, but there was something about this piece that Shann had written on servant-leadership and forgiveness that I found very touching. I went over to a pay phone—I didn't have a cell phone at that point in time, it was so long ago—and I called the number that was on the front page, he answered the phone. I told him how touched and impressed I was with the quality of what he had shared in that essay and that I very much would like to try to find a place to publish it. Eighteen months later, we did publish it as a separate essay titled, "Servant-Leadership, Restorative Justice, and Forgiveness." And, a year after that, I included it as a chapter in a book, *Practicing Servant-Leadership* [Jossey-Bass, 2004].

My initial encounters with Shann with Mike have grown and evolved over the years, and we have become friends and colleagues. In 2008, I began to teach the Servant-Leadership course that was designed by John Horsman as part of the master's program in Organizational Leadership, and to do so as an online course. I have also designed and taught a number of courses for Gonzaga's doctoral program in Leadership Studies.

I have a fondness for Gonzaga, one that is grounded in all the people I have met: students, alumni, faculty, administrators, everyone that I've encountered over the years represents servant-leadership very well. I view

Gonzaga University as a living laboratory of servant-leadership, which I think is unique. The depth of its commitment is also impressive. I look around and I see the *International Journal of Servant-Leadership*, and the undergraduate and graduate courses in servant-leadership that are being taught. All of that, plus other things, combine to make this an amazing place with which to be associated. So I'm happy to have a chance to deepen my involvement with this institution, and I'm looking forward to that.

PT: Well, I know Gonzaga is very much looking forward to having you on board in an increasing role with the university. We are absolutely just tickled to death to have you. I was delighted to hear, also, and the first thing that came to my mind is the university's mission, what a good fit that is in terms of servant-leadership—what we try to do is educate students to be people for others, with a strong emphasis on being leaders for others—with a Christian theme of serving others, and of Jesus washing the feet of folks. It kind of gave me goose bumps that we were able to connect with the world's preeminent expert on servant-leadership. So I was thrilled for that reason.

LS: Bob Greenleaf really has helped to create an opportunity for people who share this desire to want to act as servant-leaders and not to feel so lonely. We have a term, we have ideas that we share in common, and there is now a movement that is there. Greenleaf did not invent servant-leadership of course—it has been around for thousands of years—but he coined the term servant-leader in 1970 in his "Servant as Leader" essay. And so, by naming this he helped to lay the groundwork for the modern servant-leadership movement. For many years now, I have simply tried to do whatever I can to help carry his message forward into the twenty-first century.

PT: And that movement has captivated a lot of corporate America. I understand that there are a number of companies on the *Fortune* magazine list of the 100 Best Companies to Work For who are servant-led. I wonder if you could define what servant-leadership is.

LS: Sure. For me, it does start with Robert Greenleaf's definition. He said that the servant-leader is servant-leader first, and had what he called his "best test" of servant-leadership: Are those served people who wish to strive to be servant-leaders themselves, are they healthier, wiser, freer, are they more autonomous? Are they more likely to become servants? And then what is the effect on the least privileged of society? Will they benefit, or at least not be further deprived?

This is the core definition that Greenleaf used for servant-leadership. There are many definitions that have grown up around servant-leadership in the last forty-five years since he coined that term. That was Greenleaf's definition, and the one that I think has taken root in the hearts of many people. It is also the definition, which, in many ways, acts as a bridge between people of different faiths because with that understanding people are able to come together in a shared commitment to serving and leading others. I find in servant-leadership not only the inherent depth of what can be, but also a kind of bridge between people of different faiths, different philosophies. If you go to a servant-leadership conference, you find all sorts of people who are there from secular businesses as well as from faith-based institutions, higher education, foundations, health care, and other areas.

In business, there is a growing trend around companies that are working with servant-leadership, some for as long as forty years now. There are a handful of large institutions that are utilizing it in different ways: Starbucks would probably be the biggest one. The Men's Wearhouse, ServiceMaster, Southwest Airlines, TDIndustries, the Vanguard Group, and others that are trying to faithfully live it out in their workplaces. There are many smaller organizations—businesses, health care institutions, schools, and others—where it is also being practiced. The organizational preferences for servant-leadership are many and profound.

Greenleaf, though, was very clear in saying that the servant-leadership starts with the individual, so servant-leadership is not something that you can just bring into an institution, it is something that begins in the hearts of at least a core group of folks within an organization. Once it does that, it is sometimes capable of changing organizations.

PT: In what ways is it capable of transforming organizations? It sounds so counterintuitive at first, when you think of the word, "leader," it seems to thrust the self into it: "I'm the leader. The focus is on me." This sort of turns that one on its head in a sense and takes the *I* out of the leader in many ways. However, I think that's the magic of it. I wonder if you could talk a little bit about how is it better able to negotiate difficulties and lead businesses more effectively in this time.

LS: Let me take one step back and say that one of the unique aspects about servant-leadership is that Greenleaf talked about the servant as leader, not the leader as servant. I have occasionally seen an incorrect reference to Greenleaf's essay as "The Leader as Servant," rather than "The Servant as Leader"; however, to think of "The Leader as Servant" is a misunderstanding of the essential nature of Greenleaf's message. Robert Greenleaf is talking about someone who is a natural servant, and who sees the opportunity to take on a leadership role in order to help others at a higher level, to be more helpful within an organization. Now, in practice, positional leaders may also be natural servants and thus, servant-leaders. Some positional leaders understand that serving others is at the core of what it means to be a good leader.

There is a growing body of articles and case studies, doctoral dissertations, and other sorts of written material on how some of these companies that have been working with it for some time have been able to do so successfully in a difficult economic environment, and to help empower people to make more decisions on their own. It does need to begin with the individual, but there are so many things in life that begin with a single individual.

I find that servant-leaders tend to attract other servant-leaders because they recognize and appreciate what is in their hearts. I think once you begin to practice servant-leadership, it can have a multiplying effect. You may find in a short time a strong group of servant-leaders who want to become more active and be more engaged in organizations.

PT: Would it be correct to describe moving toward a position of servant-leadership, as really sort of initiating within one's heart, within one's motivation perhaps? Does it start with the motivation being other-centered as opposed to self-centered, or is it that simple?

LS: Servant-leadership does begin with the desire to want to serve others. However, that does not mean that you are forever kept from considering your own needs. Robert Greenleaf was very clear in saying that servant-leaders have the opportunity to grow in their own servant-leadership, and in who they are as people. Servant-leadership doesn't call for total selflessness; rather, it is a melding of concern for the well-being of others, coupled with deep self-awareness. I am reminded of the subtitle of Robert Greenleaf's book, *Servant Leadership: A Journey into the Nature of Legitimate Power and Greatness.* Servant-leadership teaches us that by serving and leading, we help ourselves and others to understand the meaning of legitimate power and greatness.

Part of what motivated Greenleaf to develop this idea of servant-leadership was his recognition that in organizations it is difficult for the lone chief to bear the responsibility of making all major decisions. No matter how careful, smart, and committed a single person is, it is simply not a good way—certainly for that person because there's a lot of stress, not to mention the fact that by not involving others in decision-making you are keeping them from also having an opportunity to grow and an organization from having the benefit of the thinking of many in decision-making.

Greenleaf felt that by having more people involved in important decision-making you would get, overall, a better level of quality decisions within that organization; the person at the top would have less stress upon himself or herself; and those who are involved as a team, grow as leaders in a way that might not have been possible. So, all of this is part of what goes into organizational transformation when organizations seek to practice servant-leadership faithfully.

PT: I think you mentioned some dissertations and other books that have been written about that. Have you studied or written about organizations that have indeed gone through this very distinct transformation as a result of being servant-led?

LS: I have published five anthologies of servant-leadership writings over the last fifteen years: *Reflections on Leadership* [John Wiley & Sons, 1995]; *Insights on Leadership* [John Wiley & Sons, 1998]; *Focus on Leadership* [with Michele Lawrence, John Wiley & Sons, 2002]; *Practicing Servant-Leadership* [with Michele Lawrence, Jossey-Bass, 2004]; and the fifth one, Shann Ferch and I have done together [*The Spirit of Servant-Leadership*, Paulist Press, 2011]. Each of these works include chapters about organizations and their practices of servant-leadership.

It is an interesting challenge I would say, because this focus on "It starts with the individual" is of paramount importance. Greenleaf believed that servant-leadership could become established in organizations in a number of different ways, including informally. When he was at AT&T, he used to run skunkworks projects. He would see a problem and he would try to create some sort of solution, sometimes outside the normal chain of command. That is another way in which servant-leadership can take hold. There are institutions, for instance, where there may be a particular department, but not the institution as a whole, that has embraced servant-leadership.

You can find all sorts of ways of introducing the idea. The most successful way I think, though, is how each individual who aspires to be a servant-leader, seeks to live his or her life. As you do that in a genuine, authentic way, people come to recognize that. If you see someone who, day in and day out, is trying to help others, I think it's an infectious kind of experience. We have within us a desire to serve others as well, and sometimes all we need is to understand someone whom we know. When I speak on servant-leadership, I often start by talking how we all have experiences of knowing servant-leaders, but perhaps we don't recognize them as having been that until years later.

Sometimes we have a tendency to think, "Well, it's a wonderful idea but I'm not Mahatma Ghandi, I'm not Mother Teresa, I can't do it, I'm not that great a person." The reality is that we are surrounded by servant-leaders, and that we often fail to recognize them for who they are. There are so many people around us who may have never heard the word "servant-leader" either, but who are living their lives in ways that they are trying to serve others and are trying to provide leadership.

We are aided to the degree that we can visualize ourselves as authentic servant-leaders, recognizing there are no perfect servant-leaders, that we all have our frailties and faults, but that this does not preclude our acting in a serious way in an effort to be servant-leaders, to help our institutions, to help others to become servant leaders. That is one of the things I find most encouraging.

PT: So, it can be anyone who has this orientation, this worldview of serving others. I think of my wife, for example. Do you think that there is a spiritual essence, or spiritual aspect, component, of servant-leadership?

LS: Robert Greenleaf wrote a lot about spirit. And, in some of his writings, he looked at both spirituality and religious institutions and their own practices of servant-leadership. One of his overlooked essays is one called, "The Servant as Religious Leader." It is a great essay to read in terms of looking at how people of faith can seek to act as servant-leaders, and yet it also points out that just because you are a person of you faith doesn't mean, necessarily, that you are a servant-leader. Likewise, there are servant-leaders who are not necessarily people who see themselves as people of faith, but who are clearly servant-leaders.

For Greenleaf, spirit was at the heart of his understanding of servant-leadership. He commented that it is sometimes easy to note the absence of spirit in a workplace, or in a person. Sometimes you feel it when it is present, and sometimes you may note its absence. We all have had the feeling, and many of us have the experience, of working in places where we felt uninspired in some way. Spirit is very much at the core of servant-leadership.

It is also true that people of different faith backgrounds and philosophies have been drawn to servant-leadership, so I think spirituality and faith practices can enter into it, but you do not have to be a person of any professed faith in order to be a servant-leader. Many people who I have encountered are, but I have met many people who are genuine, authentic servant-leaders who are operating within another context: a secular business framework, for instance, or in a higher-education context that isn't necessarily in a religious school setting. Throughout the decades I have met servant-leaders who were also Christian, Jewish, Muslim, Buddhist, agnostic, Secular Humanist and other faith or philosophical traditions.

PT: Which would make it even more inclusive. It seems so very inclusive, conceptually.

LS: That's right. In fact, I have a growing belief that as impactful as servant-leadership has been up to this point, sort of at the forty-five-year mark, that potentially there is still a much greater leap forward to be made through the notion that the language of servant-leadership can potentially act as a unifying force for people of different faith backgrounds—Christian, Jewish, Muslim, humanists, and others who can seem to be divided by walls. I think that servant-leadership is potentially a kind of a new bridge for people of different faiths. I think there is more about servant-leadership that needs to be explored, and I hope to be able to spend more time one on this as part of the work that I will be doing here at Gonzaga, as well as through my work with the Spears Center.

I had the opportunity to spend some time with Robert Greenleaf shortly before his death. I have always appreciated the chance that I had to do that. After his death in September 1990, his family sent me three or four boxes of his personal papers. As I read through these pieces that were in these boxes, I began to realize that there were, first, a dozen, and then two dozen, and in the end almost a hundred pieces that Greenleaf had written over a fifty-year period. These writings were virtually unknown to people, and I eventually figured out that Greenleaf had written many of them as a means of clarifying his own understanding of all kinds of issues, and without any intention of publication.

Ultimately, over fifty of those uncovered pieces of writing were published in two books in 1996: *On Becoming a Servant-Leader* [Robert K. Greenleaf; Don Frick and Larry Spears, editors; Jossey-Bass, 1996], and *Seeker and Servant* [Robert K. Greenleaf; Anne Fraker and Larry Spears, editors; Jossey-Bass, 1996]. *On Becoming a Servant-Leader* is a collection of his writings on organizational applications of servant-leadership and related ideas. *Seeker and Servant* is a collection of his writings on the nature of what it means to serve others and the search for meaning in one's life. Each of these books has come to be viewed as great sources of wisdom. I do not know whether Greenleaf ever thought of them as being published, but in going through these recovered writings, it became clear to me that many of these essays deserved a wider audience. I think many of us have grown because of our reading of Greenleaf's two books, published from the papers, after his death.

Then there were three more books of Greenleaf's writings that I put together and that were published after that (*The Power of Servant-Leadership* [Robert K. Greenleaf; Larry Spears, editor, Berrett-Koehler, 1998], *Servant Leadership [25th Anniversary Edition]* [Robert K. Greenleaf; Larry Spears, editor, Paulist Press, 2002], and *The Servant-Leader Within* [Robert K. Greenleaf; Hamilton Beazley, Julie Beggs, and Larry Spears, editors; Paulist Press, 2003]. So there are a total of five books of Robert Greenleaf's writings at this point, all published after his death.

Greenleaf had a lifetime of experience, both at AT&T and then later on as a consultant to organizations. I think his practices as a Quaker helped to inform his thinking as well. All this came together in a very unique person who looked at the world a little differently and who made the point of trying to help others by writing down his own thoughts on what it meant to serve, to lead, and to do so with spirit. In my own way, I have also tried to do this since 1990.

By the end of his life, Greenleaf was absent his ability to say much more than a word or two at a time, due to a series of strokes. A few years before these strokes, he had written a couple of letters to the Greenleaf Center board at that time, in which he said that he didn't know what the future held for servant-leadership or for the center, but that he hoped both might continue beyond his death. I like to think that Robert Greenleaf might somehow be aware of what has happened in the years since his death, and to see the ways in which the seeds that he planted through his writings in the 1970s and '80s have taken root in the hearts of people and inside organizations.

Even today, Greenleaf is not as well known as any number of other authors who have written on servant-leadership. Many of the better-known leadership authors have written and spoken about the ways in which Robert Greenleaf's writings have helped to inform and encourage their own thinking about leadership. One part of my own work since 1990 has involved bringing the ideas and writings of others more to the forefront, so that people can come to understand servant-leadership as Greenleaf wrote about it, through the lens of others who have been also influenced by Greenleaf. The servant-leadership anthologies have included contributions by people like Margaret Wheatley, Stephen Covey, Ken Blanchard, James Autry, and a whole host of others who we studied in our leadership courses here at Gonzaga University, and elsewhere.

PT: You have said that Greenleaf used writing as a higher form of thinking in many ways; to sort out his own ideas about something, would he take pen and paper, or did he sit at the typewriter or did he use computer screen?

LS: Actually, he started out writing by longhand, and then he switched to a typewriter and used carbon paper, which during those years when he was using carbon paper, it is kind of messy to sometimes make out some of the manuscripts. In the 1980s, though, someone connected to AT&T bought for him one of the very first AT&T personal computers. I believe it was an AT&T 6300 personal computer, which came out in 1982 or '83. Robert Greenleaf was in his late seventies at that point—an age at which many of us might not be inclined to want to learn some new skills involving a computer; yet, Greenleaf saw it as something of an adventure, and so he was brought a computer to his home and took the time to learn how to make use of it.

PT: So he was never tired of learning. He was obviously a lifelong learner all the way up to the very end. That's amazing, I think.

LS: As amazing as that is, there is an even more remarkable aspect to Greenleaf, the person, which I think is worth noting. At the age of forty, Bob Greenleaf heard the radio commentator of the time, Elmer Davis, say that he thought people shouldn't just retire, or at least that there were some who should not do that, and who had much more to give. Davis was encouraging people to think about preparing for the future, "to prepare for their old age," as the commentator put it. Greenleaf heard this radio message, and he writes that it spoke to him in a way that just made great sense. And so, at the age of forty he began to think about what might he do in his retirement years, and he thought, Well, I probably would take early retirement at age 60 from AT&T, and then try to do something else. He did not know what that would be, but from the ages of forty to sixty Greenleaf embarked on a very conscious effort to learn and to grow as a person, to prepare himself for whatever might come after his retirement from AT&T. He did this in different ways: he began to read more widely; he began to reach out to people from whom he thought he might learn something of value to his preparation. He wrote letters to folks, arranged meetings, went to visit people who had expertise in a whole host of areas that he was interested in. He had many phone conversations and correspondence with all sorts of people, including Eleanor Roosevelt, Karl Menninger, business leaders, military leaders, educators, religious leaders—people from various disciplines and people whom he was just curious about. While I believe that Greenleaf always had a curious nature—at the age of forty something inside him got switched on even more. He had a wide-ranging mind that led him to have all these conversations. Bob Greenleaf also developed several great friendships during this twenty-year period of seeking insight and direction.

Personal relationships, a growing intellectual sense of what might be—all these things fed into this two decades of preparation, so that by the time he retired in 1964 at the age of sixty from AT&T, enough clarity had come that he thought he might be able to be of some help to organizations as an organizational consultant. He also began to teach and to write.

I admire Greenleaf for many reasons, not the least of which is that I see in him somebody who took very seriously the possibilities and responsibility that we have to determine how we may best contribute to the welfare of others. From that perspective, he is a great example for anyone interested in personal growth and development.

PT: Greenleaf was a seeker in many ways. By seeking and by engaging with others he gained their wisdom and all this time it was percolating and being informed by all kinds of experiences. All of that was percolating in the background until the time came when he had that opportunity to start writing and to focus on that, that it was already probably formed. It is mind-boggling how powerful intentions can be, if you intend to do something for others and you're not sure what it is, but if you have faith and intentionality.

LS: Well, that is right. As I went through Greenleaf's unpublished writings after his death, I got a deeper insight into who he was as a person and began to see him more clearly. You could see how he was so firmly committed to seeking meaning in his own life, in its implications for the people he loved, for institutions, for the country, and for the world. There was a five-year gap between the initial discoveries of these unpublished writings and the publication of half of them into these two books. By the time we were into the book preparation process, it was clear that there was no other title to give to this one book other than *Seeker and Servant*, because it absolutely captured what the content of that book was about and reflected who Greenleaf was as a human being. We titled the other book, *On Becoming a Servant-Leader.*

If you look at what it means to grow as a person, sometimes you have to take risks, and I have found in Greenleaf and in his writings personal encouragement for taking those risks. There is also a richness that I find in Greenleaf's writing, and in rereading his work, that never ceases to amaze me. Some things you can read, reread, and continually find something that you hadn't picked up on before, and Greenleaf is much like that, or at least for me has been very much like that.

PT: You are now teaching online graduate courses in servant-leadership for Gonzaga University. What has that experience been like for you?

LS: I love it! I have learned so much through the experience. For one thing, I have learned that the teaching of online courses does not prohibit the possibility of creating community, nor is it an impediment to encouraging an authentic understanding and practice of servant-leadership. One of the things I like so much about the online course approach is the use of our "Blackboard" platform, and how carefully it has been thought about in the way it has been created. I have also witnessed a greater depth of exchange and engagement among students in the courses. Online learning environments seem to encourage the crafting of more carefully considered responses, replies, and sharing of ideas. When you have a little more time to think about and to respond to a question that somebody has asked, or where you can share a relevant story, there can be a greater depth of engagement that comes from that kind of learning environment.

I have had some long-standing interest in Myers-Briggs and have recently cowritten several essays on Myers-Briggs and servant-leadership that have been published. Myers-Briggs identifies a number of different distinctive aspects of personality, one of which is whether you are an introvert or an extrovert. In the classroom environment, extroverts tend to dominate discussions. Introverts usually take longer to think about their responses, and that tends to give the edge in self-expression to extroverts inside the classroom. However, in the online environment there is a leveling of the playing field so that everyone has an equal opportunity. Also, I find that the relative anonymity of the online environment encourages students to share relevant real life experiences that pertain to the topics that we discuss. That, in turn, deepens the dialogue and learning for everyone. I have become a major proponent of online learning. I think it is a very important and impactful way of learning, and I hope to do much more with it in the future.

PT: And what about the *International Journal of Servant-Leadership*?

LS: *The International Journal of Servant-Leadership* was started in 2005, and is something that Shann Ferch and I enjoy collaborating on. Shann is the editor, and I serve as senior advisory editor. It is a joint publication of Gonzaga University and the Spears Center for Servant-Leadership. As a publication, I believe that it has an important role to play in the global spread of servant-leadership. In higher education, there are many people now who have been introduced to servant-leadership through the journal. It provides an opportunity for people to understand that servant-leadership is also an area for legitimate research, writing, teaching—as a field of study, as an academic discipline. So that's part of why the journal is important to me, and part of why I get such a kick out of being involved with it.

Chapter Five

Margaret Wheatley

Interviewed by Larry C. Spears and John Noble

Margaret Wheatley writes, teaches, and speaks about radically new practices and ideas for how we can live together harmoniously in these chaotic times. She has worked in organizations of nearly all types, on all continents, and is a committed global citizen. Her aspiration is to help create organizations and communities where people are seen as the blessing, not the problem. She is president emeritus of the Berkana Institute (www.berkana.org), a charitable global foundation supporting life-affirming leaders around the world. Dr. Wheatley has been an organizational consultant since 1973, as well as a professor of management in two graduate business programs. She received her doctorate in organizational behavior from Harvard University, an MA in systems thinking from New York University, and has been a research associate at Yale University. She is the author of many award-winning books, including Leadership and the New Science *(1992, 1999),* A Simpler Way *(1996), and* Turning to One Another: Simple Conversations to Restore Hope to the Future *(2002). She is a powerful advocate for servant-leadership worldwide. Special thanks to John Noble, director of the Greenleaf Centre-United Kingdom, for his involvement in this interview.*

Larry Spears: Do you recall when you first encountered Robert Greenleaf's writings and any remembrances of your initial impressions?

Margaret Wheatley: I've been trying to remember. I think it was through Max DePree. What I enjoy most about Greenleaf's work is realizing that every time I go back, I read something that feels completely new and relevant. And each time I'll read a paragraph or an article it suddenly feels completely contemporary and relevant and it's different from what I noticed last time. In that way his work stays very contemporary and exceedingly relevant. I think that's the mark of a great thinker. It's not just that he was a visionary and saw the need for the servant as leader. It's truly great concepts and ideas that are timeless and fundamental. That's what I enjoy most. Every time I pick up anything of his to read I realize that I'm going to be surprised again. It's not the same old thing.

LS: Is there any particular thought or idea about servant-leadership that has struck you as a source of wisdom or importance?

MW: I was recently struck by Greenleaf's admonition to "do no harm." I've been saying to a number of colleagues that doing no harm is becoming exceedingly difficult. It's not just about doing good, it's actually avoiding harm. We don't see the consequences of our actions. America is in the midst of a huge "wake up call" about what is the cost to the rest of the world for us to be living the life we are living. It isn't about terrorist activity; it's about noticing that we put an extraordinary demand on the rest of the world for resources and energy, and that our way of life does not work well for most other people because of the demands we put on them. So that's what I've been feeling about "doing no harm"—we don't even know what we're doing that's causing harm. I know Greenleaf wrote that in a much simpler time, but I was really struck by that this time through.

LS: In light of the events of September 11th, 2001, have you any thoughts as to what servant-leadership has to offer to the world today that might be useful, and what we, who are involved in this work, may be thinking positively about?

MW: That's a very important question. I have been asking: "What is the leadership the world needs now, and what are we learning about leadership from actually being followers?" By this I mean some of us who have been leaders are now followers, watching our government and our military trying to lead us. What are we learning about all this? I think the questions are writ large. "What are you learning now that you are a follower? What makes for effective leadership?"

Now more than ever, we have to fundamentally shift our ideas of what makes an effective leader. We have to shift them away from this secretive, command and control, "We know what's best." We have to leave all that behind, even though it may be effective in the moment. I'm certainly learning that there are different needs at different times when you are a leader. Different styles, different modalities. But what I find in servant-leadership that I still find missing in the world is this fundamental respect for what it means to be human. And I think that right now the greatest need is to have faith in people. That is the single most courageous act of a leader. Give people resources, give them a sense of direction, give them a sense of their own power, and just have tremendous faith that they'll figure it out.

We need to move from the leader as hero, to the leader as host. Can we be as welcoming, congenial, and invitational to the people who work with us as we would be if they were our guests at a party? Can we think of the leader as a convener of people? I am realizing that we can't do that if we don't have a fundamental and unshakable faith in people. You can't turn over power to people who don't trust. It just doesn't happen. So what I think I'm learning from September 11th is that it's possible that people really are motivated by altruism, not by profit, and that when our hearts open to each other we become wonderful. The level of compassion and gentleness that became available, taking a little more time with each other, all of that, I think, has shown me the things that I have treasured for a long time in people. But I think it's very clear, and so we have an opportunity to notice how good we are. If you don't have faith in people, you can't be a servant. I mean, what are you serving? If you're not serving human goodness, you can't be a servant. For me it's just that simple. There is no greater act on the part of the leader than to find ways to express that great faith in people.

The other part about the timelessness of servant-leadership is, what do you do if you can't control events? There is no longer any room for leaders to be heroes. I think one really needs to understand that we have no control, and that things that we have no control over can absolutely change our lives. I think it will take a little while for Americans to really accept that there is no control possible in this greater interconnected world. There are lots of things we can do to prepare, but there is no control. One of the great ironies right now is that no matter how good you were as a business before September 11th and no matter how skilled you were at planning, and no matter how skilled you were at budgeting, everything has shifted. The only way to lead when you don't have control is you lead through the power of your relationships. You can deal with the unknown only if you have enormous levels of trust, and if you're working together and bringing out the best in people. I don't know of any other model that can truly work in the world right now except servant-leadership.

Even within the military, *command and control* is not what's making it work right now, and it hasn't for a long time. I was just reading about a huge fiasco with the Delta Force as they went into Afghanistan at the start of our military action there October 2001. Instead of their normal procedure, which is to operate as small teams, and work in quiet and stealth they were parachuted in—one hundred of them—because that's how central command decided they should be used. And they were furious, absolutely furious! They nearly got killed, they got out by the skin of their teeth, and they had several casualties. They exclaimed, "You can't do this to us! We know how to fight. You can't create these huge theatrical events and you can't have centralized control and expect us to do our job." So, even under the facade of command and control, one of the things I've always noticed in the military is that it works on the basis of deep relationships, long-term training, and relying on every individual soldier—especially in special operations. I can't think of any other model than servant-leadership that works in times of uncertainty. Our time is now!

John Noble: What were the markers in your life, the people and events that have shaped your thinking and helped to get you to where you are now?

MW: The list of people changes depending on where I am right now in my life. But I do believe that there were seminal events, there were a few moments that I will always remember. And the reason I don't want to go for people is that the list keeps changing. Just now, the people who inform me most are the earlier historians, like Otto Spengler and Arnold Toynbee, who had an organic theory of civilizations as living beings, which is quite similar to how I'm feeling about this time in history. It's one of decline, the winter of Western civilization.

In terms of events I think that the one that is still really pertinent to me was when I realized that as consultant, no matter what we did, we really didn't succeed. I was working as consultant to a large consultancy firm and asked them to recall a successful engagement and what made it work. I realized that people couldn't, and if they did, it was one little event in a long stream of work. I've had the same experience of feeling completely frustrated, and I wrote about this in *Leadership and the New Science*. I think it was that realization that opened me to asking if there might be another way of looking at all of this? That's when I really started looking back to my former discipline, science. I feel very grateful to have studied what I studied so that at one point I could bring it all together. I was comfortable reading science and loved the scientific imagination and also had the historical imagination and love of literature, and loved to be in philosophical questioning. And all of those weren't connected for me until I grew to notice that they could be connected. What I'm doing now is not anything I actually created. It really does feel like the work I've been prepared to do.

JN: Over the last few years we have increasingly heard the phrase "spirituality in the workplace." What does that phrase mean to you and where have you seen spirituality in the workplace particularly epitomized?

MW: For a long time I was terrified by the phrase, the combination of spirituality and the workplace. I was afraid of how we might use spirituality rather than simply honoring the fact that people are spiritual beings, people have spirit. This is not even a religious viewpoint. There is such a thing as the human spirit. It's an awareness that people have something beyond the instrumental or the utilitarian. People have deep yearnings, a quest for meaning, and an ability to wonder. This is a nonreligious view of what spirituality might mean.

When did we forget this, about being human? When did human beings become so instrumentally viewed, and when did we start to see ourselves as objects, just to be filled with information and sent to work? When did we lose that awareness? It's just mind-boggling if you think about it. I feel the same sort of puzzlement at the whole focus on emotional intelligence now. When did we forget this? It really shows you the bizarre side of our Western civilization, that we have to relearn what is so obvious in other cultures.

When spirituality became connected with the workplace in the 1990s it was initially just another way to motivate people. There were many of us saying, "Be careful here." Because, if the only reason a boss is going to acknowledge that someone has a spiritual life is to figure out how to get more work out of them, and if they don't get more work out of them, are they then going to forget the fact that we all have spirit?

Then we had a nice shift to the idea that if you don't acknowledge that people have spirit, you really can't have a productive workplace. It wasn't using spirit for productivity; instead, it was acknowledging who the person is, who the whole person is. Now I see our spirit in the questions we're asking. People are questioning the meaning of life. The meaninglessness of just working harder, consuming more, becoming disconnected from your children, these large questions have started to well up in people. *We do all have spirits.*

In terms of organizations, I look to see those organizations that describe back to me a real understanding of what is a human being. They don't have to use the words *soul* or *spirit*, but I get from them that they have a deep appreciation of fundamental creativity and caring, that they really rely on the wholeness of the people who work there. I haven't seen it in a lot of large corporations recently. Even those that had those strong values, they've been whipped around in the past year. But I consistently hear this from smaller manufacturing companies. I've had some wonderful conversations with those folks because they really understand and rely on the people who work there. They do all sorts of innovative things without consciously talking about spirituality in the workplace. What they talk about is human beings. That's more than enough for me! You know, if we can just understand what it means to be human then that brings in our spirits.

JN: *It's a Wonderful Life* has been a favorite film of mine for as long as I can remember, and George Bailey a personal hero. How did you make the connection with servant-leadership and how did you set about making that wonderful video? [*It's a Wonderful Life: Leading Through Service*, 22 minutes, Advanced Knowledge.]

MW: Well, I have to give credit to the producer, who didn't know a lot about servant-leadership and just said to me, "I think this movie is about servant-leadership." I just said, "Please let me write this." It was interesting for me knowing the lens they were going to use to go into that movie, which I hadn't really watched *carefully*—it's always on at Christmas. I think it came at the right time because I was to my own developing awareness of how confining it was to believe we knew what our life purpose was, and I had just written about that in what was a sort of spiritual autobiography.

I got into the film having already had that awakening in my own consciousness, that you really need to stay available to life and to what life wants you to do. When I looked at the movie, it was just such a great teacher for me, personally, about what it's like to be present and respond to the needs of people as they come to you. To be able to see that at the end of your life there was direction, there was guidance, but the only way you were aware of the guidance was to just surrender. And, of course, that's the highest spiritual practice.

LS: Can you elaborate a little on some of the qualities that George Bailey has as a servant-leader?

MW: What's interesting about George Bailey is his unintentional servant-leadership, which is also spontaneous and from the heart. I think it's an interesting question for any of us if we just felt free to go where our hearts led us in the moment. How do we respond to someone instead of hiding behind a role or some old rule—this is something that I think Jim Autry's poetry really captures. If, in a workplace, someone comes to you with a deep need and you can only respond with, "Well, this is the policy." Or, "I'm sorry. I'd love to make an exception, but if I make an exception for you I'd have to make an exception for everybody." It's just one of the most crippling phrases and thoughts we have in our society. You know, we just can't seem to respond at the level of the individual. We think that if we do, everyone else will be angry at us or want the same thing, yet it's not how life is at all. It is about what George Bailey did, that individual response, in the moment where he let his heart open and lead him. And when you do that you don't actually feel that you are sacrificing something. It's really interesting that when you are responding as your heart leads you, you are actually deeply satisfied even though, as in the case of George Bailey, it led him to an entirely different life. It didn't lead him away from Bedford Falls, and it didn't lead him out into the world. His heart just kept him responding to current crises at home. But I don't think in those moments that we experience it as sacrifice. We experience it as very fulfilling always to just respond to a person who needs something.

What I see in organizations are the boxes of our understandings of who we can be for each other. And those boxes in our organizations, which are also boxes of the psyche, really make it impossible for most people to act spontaneously the way George Bailey did, to just help when help is needed. When there's a crisis of any kind, whether it's a crisis like in that movie, or in real life like the crisis we've recently gone through, we don't see people hesitating to figure out how to serve. People don't hesitate; they just hope that what they're doing at a very instantaneous and spontaneous level will help somebody else.

What I think about crisis is that it's an easy opportunity to see how good we are, spontaneously. But if you look at life in organizations, it's amazing how fear-based they are, so that we are afraid of spontaneity. We are afraid of people's spirits, actually. We are afraid that if we give people any room they'll go off on some crazy direction with the work. I encounter this all the time. A manager will say, "We can't just give people choice here, we can't give people enough room to define meaningful work for themselves because God knows what they'll do." We always assume that they'll take the organization in a completely different direction. We are so afraid of each other that we want to box it into a plan, to a job description. And the loss of that, what we lose with that fear of each other, is extraordinary.

I am frequently struck by the great tragedy of how we have constructed work, the great loss. We've made it so hard to be in good relationships, we've made it so hard for people to contribute, we've made it so difficult for people to think well of themselves and then we say, "As a leader I'll come and I'll pump you up and I'll give you my vision, I'll make you feel we can do it." But it's not based on a deep love of who people are, a deep respect. As a leader, how do you pump up what has been killed?

I actually had an experience of this on a symbolic level. I was with a group of nuns in a chapel and one of them fainted, and before the medics came (apparently this was not unusual, because she had some sort of condition) nobody panicked. They called 911, but before help got there we just sat there in prayer for this person as other sisters went up and held her—it was all very gentle. And then the medics rushed in and they had oxygen and they had defibrillators, all sorts of high-tech equipment, and they surrounded this woman and just started clamping machines on to her body and then pumping in oxygen. I thought they were blowing up a balloon!

The symbology of it for me is that we are in our organizations and we've actually created a lot of death and destruction and a complete loss of people's confidence in themselves. Leaders don't have confidence in people. And then we rush in with this high-tech machinery, and just try and pump up people and motivate them with a new initiative or a new computer system or a new leadership vision. But what goes on in organizations is often not based on people being human. It's based on people being objects to be used for the accomplishment of goals of a very utilitarian kind.

"Whom do we serve as leaders?" I've asked that question of a lot of people. Whom do we serve? We are serving human beings. That is a radical shift in this culture at this time. But we are serving human beings, and the best way to know who another human being is, is to notice yourself fully, what you need, what's meaningful to you, what gives you heart in your work. If we could just notice our own humanness it would be a very big step forward to being able to relate to other people. If we are a leader, especially if we notice our own humanness, we notice that we have spirit, we notice that we have questions of meaning. I think all of the work that is done in helping leaders to wake up to their own humanity and their own spirituality is very essential work. It also keeps us away from using servant-leadership as the next instrument of control.

LS: There's one more theme in *It's a Wonderful Life* that strikes me. There is a Quaker phrase, Speaking Truth to Power. Have you found ways in your work to encourage people to lovingly confront the people in power when things are not right and need to be addressed, but in a way that also honors those in power as human beings?

MW: I have. In the past I have relied on processes that would allow people to listen to each other, and I haven't relied on what I would rely on now, which is personal courage. I was just reading a survey of fifty thousand workers in which half of them said they'd never dream of speaking up at work. And we are dealing with many, many years now of people having tried to give voice to their concerns and then being met with rebuff or ridicule or being told, "It's not your job!" And so we have had now for a long time an incredibly dependent workforce that is quite hostile. So we get *Dilbert*! *Dilbert* is the best representative of our deep cynicism for all those years of disrespect and maltreatment. People say to themselves, "Well, I'm not going to tell them anything, because they don't listen and they're a bunch of idiots, and I tried and it didn't work." We have our own internal conversation that keeps us from stepping forward. But then as employees we just get angrier and angrier and sometimes that erupts at meetings. This sometimes happens if there's a leader who says, "Well, I really want to find out what the pulse of the organization is. I'm going to start doing breakfast meetings." And then all they get is grief from people. I think it's one of the worst things you can advise a leader to do, especially if you know there's all that pent-up anger.

What I found works is if I can shift the content of the conversation and the dynamic, so as to move it from cynicism and anger to something more helpful. To do this, I change who is in the conversation. If the organization is struggling with something, and it's stayed within a certain level of employees and the boss, or we are trying to think through an issue but it's just our small little team; whenever we're stuck, then is the time to invite people in who aren't normally included.

It's the simplest solution but it's so powerful. It's actually a biological principle, which is when a living system is suffering and in ill health, the way to create more health is to connect it to more of itself. You create feedback loops from different parts of the system. It works at the level of our own bodies as a living system in that if we're suffering from some disease it doesn't help to just treat the symptom, we have to look at our whole life and look for information from other parts of our system. What are our sleeping patterns, what is our anxiety level, what's our exercise level? It doesn't work to look at just the one problem. We need information from our whole system.

This same activity also works brilliantly in organizations, to bring in customers, to bring in students, to bring in congregants, to bring in the people we think we don't need to hear from. Usually we fear hearing from them, because we believe we'll only hear complaints and anger. But in fact when you create more diversity, more plurality in the conversation, people step forward and demonstrate that they too care about the organization. As a process I rely on this now to an extraordinary degree. If we are in a certain pattern, if we are angry with each other, if we can't figure out how to solve the problem, bring in new voices. And then all the dynamics shift and you get really useful information that helps you then to see the problem differently.

I have a great belief in the power of whole systems, getting the whole system in the room. And it changes us from being angry and rigid: It changes us as individuals to realizing that, "Wow, I never thought of that!" "Gee, do you really see it that way?" We're going through that at a national level right now. I mean, there are new voices in the room. We're learning a lot about Islam, we're learning a lot about oil and Arab-U.S. relations, we're learning a lot about globalization. We have available now a lot more information that can really help us change our minds, as long as we are willing to be in that conversation.

If you want to change the conversation, you change who's in it. That doesn't mean that you have to coach people on how to be empathic presenters to a leader. You don't have to coach a leader on how not to get angry if someone's giving them terrible feedback. You just get out of those intensely personal and confrontational moments because you have a lot of new voices in the room. And people really do get interested as soon as they realize there is a fundamentally different perspective available. Most people actually get interested in that. I have been in hierarchical situations where the voice that shocked everyone with its perspective was a young woman. A new employee, female, who suddenly said something and everyone went, "Wow!" I've also seen it happen in faculties when we listen to students for the first time, or we listen to the people who hired our graduates. You never know where these comments are going to come from. They're usually so shocking that people are humbled and climb down off their soapboxes.

I want very much to say something about personal courage. One of the things that is sorely lacking in our lives is a necessary level of courage to stand up against the things we know are wrong, and for the things we know are right. There has been a kind of complacency—it feels more fear-based to me—where people, especially in organizations, are too afraid to speak up and we have become, I believe, moral cowards in a way. We give all sorts of reasons why we can't speak up. There are so many grievances in organizations that I think people have developed a sense of helplessness about it, and I understand that feeling of helplessness and saying, "I would never speak up." But I also live with an awareness that if we don't start speaking up we are going down a road that will only lead to increased devastation, and destruction. Edmund Burke said, "The only thing necessary for the triumph of evil is for good men to do nothing." Julian of Norwich said, "We must speak with a million voices: it is the silence that kills."

I think we're in that place right now, and what I find personally so uncomfortable is that as much as I want to raise my own voice on behalf of several different issues, I notice that I feel more powerless than at any time in my life. I think that's part of the tension of this time, realizing that we have to lift our voices for the things that we believe in, whether it's inside an organization, or as a nation or as a planetary community. We feel that there are serious things that require our voice, and yet we also feel that it may not make a difference. That's the place I'm in every day right now. The other forces at work are exceedingly more powerful. I wonder whether we can rally ourselves as people around the things we care about, and really make the change. The essence of my work right now is based on that belief that we can get active in time, but I also realize that this is a time when there are exceedingly strong countervailing forces from our leaders. For example, leaders pursuing aggression as the solution, or business still wanting to maintain its hegemony in the world without assuming responsibility for broader needs, or America still believing it can act in isolation: Can we raise our voices on behalf of a different form of capitalism, a different form of compassion in our foreign policy, a different form of leadership in our organizations? I know if we don't raise our voices I can predict the future and it's very dark. If we *do* raise them, well, it has worked in the past. I am hopeful that it will work now, but I'm not nearly as certain as I'd like to be.

JN: In *Leadership and the New Science* you said that vision could no longer be the prerogative of the leader or CEO, and increasingly vision would have to be the shared vision of everyone in an organization. From your experience are you seeing that happening?

MW: The deeper theory under those statements was that vision was a field and that fields are those invisible forces that shape behavior. I find a lot more credence is being given to the understanding that there are fields we can't see, invisible influences that affect behavior. People would have called that far-out thinking before, but I find that people are much more open to that today than ten years ago. Creative vision is a powerful influence in shaping our behavior, and you don't need to specify a lot of controls or roles if you have vision. People can do what they think is right and it can lead to a very coherent organization that is moving in concert toward achieving its vision. I have certainly come across a number of organizations that are working that way now, but I've also experienced in the last year or two that we've been in an enormous leap *backward* organizationally since times started to get uncertain. And now we'll just have to wait and see whether this level of uncertainty leads us forward into new ways of leading, or even further backward into command and control.

One of the possibilities is that try as we might we will realize that command and control just doesn't work because you can't control! We might be learning that. But recently, I have seen an enormously retrogressive movement in organizations based on fear, based on a weakening economy, based on what I think is a normal human reaction that when you get scared, you go backward; you default to what didn't work in the past! The power of vision to rally people or to give people a reason to live, to work hard and to sacrifice, we are seeing that at the national level right now. I don't necessarily think we're seeing it in its best form. It's true that in human experience, "if there is no vision the people perish," and whether there's a scientific explanation for that, or a spiritual explanation—I'd be just as happy these days with the spiritual definition—which is that a vision gives us a sense of possibility, a vision gives us a sense of working for something outside our narrow, self-focused efforts and therefore it rallies us at our deep human level to be greater than we are.

I'm happier with that explanation than field theory, and the reason I'm happier with it is that it is much more focused on what are the capacities in being human and how we can bring these forth. Science helps people be comfortable with that, and feel a little more trusting that you can create order through having a clear vision. But the next part of that is just as important. Once you have a clear vision you have to free people up. This is where autonomy comes in. People need to be free to make sense of the vision according to their own understandings and their own sensitivity to what's needed. If you combine the sense of great purpose and human freedom, if you can combine a vision that brings out the best of who we are and then gives us the freedom in how we're going to express that, that is how things work, in my experience.

JN: I previously worked for an organization where I once suggested that the leaders should begin to stand aside and ask the next generation of leaders for their vision and then begin to work with that in order to create a new future. My thought was that the current leaders could assume the role of stewards, supporters, servants. It didn't happen. Have you come across an organization that has worked in this way?

MW: Yes. It was the U.S. Army, under Gen. Gordon R. Sullivan. I am in absolute support of what you were trying to do. When Gen. Sullivan was chief of staff, which was in the early to mid-1990s, he said he spent 50 percent of his time thinking about the future and how to create an army for the world that was not yet known. He did simulations, he did think tanks, he did all sorts of scenario planning on what would the world be like and how could you create the army and technology to defend it. He had to think fifteen years ahead, minimally. He was really pushing out as far as he could see, using very good minds. So I did find that kind of thinking in the armed services. Then the Marines got into it seriously, and the Air Force did, too. But I think it's the only place I've seen it.

What I see in common contrast to that is organizations where to even *ask* younger people what their vision is feels like a breach of cultural norms like "They should be respecting *us*!" "Who are they? They don't know anything!" This is what I run into when I ask educators to involve students. We don't look to our younger generations as a source of any kind of wisdom, and partly I think that's because, as a culture, we so fear dying and we so fear aging. You created the role of elder there, and you were asking the senior people to become wise people who would be acting in service to the next generation. That's really countercultural in the West. You could have found support for that in most other cultures, but not in the West where we have so feared aging. As one of my African friends says, "You call your elders elderly, and that's part of the problem!" To actually ask leaders to think of themselves as elders and stewards for the future is a radical proposition. I think it's very important work and I'm not surprised it didn't go anywhere because of the weight of the culture.

One of the things I've been quite intrigued by is the number of younger leaders I have encountered who are college age, who are now intent on training high school kids to be leaders. They're not even looking to us anymore! They'd love it if we talked to them, but they acutely feel the need to steward younger people. I find that quite remarkable. I'll tell you why it's so difficult, I think, in the corporate arena. Maybe our short-term focus is shifting now, and one of at least the temporary consequences of September 11th is the realization that you just can't spin these organizations for the short term, because you don't even know what the short term is. When Gen. Sullivan retired from the army and went to serve on corporate boards, he was dismayed that nobody was thinking about the future. He said they'd spend hours figuring how to get the stock price up by half a penny, yet nobody was talking about how to develop the next generation of leaders.

I think it's for us to develop intergenerational collaboration. You were suggesting something much stronger than that. But just to call in the voices of the future into our present deliberations is not happening enough, and yet it is one of the most powerful things. Once you get people into these intergenerational conversations it is so inspiring for everyone to be talking with each other. It's the right work, but very difficult to do.

LS: In *Leadership and the New Science* you wrote, "Love in organizations is the most potent source of power we have available." What do you think that servant-leaders inside our many organizations can do to unleash love in the workplace?

MW: It's simple: *just be loving*! Why has expressing love become such a problem when it's a fundamental human characteristic? This is where I think we have overanalyzed and overcomplexified something that is known to everyone alive. Babies know how to unleash love. It's all about our relationships and being available as a human, rather than as a role. It's about being present and being vulnerable and showing what you're feeling. You know, we don't want to reveal who we are. Even the best of leaders try to be objective, rather than relational, and that's supposedly adding value to our work lives if we treat each other objectively. But it's again one of those huge things we get wrong. You can't have love if you can't have relationships, and you can't have relationships with one another if you have this curse of something called *being objective,* or *one size fits all*, as a policy, or having to go by the manual. I can feel the fear that so many of us have that, "Well, if it's not objective, we couldn't possibly live in the messiness and the intimacy that would come about by treating each human being as their own unique self." But I think that objectivity makes it impossible to be loving. Objectivity doesn't allow love, because love takes you to intimacy and uniqueness and very personal territory. We need to get away from the belief that you can run an organization using what are called objective measures or objective processes, which are actually just completely dehumanized. The fear of love in organizations is that it makes your life as a leader far more complex. But it also makes you much more effective.

I was just listening a few days ago to a woman who had recently retired as the chief of the Calgary Police Force, and she talked about what it took to be personally available and present for each of those officers, so that she was always embodying the values, finding ways for them to embody the values, and believe in the values and become the kind of police officers they wanted to be. She worked from a very clear perspective that it's not the corporate values that count, it's whether people can enact their personal values inside the corporation. I thought that was a brilliant rethinking of that. She would work with everyone on what they were trying to accomplish and the values they were trying to bring forth. And from those, of course, you get a wonderful corporate culture and very strong values. But she kept saying that this was enormously time-consuming and was very difficult work that required her to be there all the time. And so I understand why leaders don't want to go down this *love* path or the *relationship* path, because it requires so much. But that's where I think you have to want to believe in people. I believe on September 11th there were numerous corporate leaders who suddenly realized that people really were the most important thing to them, even though an hour before they'd been working a system that ignored human concerns. But then they got the wakeup call of their life. When I said that you have to want to believe, you really have to want to have relationship, and there are an awful lot of people in our workplaces, not just leaders but whole professions, who have never wanted relationships. They've wanted the work, and hopefully we are now realizing, most of us, how important relationships are.

LS: For many, serving others is inextricably tied to their own sense of spirituality. Are there practices you have found useful in terms of how we can better develop our own servant's heart?

MW: Well, I think first I would just underline where you're focused, which is we do need practices to develop this, and I would say the "this" we need practices for is to open our hearts. For most people it's not something you can rely on as spontaneously occurring. For some it is, but, especially if you're in the workplace, your heart gets pretty hardened. You shut down, or you just find that you can't express your love and compassion and so you take it elsewhere. So, even if you start out with a naturally open heart and a generous spirit toward others, there are many, many structures and processes in modern work and modern life that actually close us down. So we do need a practice to maintain an open heart.

I am a strong believer in meditation personally, but I think any process by which you withdraw from the world and focus on your own inner grounding is useful. For some people, that's running; for some people, it's playing tennis. I can get very similar grounding when I horseback ride, because you can't lose your attention for too long without losing your seat! For some people it's walking, or flower arranging. Whatever it is, it's just to notice what it is that revives your sense of feeling grounded, present, and peaceful. I have often felt that I need to leave my room peaceful in the morning because I don't expect it to get any more peaceful while I'm out doing work. So that's the first discipline—practicing what gives you your grounding and your peace, and to not let it slip away. The world just keeps pulling at you and I find that every so often I have to say, "Okay, Meg. Just notice you're spending less time cultivating your peacefulness and let's get back to serious practice." People of any religious order know the value of a routine to one's practice, whether it's a daily liturgy or a daily practice. Whatever it is, it's the routinization that really helps over time. So, it's not just episodic, or only when you feel like it. Your whole being benefits from knowing every morning you're going to pray or run or whatever. So, I find it needs to be routinized.

Once I decided that the work was really how to keep my heart open, that led me to a number of practices beyond my own meditation, although some of the meditations I work with now are traditional practices to keep your heart open. One of the ones I've loved the most is to realize that when I am suffering, whatever it is—whether it's anger, fear, feeling discounted or treated rudely or whatever—I remember that the experience I've just had is an experience that millions of people around the world have, just by virtue of being human. If I'm sitting in a hotel room one night feeling lonely, just for a moment I might reflect that, "Just like me, there are millions of people around the world feeling lonely at this very moment." This practice has been an extraordinary gift, of going from your personal experience outward to the human experience. Your own private experience is being felt by countless other human beings, and somehow this changes the experience from personal pain and anxiety to your heart opening to many others. And then when I see someone else I think, "You're feeling just the way I do." That practice has opened my heart more than any other single practice and has made me feel part of the human experience and the human family.

LS: What do you find most compelling about Buddhist practices?

MW: What I find to be enormously helpful about a Buddhist perspective on life is that it really isn't a religion. It is actually just a way to live your life. I have my own very eclectic theology. I was raised Christian and Jewish, so I started out with that eclecticism, and Buddhism has really introduced me to the day-to-day practices that I feel have really opened my heart and made me far more understanding and gentle. And, what is more important to me, it has made me far less likely to condemn quickly and far more willing to be in the presence of suffering and not to run from it. And to bear witness—to just be with whatever's going on and not to be afraid of it. All of that is not a theology, it's a practice. In my book *Turning to One Another: Simple Conversations to Restore Hope to the Future* (Berrett-Koehler, 2002), there's this very strong influence about the practice, and I have a whole section on bearing witness—of just being with another person's experience and not having to fix it, or counsel someone away from their grief. It's actually very fulfilling, and it takes the stress off when you stop feeling that you have to fix people's human experience. You just have to be there. These are capacities I didn't have, but now have, since I started doing these practices.

I have found that many Buddhist practices have helped me be with people differently and have changed my expectations of what needs to happen if I'm just with someone. Just being with someone has become really important, rather than saying the right phrase or the right word that will fix it. Now, the irony of this is that I'm still a public speaker who gets up on stage allegedly to say things that will fix things, and yet what I'm finding—and I've heard this from other speakers as well—is we are realizing it's who we are when we *are* up there, and not what we're *saying*. And so I very much want to be the presence of peace and possibility for people. I feel that is something I can be, and have been, and in order to be that, I need to experience peace fairly regularly from this much deeper place which is available to me through my different practices.

I think that the central work of our time is how to be together differently. Can we live together with our hearts open, with our awareness that we can't stop suffering, but that we can certainly be with it differently? Can we notice where we are causing harm and try at least to do no harm? And can we be together without fear of what it's like to be together, to really just not be afraid to be with other people? That would be a huge step forward for a lot of us. And we're all crying for it, we're all crying to be together in more loving ways because this is what it is to be human. So many of us were overwhelmed by the experiences of September 11th, but we saw people being together without the divisions that had separated them moments before. Buddhism is a series of practices that keep my heart open and keep me being present, rather than fleeing from what is day-to-day life. In that way I think it has also saved my life.

JN: In many organizations the word *change* has become a noun rather than a verb, and all too often phrases such as "You are afraid of change" are used to hurt one another. When you have encountered this in organizations how have you addressed the problem?

MW: There's a wonderful quote from a contemporary Buddhist who said, "Change is just the way it is!" I've worked a lot and written quite a bit on how we are actually responsible for creating resistance to change. I don't know who said it first but, "We don't resist change; we resist being changed." Most organizations fail to involve people in the design of change, in the redesign of organizations, or they don't involve people soon enough or substantially enough. What we get is something that is predictable in everything that is alive, from bacteria on up. When you do something to another living being, that being has the freedom to decide whether it's even going to notice what just happened or what somebody has done. So, the first freedom is you *choose whether you notice or not*. And the second freedom is you are then completely free to *choose your reaction to it*.

You can't impose change on anything alive. It will always react, it will never obey. This is one of the principles I've embraced for many years. Life doesn't ever obey, and yet we still think in organizations that we'll find the perfect means, the perfect vision, the perfect writing, the perfect PowerPoint presentation to get people to say, "Great! This is just perfect!" And instead, what people do is change the plan, file it away and never look at it again, or modify it. We look at all that and we say they are resisting change, but they're not. They're responding like all life does—they are reacting. And they're actually being quite creative. I've asked people to just look at that dynamic, which is so fundamental.

We get in organizations and we forget about that dynamic which we all know so well and we say, "I'll tell you what to do and you'll do it." And it doesn't happen. I must have asked this of tens of thousands of people, "Can you think of a time in your experience when you gave another human being a set of directions and they followed them perfectly?" And in the few cases where people have followed the directions perfectly I've asked, "Did you actually like that person?" Because those people are robots, those people aren't there. We've destroyed their spirits. If they do just what we say, we have killed the spirit. And we don't like being around those people. We have a profound disrespect for people who act like automatons, even though, if you look at most managers, they still think they want an automatic obedient response. So, if life doesn't obey but it always reacts, then the other principle from that is that if you want people to support something, they have to be involved in its creation. This has been a very old maxim in the field of organizational behavior, that people support what they create. I say that people *only* support what they create.

What this means for any organizational change process, most of which have been appallingly disruptive and have failed (we now know that almost 80% of them fail), is that they should make sure that they only use participative processes. That doesn't mean having everyone involved in every decision, but to be thoughtful and creative about how we are going to bring along everybody and involve people at different points so that this truly is owned by everyone, because it's their creation. It's a no-brainer; these things work! I find when I speak about participation, people still think that I mean everybody in the room doing all of the work at the same time. But it's not that.

I've worked with small teams of employees and charged them with, *how are you going to involve everyone in your network, everyone in your department?* And they are much more creative! They'll do TV shows, they'll actually create simulations to put people through the same experience that they have just had. They're enormously creative. I've also found, over time, that when you've charged a small group of employees with making sure that everyone knew about it, that the whole organization seemed to pay attention, and then it was very easy for people to know about it. I also work with the principle that participation is not a choice. If you don't get people involved, you're just breeding resistance and sabotage that you'll then spend months or years trying to overcome.

LS: *Leadership and the New Science* is generally considered to be one of the most important books on leadership to be published. Did you have a sense when you were writing it that you were on to something?

MW: I didn't have a sense of what I was on to. I didn't really understand that I was presenting an entirely different worldview. I thought it would be easier to convince people of the shifts that would need to take place because I didn't know it was about changing a worldview, and changing a worldview takes a long, long time. The original 1992 edition had a lot of questions, but as far as I can remember I hadn't the faintest idea what this work would mean. I just wrote it because it felt like the work I was supposed to be doing. I can't remember now who I was while I was writing it. I can remember some of the fear and hesitation, experimenting with a new voice as a writer, and all of that, but I don't remember what I thought.

LS: Was your move to Utah significant in the writing of *Leadership and the New Science*?

MW: It was absolutely tied to that book coming forth. I told my friends in Massachusetts that had I stayed there I'd have written deep, introspective works in the tradition of some writers there, and I realized, retrospectively, that I needed the open space. The West for me is freedom, and the wilderness is for me the deepest experience of harmony. I live in the wilderness—or it's at my back. I had no idea why I was moving to Utah at the time. I think it was just to be liberated into life, really, into the experience of what is space and wilderness and sky. And also just the incredible beauty of Utah. The red rocks of Utah are still my most sacred place to go. Again, I had no idea of why I was going—it felt really weird—but now it feels like, "Of course! That was it!"

JN: Your recent book is titled *Turning to One Another: Simple Conversations to Restore Hope for the Future*. What led you to choose the subject of conversation?

MW: Actually, I didn't choose the subject of conversation. I chose the action of *turning to one another*, and conversation is the simplest way to do that. To actually be willing to listen and talk to other human beings is the way throughout time that we have thought together and dreamed together. The simple act of conversation seems so far removed from our daily lives now, and yet we all have a vague memory of what it was like. Since September 11, we have been profoundly different conversationalists and felt the need to talk to each other and to be together. So I rely on the ancientness and primalness of human beings being together, and being together through this act of listening and talking as a way for us to surface, or to develop, greater awareness of how we are reacting to what's going on in the world. Therefore, hopefully, from that greater awareness of what we care about, what we're talking about, or struggling with at a very personal level, we will become more activist. We will become more intelligent actors to change the things we think need changing.

That idea is based on a more recent tradition in Paulo Freire's work called *critical education*, which is, you create the conditions for change by educating people to the forces and dynamics that are causing their life. You can start that work through conversation (or through literacy training, as Freire did). In conversation, people can become more aware of what their life is, whether they're happy, what they might do to change it. Then people do become activists, because it's their lives and their children's lives that are affected. Those are the deeper underlying threads that led me to write the book, which is different from anything I've written before. It's not written just for leaders or people in organizations. I wrote it for the world. I don't mean that to sound pretentious, it's just that the people I work with now are in so many different countries, all ages, and I just kept them in my imagination when I was writing, and I wanted to make sure that it didn't assume anything except our common humanity and our common desires for a world that does truly work for all of us. A world that is based on our common human desires for love and meaning from work and a chance to contribute.

The other piece that truly informed this was my experience with the Truth and Reconciliation Commission in South Africa, which was life changing for me. I only attended it once but followed the proceedings every time I was in South Africa during its three-year history. And the one day that I went was unbelievably impactful. It was when the parents of a young American Fulbright scholar who had been murdered, Amy Biel, were present. Their daughter had been slain in one of the townships after driving into a very angry crowd. Her parents were there listening to the description of her death by her killer, and they were sitting next to the mother of the killer, sitting two rows in front of us. It was an experience you don't normally have in your life, one of such forgiveness, and violence, and repentance. The primary thing I learned in observing the Truth and Reconciliation Commission hearings was that the power of speaking your experience is what heals you. The power of feeling we are heard is what heals us. It made bearing witness a much easier act. *I don't have to fix the person—I just have to really listen.* And from that experience I started to see it in so many different settings how, when we truly listen to people, they can heal themselves. My trust in conversation is that it also allows that level of listening, and there are other people who have written specifically about conversation. I am using the process to restore hope to the future; that was the underlying theme. I wrote it in March, 2001, and I had no idea of what was to come on September 11. But I could already see that the future was looking pretty hopeless, and I had a lot of people saying, "What does this mean, restore hope to the future?" And now we all know.

LS: Do you have any closing words of hope or advice for servant-leaders around the world?

MW: A few phrases come to mind from a wonderful gospel song, "We are the ones we've been waiting for." This is the time for which we have been preparing, and so there is a deep sense of call. Servant-leadership is not just an interesting idea, but something fundamental and vital for the world, and now the world that truly needs it. The whole concept of servant-leadership must move from an interesting idea in the public imagination toward the realization that *this is the only way we can go forward.* I personally experience that sense of right-timeliness to this body of work called servant-leadership. I feel that for more and more of us we need to realize that it will take even more courage to move it forward, but that the necessity of moving it forward is clear. It moves from being a body of work to being a movement—literally a movement—how we are going to move this into the world. I think that will require more acts of courage, more clarity, more saying *this has to change now.* I am hoping that it *will* change now.

Chapter Six

Ann McGee-Cooper

Interviewed by Michael R. Carey

Ann McGee-Cooper is cofounding partner of Ann McGee-Cooper and Associates, a team of futurists and business consultants specializing in servant-leadership. She is an international leader in researching and applying servant-leadership in the workplace, having been mentored by Robert Greenleaf during the last decade of his life, serving on the Culture Committee of Southwest Airlines since its beginning in 1990, and partnering in the design and facilitation of curriculum on servant-leadership with TDIndustries since 1976. She has counseled national business leaders, governmental officials, and college presidents on servant-leadership, culture transformation, high-performance teaming, life/work balance, time management, awakening genius in leaders and teams, and creative problem-solving. She is coauthor with her business partner, Duane Trammell of You Don't Have to Go Home from Work Exhausted, Time Management for Unmanageable People, The Essentials of Servant-Leadership: Principles in Practice, Being the Change: Profiles from Our Servant-Leadership Learning Community, Awakening Your Sleeping Genius: A Journaling Approach to Personal Growth and Servant-Leadership, *and* The Art of Coaching as a Servant-Leader *with Deborah V. Welch, PhD.*

Michael Carey: To begin, can you share with us something about the times that you spent with Robert K. Greenleaf?

Ann McGee-Cooper: My friendship with Robert Greenleaf was profound. I visited him several times at Crosslands, a Quaker retirement center in Kennett Square, Pennsylvania, where he and his wife had gone to for their later retirement. Esther needed some primary care and so they choose this Quaker retirement village. I got to see inside the fascinating synergy of their marriage and it was so inspiring. We had breakfast together that first morning. Robert went to get Esther from her room and brought her to the table in a wheelchair. And here they sat across from each other and their love was so vibrant, the respect and the deep affection between them was so strong. At that time they were both in their late seventies, and I was deeply moved by their strong, loving connection. They had both read meaningful books and articles the night before and were eager to share. What I was observing was a wonderfully rich example of dialogue, but at that time I was not familiar with dialogue. So what I observed was two highly appreciative soul-mates sharing their research about current affairs and obviously continuing a conversation building on earlier sharing. They would ask clarifying questions, challenge assumptions, and laugh frequently, delighting in new discoveries. History, poetry, current events, and biographies were some of the sources I remember, along with current events from more than one news source.

Bob invited me to come and see an exhibition of Esther's paintings in the hall adjacent to the dining room, and to my amazement and delight, I discovered her to be a very creative and sophisticated artist, a brilliant painter who did nonobjective art long before that was widely accepted. But here she was in her elder years, still actively painting with some powerfully refreshing and provocative artwork.

As I think back I only wish I could relive these experiences, because Bob Greenleaf had all these ways of taking my thoughts deeper. For example, he used a lot of silence. At that time in my life, I thought silence was an opportunity to speak. I had no awareness of the power of silence or why someone might prefer to sit together quietly in silence rather than to use this precious time together talking. Madeline, one of his daughters, talked about coming to visit him in his later years and just spending a lot of time sitting in silence. I remember Bob would often invite me to go out in the garden, and we'd walk out to sit quietly until I broke the silence.

I remember one time he talked about some of the ways that conversation can have deeper meaning, and he was describing dialogue. Here is how it unfolded. I had come that day with several pages of questions and I was asking each of them rapid-fire, taking notes as he spoke. And as quickly as he completed one idea I'd move to the next question. At one point he silently stood, took my hand, and walked me out into the garden still saying nothing. I was taken aback. What did this mean? Why had he stopped our interview? Had I said or done something wrong that offended him?

He walked us to a wooden bench in the sunlight and sat down quietly, still saying nothing. Then, as he was ready he said something like this. "Ann, I have been a Quaker for many years and one of the deep insights I have learned is this. Don't speak unless you can improve upon the silence." What did that mean? Was he suggesting that silence had value in and of itself? I was stunned as I pondered his words and searched for his meaning.

Then he added a second piece to this. He described them as bookends for dialogue. "The balancing piece is you have a responsibility to speak when spirit moves within you. So as you sit quietly, if there's something that comes to you and you think this really needs to be said, then it's your responsibility not to hide in silence, hoping someone else will stick their neck out but not wanting to take this risk." As I pondered this I realized what he was saying. There are times when something comes to me that I know needs to be said. And often I duck, not wanting to be "the messenger that gets punished for her message."

In all this he was awakening me to the difference between chitchat versus meaningful dialogue. Until that moment, the two had never occurred to me as very different ways of connecting with those around me.

Time with Bob was a very powerful awakener, an invitation to mature my ways of being and learning. He was my opposite in many ways—an introvert, quiet, very thoughtful, and in a different part of his life, being three decades my senior. He was so nonjudgmental. I would ask him questions and he was very good at turning them back around and getting me involved in finding the answers inside of myself. He shared eagerly and openly from his life, experience, and memories, and I always felt intellectually challenged, reenergized and a deep gladness when I left those times together.

MC: What else do you recall of your visits with Robert Greenleaf?

AMC: It was always a multimedia experience. I remember he loved music and we often listened to music. He was an avid reader; he drew richly on those resources. He was very well versed in what was happening politically, in the arts, and Esther was his teacher there, too. When they came together one special morning, I wish I had that particular conversation on tape because my eyes were big, I couldn't believe such a relevant, rich conversation was happening between this "elderly" couple. It woke me up. I realized I was choosing to live at a different and much less insightful level of consciousness. It challenged me to think that maybe I could also choose to enjoy a more profound level of relationship and I did, as a result of that.

He transformed my life repeatedly. One of the most profound ways was getting to be a partner inside TDIndustries. I'm not a partner in the sense that the others are, in that they're employee/owners, because they're employee-owned. I would be if I could, but there's no way to buy stock as an outsider, so I'm a partner in the sense that I buy stock by being there, supporting and learning with them over more than three decades. They've helped us enormously in growing our business, and when they were in financial trouble, we were glad we could be there for them with our services. And in more ways than I can recall, TD, Jack Lowe, and many of the partners have been there for us when we were going through hard times. So it's been very much a win-win. The real inspiration was when I experienced the pride in ownership they feel for what they're doing in the air-conditioning, mechanical, and plumbing businesses. Now, TD is so much more than mechanical contractors, but that was a wake-up call for me that plumbing or any of this construction work could be a calling. When I went out to do site visits and discovered that it was how they did the work, how they served the client, how they grew each other to have broader employability, I wanted some of that. We were eager and committed students from the beginning.

I also met Steven Covey there at TDIndustries. One evening Jack Lowe invited my husband and me to come for a three-hour session with Covey, where we sat with about fifteen other TD couples and learned, were challenged to go teach what we learned, then practiced what we had learned; and, of course, that was life changing. On another occasion I had the opportunity to learn from Tom Peters because of TD, and with many other thought leaders as well. TD has always dreamed big, and a top priority is to grow people. I think it's interesting that their focus is to grow their coaches too, because I was serving as a coach on servant-leadership. But it's always been very two-way because nobody is the authority on servant-leadership. I came in with an expertise around pedagogy, helping people of all walks of life become highly successful learners in the deepest sense of that word, and to be teachers in the process, because we all teach each other. But, I was starting at the beginning to learn about servant-leadership and just found it so powerful and something I wanted to claim as a part of my life and with my family, our three grown children, their spouses, and now our five grandchildren. Servant-leadership is something that if you dare to bring into your life it transforms everything about who you are and your values, how you think, your priorities, how you live your life.

MC: How do you define servant-leadership?

AMC: I would quote Greenleaf; I think he gives the best definition of it, saying that it begins with a feeling of wanting to serve, to serve first. Then by earning the trust and respect of those around you, they choose to follow you. It's not about a position, a title you're given and people not having a choice. It's about a spirit, or a way of serving, and it is about humility. To me it's a maturing.

Early on, I was the kid who wanted to be in charge and was very bright and thought if people wanted me to lead it was because they wanted my bright ideas. So, I talked first, I often talked over people, I sometimes interrupted and I could be very impatient about listening. Then I began to discover there's a much more powerful way to bring people together. The more you listen and ask respectful questions and grow people through good questions, the more they contribute to owning a shared vision. I think the difference between traditional leadership and servant-leadership is that in traditional leadership we tend to relate to people as "things to control and manage," and it's very fragmented. We even think about how we control and motivate as though others were off-on switches. In servant-leadership you listen broadly: What's happening? What's bubbling up with those around me? What needs to happen? Who cares? How can I bring this group together? Where is the leadership in this group? How can I serve these people as they find and identify their calling and then step into it? It requires humility; it absolutely requires a parking your ego. You have to model being humble by being willing to be wrong and keep an open mind and own mistakes and shortcomings. You say things like, "I apologize for my arrogance. I was imposing this on the situation as I listened to you. I misunderstood; there was something very different going on." You really step out of the way and, as you do, people step in and begin taking ownership.

Greenleaf says it best in his Test for Servant-Leadership:

"The best test . . . is: do those served grow as persons; do they, *while being served*, become healthier, wiser, freer, more autonomous, more likely themselves to become servants? *And*, what is the effect on the least privileged in society; will s/he benefit, or, at least, will s/he not be further deprived?"

MC: In what other ways can servant-leadership impact people?

AMC: I think it's very much about growing people, and in the process you grow yourself, because it's a much more difficult way to lead, much more challenging in the immediacy of it. With traditional leadership, I get to tell you what to do and if you don't do it right I can tell you that and attempt to control you because I have the power to fire you. Within this process, I'm robbing you of your self-motivation and ownership, and when I leave, ownership to get work done leaves with me. You're depending on me to keep you going, to remind you, to check up on you, and that's not very effective. In fact, it turns you into "hired hands," and I lose your heart and mind because you're not being encouraged to participate at a meaningful level, to challenge, to think rigorously, to be a mental partner in generating and testing ideas, or to make the outcome better and get really excited because you're participating in the creation of something that you know will be respected and make a difference.

I'll tell you a little story. When I taught at elementary school I had a principal, Mr. Wade Thompson, who was a servant-leader. I was the art teacher; and he'd step in my room and walk around to see what the children were doing and talk with them. Then he might say, "Boys and girls, I'm inviting your teacher to come for a cup of coffee and we're going to be gone for about twenty minutes. Is there anyone who needs help before she leaves, and can we count on you to continue doing your work and if it's close to the end of the class period do you know how to clean up?" He was really asking was, "Are you prepared for this responsibility?" As a result, in that school there were no locks on bicycles or lockers nor were any needed. A school of over 800 children who had learned how to take responsibility for themselves and each other, and they were very mature and remarkably responsible. Teachers were not police and were not mommas in the sense of having to constantly remind kids. Mr. Thompson modeled and taught self-directed ownership by all of us to create a great learning environment and appreciative community for everyone. This is the spirit of a leaderful community based on servant-leadership. Each one of us learned to feel responsible for the whole and how we could support others.

Another interesting thing happened one Thanksgiving. I took my parents over to show them the school where I taught. Thanksgiving morning there was a little fifth-grader out with a garbage bag cleaning up newspapers that had blown onto the school ground. I said, "Good morning Mark, you're up early. What are you doing?"

He replied, "Cleaning up."

"Who told you to do that?" I asked.

He looked at me with a puzzled look and replied, "No one."

I said, "So but, why are you doing all this work? Who told you to do this?"

He looked back at the school grounds and noted, "All of this paper blew all over our playground and I wanted to clean it up."

I said, "But why are you doing that?"

He said, "Because it's my school."

His clear perspective was, why would I *not* do it? Well, I think you'd agree that's extraordinary for a ten-year-old to choose that as what he was going to do early morning on a holiday when he could be sleeping in or any number of fun personal projects. And that's the power of servant-leadership. It's when individuals of any age begin to see their broader calling in life and begin to find meaning in that, and you can't push them away from it.

But you do have to learn to share the spotlight and you do have to mature yourself, because you are giving up control and giving up the opportunity to personally take credit for as much as possible. I confess that I'm not yet measuring up to this level of selfless collaboration 100 percent of the time. I do have my moments when I realize, painfully, that what I really want is to receive full credit for all my ideas and work. My ego has crowded back in and it's going to interfere with the collective Thou.

MC: How do you approach working with organizations around servant-leadership?

AMC: In a contract with a business client, I often don't use the term *servant-leadership*. If for any reason the term, *servant-leadership*, becomes a barrier, we find another suitable name. It's not the name that is important—rather, it's what you're doing. So, sometimes we might call it high-performance teaming, or collaborative leadership. It's always about culture change, inclusive ownership, getting everyone to think and act like an owner of a shared vision and mutual goals, and to feel the satisfaction of being a true owner on the team. It's clear to me that servant-leadership is now a part of everything we're doing in our consulting work. We've worked with a broad range of clients, and we always go to where the workers work. In Southwest Airlines we've done lots of hours in the hangers where they do maintenance, and in flight simulators, I've gotten to experience flying in the flight simulators, or to go where they load luggage. Part of what we do on the Culture Committee of Southwest Airlines, is appreciation events, and so we get to be behind the scenes and that's really a lot of fun.

It takes a lot of courage to let go of power and trust every person in the organization to step up and do the right thing, but that's really what we're talking about. When you think about it, nobody gets up in the morning and says, "I'm really going to mess up this day for myself and everyone else." Everyone wants to produce good work and make a meaningful difference. I think we have inadvertently bought into a hierarchy by believing that only the few at the top are smart enough to hang onto all the myriad details to figure out the business strategy and lead implementation. So, those few will tell others what they need to do and those reporting to them will be obedient and that's efficient. Well, it's not efficient or effective, whether you're a principal of an elementary school, a supervisor or project manager. I once had an opportunity to coach on a NASCAR team, and it was about helping them come together and define their collective goals and then figuring out what was preventing them from succeeding.

A servant-leader is helping people come together around creating a vision and goals, and then identifying the gaps and coming up with solutions. The most effective and efficient way for this to happen is through respectful, rigorous, healthy dialogue

MC: Tell us more about your experience of working with NASCAR.

AMC: NASCAR is not respectful to women, and women were not invited into NASCAR. I was because our team had coached on a construction project made up of five competitor contractors building a nuclear steam generation station, and we had broken records in terms of bringing that project in on budget and on schedule, much to everyone's surprise. This was a critical goal because Unit One had broken records to the negative and almost took the company under. Unit Two broke records to the positive, not only on budget and schedule, but with their Quality Assurance, Quality Control numbers. The owner of the Bechtel lead team also owned a NASCAR race team and thought, Gee, if it works in construction maybe it would work in NASCAR. As a researcher I thought, Well, it will be interesting. Everything speeds up and I can test my assumptions a lot faster, and that was true. It was amazing what happened. But I also learned that the stress is so intense, I couldn't do that work and the work we're doing in business and nonprofit organizations. Clearly, our client work teaching servant-leadership was my first love and brought far more meaningful value as a legacy. So that was my choice, and clearly, that's where my heart is.

But a funny story I was going to tell, was that the pit crew chief was less than thrilled that this woman from Texas was being invited in. So he said really grumpily, "No tits in the pit." I replied, "Well tell me where to hang 'em, because I can't help you if I can't observe what's going on." He kind of laughed, and that was over and so, I was able to join the team and learn a lot from them and help them make remarkable progress as a result of servant-leadership although we never used that term. The heart of this kind of coaching is about making it safe to have honest, respectful conversation about the kinds of things that usually are left unsaid. Too often in organizations we go talk to a third person and dysfunctional triangulation begins. We discover that we don't have the skills, and maybe the courage, to bring our shared problems and concerns out in a way that we can really hear each other.

Early on I had an opportunity to work in NASA as part of a research project I was invited to join, and that's where I learned some of the amazing skills about working with all of the brain and not just the logical, rational part of the brain. When your goal is to put an astronaut on the moon, you are challenged to find ways to test all your assumptions prior to launch. You use your creative imagination to try to imagine, before you get there what might happen, and then plan toward that. A great deal of that early work in 1968 is what I'm bringing now into servant-leadership and merging with the work of Peter Senge with building learning organizations and the very important work from Greenleaf on learning to grow leaderful organizations through servant-leadership.

MC: How do you deal with resistance to servant-leadership?

AMC: With great respect and great humility. When someone is coming at me with, "You know this is too soft and a big waste of time and you just don't understand our business and it'll never work," those kinds of things, I try to start by reframing what I'm hearing. "Help me make sure I'm understanding you accurately: I'm hearing you say that you're feeling overwhelmed as it is, and you've got more to do than you can possibly do. You're working long hours, your budget has been cut, and now they're bringing in this woman and you're being told that you are going to spend all day, six times over a year in skill-building sessions, and it makes you angry! Am I hearing you right?"

They'll either say, "You're dad-gum right." Or they'll add more to it. But it's very important that they know I understand, intellectually and emotionally, their concerns.

Then, I try to be very aligned in terms of saying, "Are you aware of why we're doing this?" They may or may not be, but typically, I would go in and if I were going to help a leadership team, or let's say, I'm now helping a team at the top of a very large organization and they are responsible for legislative issues and regulatory issues. I would preferably interview each person who is going to be part of this growth process and ask them what they would see as the three greatest challenges for the organization, and what are critical barriers. I do that one-on-one, and then our team puts this data into a confidential internal document, carefully removing all names, but then sharing it for everyone to study. Often people are shocked that this is in print. It is a confidential document, but its purpose is to help each person know, for example, on a team of eighteen, that they are not the only one that thinks we've got problems with big egos and arrogance that's causing us to not come up with the right or the best decisions. Or that we're stuck in silos and we're fighting internally and that's keeping us from partnering effectively. At the expense of great customer service, our focus is internal in-fighting rather than searching for more effective ways to serve our customers. Then I would ask, "How accurately did I capture what you see as the real issues?"

Usually they've said, "That's it." But it's almost like it's overwhelming.

I'd then say, "I don't pretend to have the answers, but I think you do, and if we could help you with a process that made it safe for everyone to represent their position so that we could get aligned and park our egos in favor of the best possible solutions, and if we could give you tools so you could work in that way, would that be worth your time?"

I don't mean to imply that there's one conversation, or one right way, but another thing we use with great sincerity and humility is the knowledge that you can't con people. That would be disrespectful and manipulative. Instead, I might say, "You're a critical player." You might be the CFO. "And you and I are wired very differently because my brain is about the future and people, yours is about numbers and strategy. Both are important, but I'm aware that you're being asked without a choice to be part of this, and we need your best thinking. Will you be my coach? And if there's anything that's happening at anytime that you think is a waste of time will you raise your hand and let me know and/or tell me at break and help me and our team make sure we're not wasting your time or anyone's time, because your time is valuable?"

I find that as I open the door honestly to a two-way relationship, everything changes.

MC: What other thoughts and examples can you share with us about handling resistance to servant-leadership?

AMC: It's important to make clear that when we work we always work as a team. I bring some important skills, but one of the most important aspects that we teach and model is that there is strength through difference. I am blessed with a very gifted cofounder and award-winning teacher, Duane Trammell. We have collaborated in all this work for over thirty years, and I want to give him generous credit for our ongoing success teaching and modeling servant-leadership.

To your question regarding approaches to dealing with resistance to servant-leadership, I would be open in saying, "If someone is not finding value, I think we should respect their decision to leave," because it changes the receptivity and mood in the group when anyone is not given free choice.

By the end of the first session, there are very few holdouts, because we've started with the issues paper I described previously and we start by looking at how our brains are wired. We use the Herrmann Brain Dominance Instrument (HBDI), and we look at those differences. Usually, we put those up, so everyone can see everyone else's. We then explore classic polarizations that can occur as a result of our different strengths and preferences and they might say, "Oh my gosh, it's not because you're an uncaring, hard-hearted guy, but because you're thinking tactical bottom-line, and I'm thinking strategic future, top-line."

Both are important, but we haven't respected how those come together. Then, we always end with dialogue, and that's learning how to make it safe to really hear each other at a deeper level. By the end of the first learning session, usually everyone's on board. We might have some cynics and skeptics and I check in by phone or in person and ask, "How did you feel about the session?" We always respect their concerns and see these as opportunities to demonstrate the true value of this approach and the benefits of growing a leaderful culture based on mutual trust and a shared vision.

And they give us written feedback at the end of every session. If someone really pans the session, I sit down with them and ask, "Please be my teacher. Help me know how you saw that and how we can make it better."

In my mind that's modeling servant-leadership; and, when I do that, I find that I learn a heck of a lot. Those people that might be seen as troublemakers or detractors become my most powerful and valuable teachers. When the group sees me honestly following the lead and learning from that person and honoring their pushback, they get it.

I learned early on when I was working in juvenile detention centers and on the streets in inner-city youth programs that I needed to find the internal leader of this group of youth, the person least likely to buy what I was offering; and, if I could find a way to get them to be my partner and I was honestly respecting their point of view, I'd learn a lot and we'd be successful. If I tried to force or coerce, ignore or trick them, I'd just never win because they had the trust and confidence of the group and knew the culture and I did not. By demonstrating my vulnerability and trust in them I could usually earn their trust over time. And together we could create winning programs for mutual benefit.

Having confidence in what you are teaching—it is a leap of faith; it's constantly a leap of faith. I would say this, we never work with clients without getting very centered, and I use a little personal meditation. What I'm doing with that is parking my ego, hopefully, and inviting spirit to move through me. Simply, I'm inviting the spirit of Robert Greenleaf, the spirit of whatever wisdom there is that's greater than me to help me listen in the right way and to be able to connect with that person and hear what they need to say to me. And there's an amazing difference when I am working from that state of expanded consciousness versus trying to go in and control the situation. Personal control always falls short, and I find what I was describing, expanding my consciousness, that's when the miracle happens. That's the leap of faith, the something I can't predict, the something I don't know to make happen but it unfolds between and among us and something changes for the better.

Often, at the end, some person will come to me privately to thank me for some story I told about some challenge in my life that I worked through. Maybe it was a story I brought in about being profoundly dyslexic, or my own personal tragedies like being divorced and a single parent. In the moment as I am speaking I might think, Oh, maybe I shouldn't share this. But then later I receive a very sincere and often tearful comment, such as, "Thank you for telling us about your divorce. I felt like such a failure in my own, and it was so affirming that you were willing to share your own pain and struggle and that you've sought counseling." That to me is the divine message. I didn't plan to do it, but intuition just caused that to come forth. I guess for me, *intuition* is another word for *spirit*. It's that divine knowing that's in all of us, and as I learn to trust it, so much more happens.

MC: Would you share your thoughts on vision and creativity?

AMC: There's a term I learned from Parker Palmer that really helps me called, *functional atheism*. What that means is playing God or trying to be all things to all people and not trusting God to delegate some of the responsibility to others. I fall into that often, and that is when I imagine that if I don't take responsibility for something, it won't get done. It's the arrogance of trying to be all things to all people. There can be an addiction to staying busy which takes away open time to reflect, meditate, and listen for deeper wisdom. I find consistently that I do my best work when I slow down to get centered and use this prayer frequently, "I will to will Thy will." When I stop trying to control everything and simply show up with an open mind and heart, the results are much more successful and typically involve the many gifts of others.

This was one of the many important habits I learned from Greenleaf, who incidentally, chose not to fly, not because he was afraid of flying, but because he knew he needed this time to meditate and to step back from any pressing situation to think big picture. We would call this systems thinking today. He was searching for how all the small pieces of complexity might fit together in a bigger, connected dynamic. So he took the train and used those days going and coming to be very reflective. He really taught me to expect the answers to find me. You can't force it. The same is true for creative problem-solving. You can't say, "I'm going to be creative in the next three minutes."

There are things you can do to invite creativity, but you can't time it or force it. Greenleaf has a quote where he says the true servant-leader starts inside of oneself to find solutions, not out there fixing others. It's not about working to improve other people, it's about transforming yourself. I think the biggest responsibility and the hardest one is to stay balanced. It's about doing the things that keep my life in balance, such as walking at least twenty minutes daily. I practice yoga daily for an hour and a half in a yoga class when I'm in Dallas. In my room, if I'm traveling, I meditate, journal, and read inspirational material. I'm vegan (which means to eat no animal products or lower on the food chain). It's a spiritual choice. When I learned that sixteen people can be fed from the same food stuff it takes to feed one meat-eater, I thought, all my life I've cared about all of the starving people in the world and three times every day I can make a difference for fifteen other hungry people. It is up to me to set my own priorities, to have the courage to say no to some things, to get clear about what I can do and what I can't do, and what I shouldn't do. All of these personal practices enhance my capacity to be creative and visionary.

One of the things that helps me is realizing the two things I love most, teaching and speaking, I learned because someone else said no, or couldn't. When I was a little kid, growing up in a small Methodist church, the minister was doing one of those impassioned pleas to the congregation for Sunday school teachers. He was talking to parents saying, "We need some volunteers to teach these kids' classes," and everyone was sitting on their hands and trying to be invisible. I was twelve years old and walked down to the front to volunteer. He couldn't say, "Go sit down kid." He didn't know what to say. But no one else said anything, so I started teaching Sunday school classes for six-year-olds when I was twelve, and I'm sure that they were just kind of baffled—"What do we do about this?" But I never knew I shouldn't or couldn't. So that's when my calling as a teacher took root.

I remember some years later, I went to a PTA meeting. I was a teacher at that time. It was a stormy night, and in the hall I could hear the PTA president and the principal wringing their hands saying, "The speaker called and has been in an auto accident and can't be here. What in the world are we going to do?" I thought for a few minutes and thought, well, I would be very happy to talk to the group. I think I could do something that might be worthwhile. So I volunteered and again, how could they say no? I've been speaking professionally ever since.

But that helped me realize both the gift and the shadow of confidence/arrogance and ego. It feels very good to get to do all of these things, and we flatter ourselves when we jump in and say, Yes, yes, yes. But really the question is, who am I saying no to when I say yes? And, to think about our energy and our talents as our sacred gift and how are we going to invest these gifts? Then staying keenly aware that we are not the only one with gifts to be shared.

I've told about my discovery that two of the things I enjoy most were discovered quite by accident when no one else volunteered. This has helped me to see the gift I can give another by limiting what I take on and considering who might welcome the opportunity in lieu of me. For example, perhaps a younger consultant might welcome an opportunity to lead a seminar when I am overbooked. There might be someone new to our community searching for a new network of colleagues who would benefit from and welcome an opportunity to speak when I am booked. And their topic might be even more relevant than what I had in mind.

There is one final insight about creativity and visioning which is very, very important. Neither of these are best done alone. The essence of creating a powerful vision is to engage the hearts and minds of everyone involved on a team or project. It's not one person's job to bring the vision for everyone else to follow. One person may bring a very powerful and compelling vision. But a key ingredient that often gets overlooked is getting the buy-in from all stakeholders. And this is done most effectively by creating time and space for all these bright minds to enhance the beginning ideas with their own insights and bold dreams about the future. People support what they help to create. This truth is important to keep in mind when searching for the most powerful creative new ideas and a guiding, unifying, and inspiring vision.

MC: How do you go about creating a shared vision within your own organization?

AMC: We invest a good deal of time thinking ahead three to five years. We have a Team Advance each year to step back out of the day-to-day and reflect on the future. Sometimes we invite some of our clients to come share their strategic plans for the next few years or their most critical future challenges. Other times we might do our own research and draw from a collection of powerful new books or other research. And we always use some creative activities to awaken our sleeping genius. Sometimes we use some of the material we are designing for clients and want to live into it before facilitating with others.

Another activity that keeps future visioning alive for each of us is the practice of making a list of ten outrageous dreams as a way to dare to listen to our hearts. It's been amazing over the years to discover that many things we write down in a playful spirit surprise us by coming true sometime later. Would this have happened without first daring to write about our dreams? We'll never know but I do know that the dreams seem to fuel our hearts and minds and bring refreshing new energy to everything we do.

Another important dimension of personal and team growth links to trustworthy, caring feedback. It's part of our team values to give each other respectful, encouraging, and instructive feedback. This happens daily. If I'm beginning to get a little overbooked, scattered, dropping pieces, too tired, they give me feedback. A person won't have the mental energy to be intuitive if in burnout. And really, burnout is a symptom that I'm attempting to go it alone, I've lost my connection with a Higher Power. It's interesting to note that when we're in burnout it's hard to tell the difference between intuition and wishful thinking. It's dangerous when you slip into that. If you really want higher wisdom to be clear to you, then you need to slow down. I take that very seriously.

I had the privilege of studying with Margaret Mead, who had a wonderful spirit, and she too had no plans to retire. She really wanted to live fully, as much of her life as she could, as long as she could make a difference, and for me, this is calling, fun, joy, and a gift. As long as I have something to contribute, that's really what I want to do. I think we each must daily be accountable to question whether we are doing something for our own self-fulfillment or perhaps ego fulfillment, versus what it is that we are called to do for the betterment of all. Who is it I am to be and what is mine to do? Robert Greenleaf asked a very provocative question and talked about knowing who you are and daring to be that and not all things. Greenleaf told the story about John Woolman, and even Thomas Jefferson, not trying to do everything that was needed by this young nation but knowing what his talents were and respecting to only do that. As a result, while others were leading the revolution he was writing new statutes embodying the new principles of law for the new nation. His influence would later become an important part of the Constitution and Declaration of Independence.

John Woolman was the Quaker who went up and down the East coast for thirty years visiting other Quakers who owned slaves and simply asking the question, "What does the owning of slaves do to you as a moral person? What kind of an institution are you binding over to your children?" And, "Is it consistent with our Quaker faith that one man should own another?" By the end of that thirty years no Quaker owned slaves. All had voluntarily chosen to end that practice as a moral choice. Greenleaf asks, "What if there had been ten other John Woolmans?"

A hundred years later, we had a civil war which solved very little, because there are still many people in America who, in their hearts, still feel entitled to "own slaves." They may not be African American, but in our corporations we have a lot of slavery, and a lot of patriarchal, dismissive, arrogant, self-serving attitudes. I think that addressing that challenge is really what servant-leadership is all about. It's freeing ourselves from the slavery paradigm of hierarchy which some perceive as giving permission to be dismissive and abusive in the service of creating financial profits. This belief tends to erode mutual trust and moral fiber.

MC: Are there any special incidents around servant-leadership that seemed especially meaningful to you?

AMC: Yes, there are many. I'll tell you this one. I have been honored to participate as a member on the Culture Committee at Southwest Airlines three or four times a year for a day, since 1990. It's rare to participate in one of those days without tearing up because I'm so deeply moved by the stories I hear. One I'll share that took me by surprise, and they often take me by surprise. A gate agent told a story of being in Las Vegas, and the Southwest Airlines' gate is right next to the Alaskan Air gate. On this particular morning, there was a work slowdown at Alaskan Air and only one employee showed up and they (Alaskan Air) had a full flight, first flight out. Right next to them Southwest also had a full flight, first flight out. One of the Southwest gate agents noticed that the Alaskan Air employee was being bombarded by this hoard of angry customers who were furious because nothing was happening. The Alaskan Air employee came out from behind the reservation desk to apologetically offer, "I am so sorry, but we're having a work slowdown, and I'm the only one who showed up to work this morning."

She began to cry as she explained, "I don't know how to get into the computer, and I can't load the luggage, and I don't know how to do all of the things to push the plane, and I'm so sorry but I don't have any way to do everything necessary to get you boarded!"

She literally didn't know when the next flight would be available, or who was going to show up, and the customers were yelling back in anger and frustration, taking it out on her. Instantly, my friend said, they called down to the Southwest team below who handled the luggage, provisioning, refueling, and all those responsibilities and explained the situation. And just as quickly, the Southwest team split in half at the gate and down below. They quickly figured out how to open the Alaskan Air computers and figured out how to use their system, (which was different than Southwest), boarded the passengers, and miraculously, both planes pushed back on time with the passengers cheering on both airlines and the team cheering and hugging this young woman from Alaskan Air! That just really causes me to feel tearful in this moment, and that's a great example of servant-leadership in action. When you focus on how you can work to improve the situation for all stakeholders and create a true win-win, you always achieve a win for others outside that circle. Anyone hearing this story will be touched by the generosity of spirit modeled by SWA of reaching out to help a competitor in a crisis.

MC: Your experiences with Southwest Airlines are remarkable. Are there other insights and experiences that you can share with us?

AMC: Sure. I was one of the first passengers to fly once Southwest was back in the air after 9/11/01. I went to Dallas Love Field and, if you remember, the skycaps were out of business because of the new security regulations. You could no longer check your luggage at the curb. You were now required to take all your stuff inside the airport to be searched, etcetera. So, when I drove up to get out at the airport, there were four skycaps sitting on the curb and one of them immediately jumped up and helped me take my things in. I was asking him, "What's happening for you?"

He said, "You won't believe this, but Southwest has created salaries for us." Now, all of the other airlines were furloughing hundreds of people. In sharp contrast, Southwest did not furlough one person! Not only that, they thoughtfully created salaries for skycaps who couldn't possibly make it on tips now, to get them through this unpredictable period.

My skycap went on sharing what he had been told "We're going to do whatever it takes. If there's not a role as a skycap they promised there'll be other roles internally, and they're really there for my family and me, and *we're going to be there for them!*" This is what so many leaders fail to realize. If a company considers the impact on all stakeholders in difficult times and goes the second mile to make sure no one gets lost or forgotten in a shake-up, this is one very important way to earn employee and customer loyalty. This is one of many reasons I proudly search for every possible way I can to support SWA as a loyal ambassador. They do such a great job of living the spirit of servant-leadership, especially in bad times!

I was just so moved. These four skycaps were asking, "How can we bring value?" And all over Southwest Airlines, people were thinking ahead. Nobody knew what the security regulations would be, or when they would be given clearance to fly, or how it would impact them. But, they had fifty-seven locations across the nation with teams simultaneously doing creative problem-solving and scenario planning. And, indeed, once they were up in the air they had all of these creative solutions. Because each location is different in terms of how things are laid out physically, and even the regulations and the people, all of it is different, but things happen when you have that kind of rich pool of talent and that strong, consistent sense of ownership. I was so moved by that moment and looking into the eyes of that young man and seeing not only no fear, but instead great courage and commitment.

Southwest was the only airline not to lay anyone off, the only major airline to make a profit in that quarter, and every quarter since, and the only airline to not cut any of their flights! Not only that, they hired another 4,000 employees in the next six months, and they added flights, and they're now beginning to add locations. Well, that comes from the spirit of the people. You can't buy that deep loyalty and courage with money and you can't boss that. You have to inspire hearts and minds to rise to this amazing level of unmatched performance.

That is why I get up every morning, making my commitment to keep working, eager to learn how to be a more effective servant-leader and partner in this journey with those around me. Everyone wants a better life, and more trusting relationships, and a more successful planet, and a healthy eco-system. All of that is about servant-leadership; about how we take responsibility for our footprint on the environment and how we bring about change that doesn't leave people behind. I think we need to be noticing who is going to be left out, who won't have a place at the table, and asking ourselves is that really alright with us and what might we do to make sure that everyone's needs are met? We can achieve this with a mentality of shared abundance!

Robert Greenleaf said, "*Nothing much happens without a dream. And for something really great to happen it takes a great dream.*"

Margaret Mead said, "*Never doubt that a small group of thoughtful, committed citizens can change the world. Indeed it's the only thing that ever has.*"

Gandhi said, "*We must be the change we want to see in the world.*"

They speak of servant-leadership.

Chapter Seven

Ken Blanchard

Interviewed by Larry C. Spears and Shann Ray Ferch

From his phenomenal bestselling book, The One Minute Manager®, *coauthored with Spencer Johnson, which has sold more than thirteen million copies and remains on best-seller lists, to favorites such as* Raving Fans, Gung Ho! *and* Leading at a Higher Level, *Ken Blanchard's impact as a writer is far reaching. His sixty books have combined sales of more than twenty-one million copies in more than twenty-five languages. Ken has received many awards and honors for his contributions in the fields of management, leadership, and speaking. The National Speakers Association awarded him its highest honor, the Council of Peers Award of Excellence. He was inducted into the Human Resource Development (HRD) Hall of Fame by Training magazine and Lakewood Conferences, and he received the Golden Gavel Award from Toastmasters International. Ken also received the Thought Leadership Award for continued support of work-related learning and performance by ISA—the Association of Learning Providers. Ken is the cofounder and chief spiritual officer of the Ken Blanchard Companies, an international management training and consulting firm that Ken and his wife, Margie, began in 1979 in San Diego, California. In addition to being a renowned speaker, consultant, and author, Ken is a trustee emeritus of the board of trustees at his alma mater, Cornell University. He is also cofounder of Lead Like Jesus, a ministry committed to inspiring, challenging, and equipping people to be servant-leaders by living and leading like Jesus.*

Larry Spears: In your forward to *Focus on Leadership* in 2002, you mentioned meeting Bob Greenleaf for the first time at Ohio University. Would you share with us your recollections of that meeting and any sense you had of Greenleaf at the time?

Ken Blanchard: I went to Ohio University because Vern Alden had gone there from Harvard to be president. He had a dream that Ohio University was going to become the "Harvard of the Midwest." He brought in some interesting people. Les Rollins, a fascinating character, was one of Vern's mentors who had worked with him at Harvard, and Les was a good friend of Bob Greenleaf. Bob came for a weekend in the mid-sixties when my wife, Margie, and I were there—so we got to spend a weekend with Bob, Les, and a group of student leaders who were part of a program they called the Ohio Fellows Program. I was an adviser to that group at the time. It was a wonderful weekend.

The biggest memory I have of Bob Greenleaf is how humble he was. He seemed to be so unimpressed with himself, and yet his accomplishments at AT&T and other things he had done were pretty amazing. He was more interested in what the students had to say than in talking about himself. I got a good sense of servant-leadership as much by his behavior as I did by his thinking, because he really wanted to bring the best out in everybody who was there. It was a great experience.

Shann Ray Ferch: Ken, I've really admired your influence coming from a tradition of spirituality and faith. You've become a profound influence around the world. Can you talk about the role of servant-leadership in your life, and about your faith?

KB: Well, Shann, I was a latecomer to my faith. I was in my late forties when I decided to turn my life over to the Lord. Being a behavioral scientist, I was interested to know what Jesus did. So I went to Matthew, Mark, Luke, John, and Acts—I was looking for the red print. I had to laugh as I read those Gospels, because that's when I discovered that everything I had ever taught or written about leadership, Jesus did—and he did it perfectly with this inexperienced, incompetent group of twelve guys he was given. It turns out he was the ultimate servant-leader ("Even I have come to serve, not to be served") and, in many ways, the greatest leadership role model of all time.

I first started thinking about Jesus as a great leader when I was on the *Hour of Power* with Rev. Bob Schuller in 1983, after *The One Minute Manager*® was published. My recollection is that Schuller said, "Ken, I love *The One Minute Manager*®. You know who was the greatest one-minute manager of all time?"

I said, "Who's that?"

He said, "Jesus of Nazareth."

I said, "Really?"

He said, "Yeah. He was real clear about goals. Isn't that the first secret—one-minute goal setting?"

I said, "Yeah,"

Bob said, "You know, you and Tom Peters didn't invent management by wandering around, Jesus did. He wandered around from one little village to another. If anybody showed any interest he would praise them and heal them. Isn't that the second secret—one-minute praising?"

I said, "Yeah."

He said, "And if people stepped out of line, he wasn't afraid to give them a little bit of a reprimand or redirect them—he threw the moneylenders out of the temple. Isn't that the third secret—one-minute reprimands?"

I said, "Yeah."

And he said, "So, Jesus was the greatest one-minute manager of all time."

Once that sunk in, I started to examine how Jesus's leadership approach related to other concepts we were teaching, such as Situational Leadership® II (SLII®). According to SLII, there is no one best leadership style. It all depends on the development level—competence and commitment—of an individual on a particular goal or task. As a person develops over time, the appropriate leadership style is changed from Directing—appropriate for an Enthusiastic Beginner, to Coaching—appropriate for a Disillusioned Learner, to Supporting—appropriate for a Capable but Cautious Performer, to Delegating—appropriate for a Self-Reliant Achiever.

As I began reading the Gospels, it was clear that Jesus was a classic example of an SLII leader. When Jesus went out and got the twelve disciples he said, "Come with me. I'm going to make you fishers of men." They were all excited. They just picked up and followed him. But they didn't know anything about being fishers of men—they were Enthusiastic Beginners. So what did they need? They needed a Directing leadership style. The first commission is all about directive behavior: "Stay here. Wear this. Do that. If they do this, dust off your feet." It's amazing.

Then you see Jesus's leadership style, over time, move from directing to coaching to supporting. And then, at the end of the book of Matthew, what did Jesus do? He delegated and said, "Go and make disciples of all nations and baptize them in the name of the Father, the Son, and the Holy Spirit." He moved his disciples from dependence as Enthusiastic Beginners to independence as Self-Reliant Achievers as he changed his leadership style. That's what Situational Leadership® II is all about.

To prove the point, in Acts, Peter—who was kind of a problem child among the disciples—saved a crowd of 3,000. So he really did become a fisher of men.

I got fascinated, but I found that nobody was teaching about Jesus being the greatest leadership model of all time in the divinity schools or in the churches. I thought perhaps this was the reason why I had been given some recognition and fame. Once I suited up for the Lord, I thought, Why not go to the greatest servant-leader of all time? After all, I realized that servant-leadership was the only approach Jesus endorsed for his followers. So that's where servant-leadership and the role of faith fit together in my life.

I hadn't thought much about servant-leadership since the time I had spent with Greenleaf, although in studying Jesus as a leader, I realized that in essence, both *The One Minute Manager*® and Situational Leadership® II were great examples of servant leadership in action. But I really didn't get it until I started to look at the Gospels and realize what an incredible servant leader Jesus was. Look at classic leaders such as Abraham Lincoln, Mahatma Gandhi, and Martin Luther King—they all credited a lot of what they practiced to studying Jesus's behavior.

I cofounded the Lead Like Jesus ministry with my old and dear friend Phil Hodges, not to convert people, but to help Christians set an example as leaders that would make Jesus smile. I feel that if we want people to believe what we do, we ought to behave differently. I think the next great evangelical movement has to be demonstration, not proclamation. And when it comes to how we should lead, what better role model is there than Jesus?

LS: Ken, Robert Greenleaf wrote in a number of places about some of the characteristics of a servant-leader. There are three I would like you to speak about in turn: listening, empathy, and foresight. Let's start with listening.

KB: Listening is probably one of the most powerful aspects of servant-leadership. I love the saying, "If God wanted us to talk more than listen, he would have given us two mouths." Listening is crucial if you're going to build a trusting relationship with people. My friend Ichak Adizes, a great teacher of leadership, has an interesting concept. He says trust begins with respect. If you respect somebody, you face them, because you want to hear their opinions and you care about what they have to say. If you don't respect somebody, you turn your back on them, because you don't care what they have to say and you're not going to listen to them.

A lot of people ask me, "In these tough economic times, how do you build a trusting relationship?" I tell them it starts with respect. You start by saying, "I want you as my business partner. I want to know what you think." Servant-leaders are there for their people and want to hear what they have to say. Listening is important.

The type of listening is important, too. I learned from Tony Robbins that there are two ways people can listen: one is to sort by self and one is to sort by other. People who are self-serving leaders sort by self. If you say to them, "Gee, it's a beautiful day," they'll say, "You should have seen the weather I experienced last week in Michigan." They take the conversation away from you—and that's not really listening. When you're with a person who sorts by others and you say, "It's a beautiful day," they might say, "Tell me what it is about beautiful days that really excites you and makes you feel good." They'll keep the ball in your court. Servant-leaders really care about their people and want to hear their views.

LS: What is the role of empathy in servant-leadership?

KB: Empathy is the capacity to put yourself in someone else's shoes. Servant-leaders are there to serve the people they're attempting to lead. Therefore, they really want to have an understanding of the other person's viewpoint, their feelings, and where they're coming from, so they can bring those people together around a vision and a direction that really makes sense. If you have no capacity to understand your people's viewpoints, you're really in trouble.

I was with a fellow recently who had an interesting model around personal relationships. He said relationships start with self-awareness and that's followed by relationship awareness. First you have to know yourself, then you have to be able to understand the other person. Because if you don't understand someone, it's hard to get them to commit to your vision. I think empathy is a very important thing—the capacity to put yourself in somebody else's shoes and see the world from their viewpoint.

LS: Greenleaf called foresight "the central ethic of leadership" and spoke about it as something leaders frequently seem to overlook. He described foresight as the ability to look at what has happened in the past, place that in the context of what's going on now, and then combine those two things and look into the future to try to make your best guess as to what the likely outcome will be of a decision. Ken, what has been your observation about foresight?

KB: I think the capacity to understand what's happened in the past is part of empathy, that's part of understanding, that's part of listening. If you can understand what's in the past and how it impacts what's happening now, then you've got a better chance of moving people successfully into the future.

I started a Golf University years ago, and one of the things I tried to teach people was that when you're behind the ball, you're really planning the future: "Okay, here's where I'm trying to head, and here's what I want to try to accomplish." When you stand over the ball, you should move into the present, which is, "I'm right here, right now." Then, after you hit the shot, you analyze the past. Here's where people get in trouble, both in golf and in life. Let's say you're golfing and you miss a short putt on the second hole because the maintenance guy didn't cut the cup right. Eight holes later you're still saying, "Aaargh, I can't believe I missed that putt!" and you're blowing your future because you're still hung up on the past. Or somebody gets to the sixteenth hole and all they have to do is get three bogeys in a row and they'll have the best round of their life. But all of the sudden they start picturing themselves in the locker room bragging to everybody about their great round. Then what happens? They go double-bogey, double-bogey, double-bogey.

I wrote a book called *Mission Possible* a number of years ago with Terry Waghorn. In that book, Terry and I emphasized how the future and the present are banging into each other nowadays. As a result, you have to manage the present and create the future at the same time. We felt you shouldn't have the same people planning your organization's future who are managing the present, because they'll kill the future. They're either overwhelmed with the present or they have a vested interest in it.

After we did the book, my wife, Margie, stepped down as president of our company and formed a department called the Office of the Future. She heads it, and has three or four people who work with her who have no operational responsibilities. Their full-time job is to look at what's going on in the world with big-picture questions: What's happening with technology that we need to get into? And what do we have to watch for that could put us out of business? When 9/11 happened and the whole training industry went downhill, we were prepared because Margie's department already knew all about virtual training through webinars, so people who wanted to train with us didn't have to get on a plane. We knew about that because we had somebody looking to the future. In fact, when Margie gets a really good idea in her group they usually give it to our board of directors and then we talk about whether we should pass it to our president to implement. It's been very helpful. It doesn't mean they don't analyze the past, but they're always studying things that could impact our future.

I've found so many times that we mix things up. I worked at universities for ten years, and the worst thing you could do was ask the faculty to plan the future—because you knew they were going to kill it. In fact, when we got involved with Grand Canyon University in Phoenix, we wanted to make it a for-profit university right away—not to make more money, but so we could make decisions. At our first faculty meeting we said, "We have good news and bad news. The bad news is that the university will no longer be run completely for the benefit of the faculty. The good news is that you're going to be paid well, because we're a for-profit university."

I think what Greenleaf was saying was that servant leaders know how to understand a lot of different time frames and somehow work them all so that they can move forward. They're not denying what happened in the past or turning their back on the present, they just understand how to use the past and present to move toward the future.

SF: How can servant leadership help an individual deal with personal weaknesses?

KB: One of the key aspects of being a good servant leader is not only to have empathy for others but also to have empathy for yourself. I think it's about being willing to be vulnerable. My father was an admiral in the U.S. Navy but he was a "Mister Roberts" kind of guy. He told me, "They used to teach us, 'Keep your distance from your men. You might have to put them in harm's way.' That's such craziness. If you act like you're not scared and you've got everything under control, your men will know that's not true. But if you're vulnerable with them, they'll be willing to be vulnerable with you." My friend and coauthor Colleen Barrett, president emeritus of Southwest Airlines, with whom I wrote the book *Lead with LUV* (Southwest's stock symbol is LUV), has a wonderful saying: "People admire your skills but love your vulnerability."

I think it's really important to get in touch with your own humanness. The neat thing about servant-leadership is that it's not all about you. It's about "us" and "we" and the team and what we can do together. If you act like you've got it all figured out, then your ego's in the way and you're going to be a self-serving leader, not a servant-leader. If you want people to be open, you have to be open with them.

I always loved the Johari Window. People think it sounds like something mystical. It's not, it's just a theory developed by Joe Luft and Harry Ingham—Joe and Harry—so they called it the Johari Window. It says there are certain things about yourself that you know—such as the color of your eyes—and certain things about yourself you don't know—such as if you've got bad breath. There are things about you that are known to others, such as how tall you are. And there are things about you that others don't know, such as fears you might have. The theory is that if you want to create an open environment where people can be truthful with each other, you have to open your public window. The public window is where what you know about yourself and what other people know about you are the same. What you know about yourself that they don't know is your private window, and what they know that you don't know is your blind window. And then, very creatively, what nobody, including yourself, knows about you is the unknown.

The way you open the public window is, first of all, through feedback, where people will share with you things you might not know. For example, my executive assistant Margery Allen came to me recently and said, "Ken, I know you've been really busy lately, but you haven't been taking the time to walk the halls as much as you used to, and I just want to tell you that people miss that." And I said, "Wow, that's so helpful." She took something that was a blind to me and brought it into the public window.

The way you open your private window to the public window is through disclosure, where you tell people about concerns you have. For example, I believe you should treat your people as your business partners. Our people don't know what's happening with the finances of our company unless we share with them. We brought in a guy in a number of years ago who taught everybody in the company how to read a balance sheet. Every quarter, we open the books to everybody, and we not only share what's happening in sales and profit margins and all that, but we also share how we're doing with our bank loans and that kind of thing. Why do we do that? We have a goal that if there are problems with the company, we want everybody to lose sleep, not just us! Ha! We did it before and after 9/11, and we do it now, because we want to keep our people. They know where we can cut costs and they know where we can increase income. If we kept everything to ourselves, it would never get out there in public where our people might be able to help us and give us some feedback. If you can create an environment where you have disclosure, feedback, disclosure, feedback, all of the sudden you start opening that unknown window. You both say, "Wow, that's really interesting, I never thought of that." "Neither did I." And now you've created synergy—where one plus one is a lot more than two.

LS: Robert Greenleaf said that, fundamentally, with servant-leadership one should be a servant first and a leader second. He had the best test to observe the growth of people: Do they, while being served, become healthier, wiser, freer, more autonomous, more likely themselves to become servants? And what's the effect on the least privileged in society? Will they benefit, or at least not be further deprived? This idea of the impact of servant-leadership on the least privileged of society—and will they benefit or at least not be further deprived—seems to me to be, in some ways, very radical and sometimes overlooked. But I think it's perhaps one of the most important parts of servant leadership. Could you share your thoughts about this, in relation to your Christian faith and also to our responsibility to the poor and others who would meet this definition of the least privileged of society?

KB: Our company's mission is to help individuals and organizations lead at a higher level—and in many ways leading at a higher level is all about servant-leadership. We say it's a process of helping people accomplish worthwhile goals while taking into consideration the concerns and well-being of all involved. So, for example, we don't think that making a profit is a worthwhile goal; it's really a byproduct of how you treat your people, how they treat your customers, and what kind of citizens you are in the community. Profit is the applause you get for creating a motivating environment for your people, who take care of your customers. Being a good citizen in your environment is to be caring about everybody there.

A colleague of ours named Owen Phelps wrote a book called *The Catholic Vision for Leading Like Jesus*. In the book, he says that we did a really good job on the *servant* part of servant-leadership, but we forgot two other aspects of leadership—the *steward* and the *shepherd*.

The servant aspect has a lot to do with these questions: Why are you leading? And are you here to serve or be served? The steward aspect is about whether you are a good steward of the resources that have been given to you—people resources, financial resources, et cetera. It's the philosophy that you don't own anything—it's all on loan. What you do with the resources that are on loan to you and your people is important. A good servant-leader is also a good steward of resources. Phelps's third aspect of servant-leadership is the shepherd. In the Bible where the shepherd has the ninety-nine sheep and one is missing, what does he do? He goes off to find the one, because everyone is important—every single human being.

My father taught me that you can really tell a lot about a leader by how they treat people who have no power—people who can't do anything for you. At our company we have profit sharing but we also take 10 percent of our profits and give it to our employees across the board for them to donate to causes they like. It has to be a 501c nonprofit organization. We want them to get used to tithing, to serving. We also allow people to take time off, up to forty hours per year—we call them *Ambassador Hours*—to serve in the community in various ways so that they understand the importance of serving.

To me, generosity isn't just about treasure, it's also about your time and talent. And I think there's another component of generosity, from a book called *The Generosity Factor* that I wrote with Truett Cathy, the founder of Chick-fil-A. It's *touch*. That's about reaching out to help others. A servant-leader thinks everyone's important. They want to know how they can help the greatest number. I don't think you do that by just giving people handouts for nothing. I think you try to help them get on their feet. Your main goal would be to help someone become self-sufficient so they are employable and able to take care of their families. I think that's so key, that whole service mind-set.

Every so often we take a group of people from the company down to Mexico to build homes, and that's a powerful experience—to work alongside a Mexican family that had to raise enough money to buy the land. The group we go with is called Youth with a Mission or YWAM. They provide the materials, but it's our labor and we work alongside the family. It's a powerful thing for people in our company. We are so privileged, we sometimes forget that not everybody has what we have. We also forget that maybe people around us need help. That's really important. It's not about you, it's about the people you want to serve and the people around you who need the impact of your servant-leadership.

SF: What does it mean to you to be a servant-leader in your family, with your wife, your kids, and your grandkids?

KB: In *Lead Your Family Like Jesus,* a book I coauthored with Phil Hodges and Tricia Goyer, we talk about how leadership is a transformational journey. Being an effective parent and an effective spouse starts with the self, and answering the basic question, "Am I here to serve or be served?" You have to begin by looking at yourself and getting perspective. Phil contends that when it comes to one-on-one leadership, it's all about the husband and the wife. Although your kids are your most important project, you need to focus on each other—because someday the kids will be gone and all of the sudden it will be just the two of you. With your kids, you're building and leading a team together—a community. And then the extended family has more of an organizational feel in terms of what you do and how you relate with the relatives and in-laws. It's important to manage those relationships. How do you bring the extended family into your family? That's really managing an organization. So it goes self, one-on-one with your spouse, the kids make it a team, and then you've got the extended family, which is the organization.

I was once on a program with Tom Landry, the great Dallas Cowboys coach, and someone asked him, "Coach, how do you stay so calm in such a crazy game?" He said, "It's really easy. I have my priorities in order. First, comes God, second comes my wife, third comes my kids, and fourth comes my job. So if I lose on Sunday, I've got a lot left over." He said, "There's coaches out here who have nothing left over if they lose on Saturday or Sunday, because they *are* their wins." He said, "The reason my wife is second is because the best way I can show the kids I love them is to love their mother, and the best way my wife can show the kids she loves them is to love their father."

What often happens in relationships is after men get married, they say to themselves, "The marriage job is done and now I can get back to work." And work becomes number one. What often happens to women once they have kids is that the kids become number one. Before you know it, the couple doesn't have a relationship with each other. So keeping that relationship fresh is really important. Peter Drucker was quoted as saying, "Nothing good happens by accident." In other words, if you want something good to happen, you need to put some structure around it. If you want a good marriage, you have to schedule some time for each other. I'm just thrilled with the things I hear about what couples are doing nowadays to keep their relationship fresh. Margie's brother, Tom, is the chairman and CEO of our company; he's eighteen years younger than Margie. Tom and his wife have a date night once every week or so. They don't break that date night. On that night, he can't talk about work and she can't talk about the kids—they talk about their relationship and "How are *we* doing?" That's a very powerful structure for them to have to keep their relationship thriving. Some people are smart and put as much money aside for coaching and family counseling as they spent on their wedding.

Does servant leadership apply to marriages and families? You'd better believe it. But two things can get you away from being a servant leader. One is false pride—when you have a "more than" attitude. You think more of yourself than you should. As a result, you're promoting yourself, thinking you're smarter, you're brighter, you're quicker than everyone around you. The other is fear or self-doubt—when you have a "less than" attitude. Now you think less of yourself than you should. Both of those things are very self-oriented: one, you think you're a really big deal and the other one, you're less important than you should be.

Let's say I'm working with Larry and I have a servant heart and Larry has a servant heart, meaning Larry wants *me* to win and be successful as much as I do, and I want *him* to win and be successful as much as he does. We have each other's best interests at heart. In this case, I guarantee you that if we're working together on a book or a project, and we both come with a servant heart, we're going to get the work done well and our relationship will build. If we're trying to work together and we've both got false pride where we're concerned with who's going to be the senior author, who's going to get more royalties, and "I've done this" and "I've got this background" and all, we're going to have conflict because we're both coming from a "more than" philosophy. If we're both coming from self-doubt and fear—"I don't know, I'm not sure that I'm as bright as he is" and "He's got all this and all that"—we're going to keep our distance from each other. The tough thing about life as a servant-leader is what to do when someone you're working with comes at you with either false pride or self-doubt. They can hook you into their territory.

I was working with a group of parents recently and gave a classic example of a teenage son who all of a sudden stands up at the breakfast table and says, "I'm so sick and tired of how you run things around here! I'm out of here, and I wish I didn't have to come back." When he storms out of the house, what would you do? You might shout out, "Who do you think you're talking to, young man? You get back here!" If you did that, now you have a false pride/false pride ego fight. But if as a parent you would stay in your servant heart, you'd call out to your son, "I can see you're really upset, and it looks like I might be part of the cause. Tonight when you come home, can we talk?" You'd be amazed to see how your son's whole body language changes.

If you're a leader and someone comes to you from self-doubt or fear and says, "You know, you've given me this job and I'm not really sure about it," and you say, "I'm not really sure either," you're going to send each other downhill. But if you stay in your servant heart, you might say, "I can hear your concern and your worry. I think you can do this but I don't want to deny that right now you're feeling a little inadequate. What can I do to help?" You can lift that person straight up into problem solving. The hard thing for us as servant-leaders is to lead with a servant heart.

Sometimes it's the follower who has a servant heart and is dealing with a false-pride boss. How should you deal with that boss? You go in and catch the boss doing something right, praise her, and try to serve her in a way that eliminates her false pride and makes her feel more secure so that you can work together.

We're all leaders in our interactions with other people. We have to remember that if we keep a servant heart, anything we're doing will get done and our relationship will blossom. I think that's so true with couples. The biggest ego problem in marriage is when the man thinks, "I should be in charge." Get a life! Both people in a couple should be there to serve, even though they have different roles. It's been found that one of the biggest negative forces in a marriage is a man who refuses to take advice from his wife. But if I had never taken advice from Margie, I would have been in a lot of trouble many times. She's a lot brighter and can see things I don't. It's the understanding that we're a team—how do we do this thing together? This year we'll celebrate our fifty-second anniversary. Margie said recently, "This is a really sweet time in our relationship. The kids are grown up, they're in their forties, and we get the grandkids once in a while but we can give them back. It's just a sweet time." The reason it's sweet is because we both happen to be married to our best friend. That doesn't come from just saying it—it comes from that give-and-take relationship over time.

LS: Ken, you've inspired individuals and companies, and you've spoken eloquently in the past about servant-led companies like ServiceMaster, Chick-fil-A, Nordstrom, Southwest Airlines, and others. What do you see as some of the similarities, the common threads, that run through these exemplary servant-led institutions?

KB: Jim Collins nailed it with his research in his book *Good to Great*. He found that great leaders had two characteristics in common. Whether it's Truett Cathy or his son Dan Cathy at Chick-fil-A; Herb Kelleher or Colleen Barrett at Southwest Airlines, Bill Pollard when he was running ServiceMaster; Jim Blanchard and his partner Bill Turner running Synovus; or the Wegman family—all these leaders had the two characteristics that Collins talks about. The first is *resolve*, which is determination to accomplish a goal, to live according to the vision and be the very best. What drives Truett Cathy and everyone at Chick-fil-A is to use the talent that God has given them to have a positive influence on everybody who comes into contact with them. They've just resolved, "We're going to do that. We're going to have an impact on people."

A lot of people think servant-leadership is kind of soft leadership. It's not—they don't know that there's two parts to it. One is vision and direction. It's about going somewhere. If you don't know where you're going, how can your people follow? The *leadership* part of servant-leadership is vision and direction, and that's what the resolve piece from Collins's research is all about. Servant leaders have a real vision—a sense of where they're going. The traditional hierarchy can be alive and well for the vision and direction piece. Look at Jesus. Where did he get his vision and direction? From his Father, the top of the hierarchy. The second part of servant leadership is about how to live according to that vision and accomplish those goals. That's when you start to philosophically turn the pyramid upside down. Now you're moving to the *servant* aspect of servant leadership. When Jesus washed the feet of his disciples, he was transitioning from vision and direction to implementation.

He had a slow group. It took almost three years for them to understand what he was really there for, and then when he realized he was going to be leaving, he had to get them ready for how they were to carry on. When he washed their feet, what did he say? "Just as I have done for you, do for others."

Take Herb Kelleher, the cofounder of Southwest Airlines and Colleen Barrett, now president emeritus. Do you know what Southwest says their business is? They're in the customer service business—they happen to fly airplanes. They also have four operating values. Given their business, their first value is Safety. Then they have three values they want everyone to engage in every day. First, a Warrior Spirit, which is that drive to get the job done, the resolve to be the best. That's why they can turn a plane around faster than any other airline. Second is to have a Servant's Heart. They hire for character and then train for skills. It's right in their basic values. And then the third is a Fun-LUVing Attitude. When they interview people for frontline positions at Southwest Airlines, they record the interview. They don't record the person being interviewed, they record the people who are doing the interviewing. What they care about is, how are these people responding to this applicant, because they want the people they hire to have a Fun-LUVing Attitude. So if the interviewers aren't laughing and having a good time, they don't hire that candidate.

So, according to Collins, the first characteristic of a great leader is *resolve*—the determination to live according to a clear vision and set of values.

The second characteristic of a great leader is *humility*. Collins never anticipated humility being a major characteristic of an effective leader, and yet that is what he found. Some people think people who are humble are weak. In the book I wrote with Norman Vincent Peale titled *The Power of Ethical Management*, we said, "People with humility didn't think less of themselves, they just think about themselves less." People who are humble feel good about themselves but they don't think they have to raise their hands and make themselves important. The second definition I love of humility comes from Fred Smith, who wrote a wonderful book called *You and Your Network*. He said, "People with humility don't deny their power or skills, but they recognize that these things pass through them, not from them." Any skill you have is on loan. It's not about you.

Those two things are so powerful when you look at them. The people I admire have low ego needs. I spent some time with Bill Bright, who founded Campus Crusade for Christ, and whenever I was with Bill you'd think that I was the most important person in the world. He wasn't looking to see who else he could talk to, he wasn't wondering who was on the phone. He was focused on whoever was in front of him. I found this characteristic also with

Norman Vincent Peale, Bill Pollard, Herb Kelleher, and Truett Cathy—when you're in front of them, you are important. They want to hear you. They want to know what you're thinking. It doesn't come from not feeling good about themselves. It comes from their desire to develop you.

One of the ways you can tell self-serving leaders is that they don't want anybody around them to look good because somebody might think that person ought to be the leader. Servant-leaders want people to develop. If a leader rises up, they're willing to partner with them, maybe even move and take another role because to them it's what it's all about—the development of people.

I think servant-leaders don't fire people; I think they fire themselves. I wrote a book with Garry Ridge, president of WD-40 Company, called *Helping People Win at Work—A Business Philosophy Called "Don't Mark My Paper, Help Me Get an A."* At WD-40, at the beginning of the year each manager sits with each of their direct reports and goes over their job requirements. Then they come up with three to five observable, measurable goals. If they accomplish those goals, they'll get an A. It's the job of the manager to help the person get an A. A lot of people say that if you do that, you'll be thought of as an easy marker. That's not true if you make sure the goals are observable and measurable. But a lot of organizations rate people on stupid stuff that nobody understands, like initiative, willingness to take responsibility, promotability. Nobody knows what that means. So what do they do? They suck up to the hierarchy.

What they do at WD-40, and what a servant leader does, is "Here's what we're trying to accomplish. Now that that's clear, I'll work with you to help you to win." No matter how you work with somebody, it's obvious if the work they do is not in their sweet spot. Then you and the person are both going to know that it's not the right job for them. What they do at WD-40 when that happens is if the person is a good values player—in other words, they're trustworthy and good citizens—they'll try to find another position in the organization for them. If they're neither a good performer nor a good values player, they will "share them with the competition." That's the term they use, not "you're fired." People who are separated from WD-40 are not angry; in many cases they know that it's the best thing because it's not the right spot for them.

LS: Are there particular titles, essays, books by Robert Greenleaf, or particular ideas that have stayed with you from your reading of Greenleaf's writings?

KB: The book Margie and I use when we teach at the University of San Diego is *Insights on Leadership*. I think that's a fabulous book. The reason we love it is because it applies servant-leadership to all kinds of organizations: profit, nonprofit, everything. It also has a very powerful article about followership. What's the role of the follower? If both leader and follower have a servant heart then something's going to happen, but if the follower is just waiting around for the leader to do everything, that's not coming from a servant heart, and the servant-leader's going to get a little impatient with that. Some people think servant-leadership is only for the church, but it's for all organizations. As I said, it's both vision/direction and implementation.

My son, Scott, and Drea Zigarmi, who heads up the research in our company, and some other colleagues wrote a white paper called "The Leadership-Profit Chain." They reviewed 200 studies of leadership and its relationship to what they call organizational vitality, or success. They wanted to see the relationship between leadership and organizational vitality, and they took into consideration employee passion and customer loyalty. They looked at two parts of leadership. One was strategic leadership, which to me is the *leadership* part of servant leadership—vision and direction and values. The second was operational leadership, which is the *servant* part of servant leadership.

Very interestingly, they found only an indirect relationship between strategic leadership and organizational vitality and success. The reason why it's an indirect relationship is that your people and your customers often don't know what the strategy is. They don't know where you're heading. All they know is how they're treated by the leaders throughout the organization. A servant-leader wants to build leadership capacity throughout the organization. If you have an organization where the vision, values, and direction are clear, and then they turn the pyramid upside-down and empower all the frontline people, supervisors, and middle managers to make it happen, all of the sudden people feel empowered. What happens when people get appreciated and empowered? They get passionate about their work! And what do passionate people at work do? They go out of their way to serve customers. That makes their customers loyal. The customers start bragging on the people, which reinforces them. It's this interaction between passionate employees and loyal customers that really has the biggest impact on organizational vitality. It's driven by operational leadership, the servant part of servant leadership.

My goal is to make people understand that servant leadership is not the inmates running the prison. It's not about pleasing people. It's not some religious movement. It's the only kind of leadership that makes sense, that takes into consideration, in Jim Collins's words, both people and results. It's not either-or; it's both-and. And that's where the action is.

LS: I love where Greenleaf talked about the Latin root of religion, *religio*, meaning "to rebind." Through the Center for Faithwalk Leadership and now through Lead Like Jesus, you've brought a powerful expression to servant-leadership through the meaning of Christ in your life. I've met people of many different faiths and philosophies who are sincere, humble, practicing servant-leaders. And one of the great challenges of life through the history of humankind has been the way in which our faith and beliefs sometimes seem to set us at odds, when perhaps there are more things linking us together if we spend time looking at it—bridges rather than walls. I wanted to get your sense of where you view servant-leadership in relation to different faiths and philosophies of the world. I guess the question really comes down to this: From your perspective, is it possible for someone of any faith or belief to be a sincere servant-leader?

KB: I think it's an interesting question, whether somebody can be a true servant-leader if they are not be a person of faith. I think they can be, if they have it in their heart. I think if they have it in their heart, God's already there; they just haven't picked it up yet. It really comes from the heart. One of the things that excites me again about Jesus is that he didn't want people to be loving; he wanted them to be loving human beings. He didn't want them to be kind; he wanted them to be kind human beings.

When I was working with Bill Hybels, the Willow Creek pastor, on our book *Leadership by the Book*, he said to me, "Ken, what's your biggest disappointment in your work?" I said, "The biggest disappointment is that more people don't use the information I'm trying to give them. I get people coming up to me all the time and saying, 'Oh, Ken, I just love your books. I've read them all.' I try to be polite, but I really want to say, 'Have you ever used any of it?' I still go around the world and ask people, 'How do you know whether you're doing a good job?' and the number one response, 80 to 90 percent of the time, is 'Nobody's yelled at me lately. You know, no news is good news.' So I know people aren't being caught doing things right."

Then Bill said an interesting thing. He said, "Ken, I think you're making the same mistake I did. You're trying to change people from the outside in. I used to do that. I used to preach the Golden Rule and the Ten Commandments, until I realized that what Jesus wanted is to give us a 'heart attack.' He wanted to really get inside us." I think people who are servant-leaders, whether or not they recognize the Spirit in them, have some unique energy in them that says to them, "I'm here to serve, not to be served. That's my belief, that's who I am."

I got interested when the Pharisees essentially said to Jesus: "Ten commandments are too many. What are the biggies?" And he said to love God with all your heart, all your soul, and all your mind, and love your neighbor as yourself. If you have those as your values, you don't need commandments like thou shalt not kill, thou shalt not commit adultery, or thou shalt not steal. If people really have in their heart that they are here to serve and not be served, that's who they are. I don't think we need to teach them a lot about listening or empathy. I don't think we need to teach them a lot about anything. I think that's who they are and they're going to be seen as who they are. Where people get in trouble as servant-leaders is when they're trying to become servant-leaders from their head, not from their heart. But I want to tell you, when push comes to shove, under pressure, if it's not who you are, it's hard for you to do even what you think is right because your ego is going to get in the way—your false pride and your self-doubt. But if it's who you are, then that's who you're going to be on a day-to-day basis.

In our Lead Like Jesus ministry (www.leadlikejesus.com), we think being a great servant leader has four aspects. One is the *heart*, which is about your character. This is where you ask the questions Who am I? and Whose am I? Second is the *head*, which is where your beliefs about leading and motivating people are. The third is the *hands*, which is how you behave. Unfortunately the heart and the head nobody can see, but people can see your behavior. If your heart and your head are in the right place it's going to come out in your behavior. But even if it's in your heart, there are temptations and pressures in life that are going to get you off track, so the fourth thing we look at is *habits*. I had never studied habits before, just like I'd never studied the heart before. I mainly was a head and hands guy—leadership theory and leader behavior. Through Bill Hybels, I really started to look at the heart—intentions and character, and habits—how to recalibrate, on a daily basis, who you want to be in the world.

Jesus had five habits. One was solitude. He wasn't afraid to get off by himself. It's really interesting if you trace when he went off by himself. After he was baptized he went off for forty days—that's a long period of time. How many of you have taken that much time away? So Satan made a mistake to tempt him then because he might have been hungry, but Jesus knew *who* he was and *whose* he was. He went off by himself after he found out John the Baptist was killed, I think to deal with grief. He went off by himself after he fed the 5,000, I think to deal with ego and pride—remember, he was both human and God, and they wanted to make him king. The story I got the biggest kick out of was when he was healing the sick one day and the disciples were getting excited: "You know, this could be a really good business!" The next line of the Bible is "Early the next morning Jesus went off by himself to a solitary place to pray." This is the second habit—prayer, a conversation with someone more powerful than you. And when the disciples woke up, the crowd was there but Jesus wasn't there. So they went and found him and said, "Come, they're waiting for you." Now, did Jesus care about these people? Sure he did. I don't think there's been a more empathetic person on earth. Remember, you are going to be tempted by stuff that seems attractive. You'll get tempted by lousy decisions. You'll get tempted by attractive options. And Jesus said, "No, let's go to the next village so I can preach, for that is why I've come." He didn't come to be the greatest healer of all time; he came to spread the Good News and the Gospel.

So he had solitude, he had prayer—he was constantly in prayer, even at the end, saying, "Do I have to do this?" Third, he understood Scripture. I always say to people, "What do you read? Are you reading junk or good stuff?" When Satan tempted Jesus, he could've blown Satan off and said, "Hey, baby, I'm number two, at least. You'd best get out of here." But what did he do? He said, "It is written." How many times did he quote Scriptures? And boy, you need those sometimes.

My friend Bob Buford, who wrote the wonderful book *Halftime*, got a call years ago that his son, Ross, was missing. Ross had been camping out on the Rio Grande River with a couple of buddies and they got this crazy idea about what it would be like to be an illegal alien—so they swam across the Rio Grande River, except it was January, and only one of them made it. Bob got everything money could buy: helicopters and trackers and all. That afternoon he was on a bluff with an old guy who had been tracking illegal aliens for over thirty years and Bob said, "What are the chances I'll ever see my son again?" The guy said, "Not good." And Bob said, "I was thinking of jumping off the cliff." Ross was his only child; he loved that kid more than anybody could love anybody. And all of the sudden he remembered Proverbs 3:5, "Trust in God with all your heart and lean not on your own understanding," because it doesn't make any sense for a twenty-three-year-old kid to die. And Bob said, "That saved my life because I thought, well, I just missed out on thirty years with Ross, but what's that compared to eternity? There's important things to be done."

A fourth habit Jesus practiced was having a small group he could be vulnerable with. He took Peter and John and James away. We all need a small group that we can be vulnerable with, a group that can also be honest with us. Do you have a small accountability group?

And then, finally, undoubtedly the greatest habit of all, is trusting in the unconditional love of God. I say to parents all the time, "How many of you love your kids?" They all laugh and put their hands up. "How many of you love your kids only if they're successful, if they're good athletes, good students?" People don't put their hands up. And so I say, "So you mean you love your kids unconditionally? What if you accept that unconditional love for yourself? What if you realized that you can't earn enough, you can't perform well enough, you can't sell enough, you can't do anything to get any more love. You've got all the love there is." Then you're going to have a different perspective on life.

One of the things I think is so important for people who want to be servant-leaders is to find a way to enter their day slowly. Norman Vincent Peale and I said we all have two selves. We have an external, task-oriented self that's used to getting jobs done, and then we have an inner, thoughtful, reflective self. Which of those two selves wakes up quicker in the morning? It's the external, task-oriented one. What happens? The alarm goes off. Have you ever thought about what a stupid term that is? As my friend, teacher, and well-known author John Ortberg says, "Why isn't it the 'opportunity clock' or the 'it's going to be a great day' clock?" No, it's the *alarm*! Boom, bang, you jump out of bed and right away you're into your task-oriented self. You're trying to eat while you're washing and you jump in the car and start talking on the phone. You've got yourself running to this meeting, that meeting, here, there, and all, and finally you get home, eight, nine, ten o'clock at night, absolutely exhausted, fall into bed, and don't even have enough energy to say "Good night" to somebody lying next to you. The next day, *boom*, you're out of there again. I find that a lot of good-intentioned people are caught in a rat race. Lily Tomlin, the comedian and actress, once said that the problem with the rat race is that even if you win it, you're still a rat. That's why I think we need to enter our day more slowly and maybe recalibrate who we want to be in the world so that we have a higher chance of succeeding. But if we don't, we're just going to race around.

I met a CEO once who had an amazing approach to problem solving. Whenever his organization had a problem, he'd gather information about it. Once he had all the information, he'd say to his people, "Okay, we're going to go to solution now. But before we do that, I want you to spread out around the building and sit quietly, or take a walk for about a half hour. Whatever you do, I want you to quiet yourself. No telephone, nothing to read. And I want you to look for the answer within." He told me it blew his mind to see how people's clarity and decision-making capacity would come back when they had a chance to quiet themselves and think through something without all kinds of distractions. I think half our problem of not behaving on our good intentions is that we don't give ourselves any space to recalibrate who we want to be.

I never was a journal writer; I have friends who do journal writing in four colors and write poetry, and I'm competitive enough that if I'm going to write a journal I want it to be one of the best journals around. Bill Hybels told me he resisted journal writing for the same reason until he was a chaplain for the Chicago Bears. As part of his role, Bill would lead a Bible study on Monday morning. After Bible study, the team would watch the game films from the weekend. They would identify what they thought went well, what they thought didn't go so well, and what they needed to change. Bill said, "Man, *that's* a journal."

Write in a journal at the end of the day and start it off with praisings—what you did today that's consistent with who you want to be—and pat yourself on the back. Then write some redirections—what did you do today that you'd love to have another shot at. Maybe it's something you ought to apologize or ask forgiveness for. But if you kept track, started your day slowly, got a chance to really set a vision of who you wanted to be, and then gave yourself a score at the end of the day, that's a powerful way to run your life.

Servant-leadership is not only powerful for everybody around you, it's also powerful for you. It's a win-win. I see people who are servant-leaders with inner peace, with a quiet joy in them, and I think, Why? It's because they're doing good things. But they're also constantly examining themselves. They want to behave on their good intentions. I think that's so key. And that gets back to the heart. I think the heart and the habits are just two pieces that I wasn't into before, but man, are they powerful for people who want to be servant leaders.

Chapter Eight

Mary McFarland

Interviewed by Michael R. Carey

Dr. McFarland is the director of Jesuit Commons: Higher Education at the Margins, providing higher education to refugees throughout the world. Prior to her work with Jesuit Commons, Dr. McFarland was the dean of the School of Professional Studies at Gonzaga University and represented Gonzaga at JesuitNet, which is a partnership of twenty-five Jesuit universities committed to the design and delivery of distance learning. Dr. McFarland is cofounder of the Gonzaga University Renaissance Center for Leadership, and serves as a consultant in the area of leadership development. As a full professor, her teaching focus was on health-care policy, nursing education, and leadership in corporate and higher-education settings. Dr. McFarland's research foci includes international refugee educational formation, visionary leadership, and effective leadership strategies during times of corporate organizational transformation. She serves on the Board of Directors for Regence BlueShield of Idaho and is a member of the Quality Care Committee of the Board of Directors of Saint Alphonsus Regional Medical Center in Boise, Idaho. Her career in nursing has included critical care, hospice, adult nurse practitioner, and nursing education. Dr. McFarland is a Robert Wood Johnson Fellow and previously completed a three-year funded project in the Nurse Executive leadership program.

Michael Carey: Your own research work and thinking was in the area of visionary leadership. Please talk about how you understand servant-leadership connected with visionary leadership, focused on foresight.

Mary McFarland: When I first started to read about servant-leadership foresight really caught my attention. I had done my dissertation study in visionary leadership and there was such a correlation from my understanding of the concept of foresight to the important role that visionary leaders have, the sense of how to track driving forces to bring organizations and people to a better direction. Driving forces as those things that are very evident to us, we sense them, we see there are trends emerging, but we haven't felt the full force yet. So from a servant-leadership perspective, at a corporate or organizational level, how do we help bring attention to that so that people can prepare and continue to be very productive toward a new direction? The servant-leader as a visionary leader understands the sense of the future needs to come from doing the homework—reading, studying—but that it is only going to be meaningful if you truly bring in the collective ideas of people. Key to servant-leadership, is the responsibility to begin to articulate what this future is, the sketch of it, so that you can ignite people's hearts and ideas and minds so that they contribute to the foresight, and eventually life becomes this whole collective journey that we all want to be on. The process is not linear, it is not singular, but truly, a very profound question comes with it: Are others better off having been served by that leader? A leader that can help a group anticipate what is coming down the road—not dictating it, but truly feeling the way with others—that, for me, is the connection.

MC: For a servant-leader today in American society, what are the key issues in building the foresight necessary to prepare people for what we need today?

MM: I think for people striving to engage in servant-leadership today in America there are so many things we need to have our eye on about the world. The Internet, communication strategies, and all the ways we can connect outward are so profound right now that a person can feel bombarded, and maybe the weight is too much: How do we figure it all out? In servant-leadership, how do we help people become healthier in mind, body, and spirit, understanding that the world really is at our doorstep right now?

Leaders in America have to come to new strategies of how we understand the world if we are truly going to engage in productive outcomes regarding foresight. So what are we reading, who are we talking about, what is capturing our imagination so that we can be informed and have better questions that we ask of people, that we ask of ourselves, questions that are informed beyond the boundaries of our own country, state, home? What do we expect of the news? What do we expect of our politicians? From a framework of servant-leadership, this connection to foresight and stewardship is huge. What kind of stewards are we going to be of the air, of the water, of the people of the world who are least privileged?

I want to give one particular example. I've just come back from several months of traveling over a period of time and about a month working in Kakuma Refugee Camp, just south of the Sudan border, and had a great experience of teaching a section of servant-leadership. So I thought about Larry Spears and Mike Carey, Shann Ferch, all the people that are so engaged in this work and was wishing everybody could be there to hear these students who come from seven different countries—some have lived in the refugee camp for a few years, some almost from birth, some relatively new. We're doing an introduction to the concept of leadership using servant-leadership as the framework. On the concept of foresight, what the people there helped me understand was that our view of the future is very different because we believe we have a future. And there are places in the world where people need to focus so much on what is happening today, at this moment, that their idea of the future is very different. And as we talked about servant-leadership and the characteristics that Larry Spears has identified and in small groups they tackled each characteristic to see, from their own cultural perspective, what each characteristic meant to them. With foresight it was difficult because people around the world don't always know they have a future, so then how do they prepare for it? Now this is part of a program that is just beginning, it's an initiative of the Jesuit universities worldwide and as part of the admission process students were asked to articulate what they thought they could do if they entered into tertiary education, and without fail the students, even those not admitted, talked about the hope that they had to go back to their home country and if they became educated they felt they would be better prepared to make a difference to their people, to their community. And so I brought that perspective back into this class conversation now with the group that's been admitted. That helped because there is a belief and a hope in people from the countries who have a chronic history of war that the people can go back and actually be of service to others, including those who have significantly oppressed them. So I think there is enormous potential as we understand more about foresight.

In our doctoral program at Gonzaga we have doctoral students who complete their dissertations on the concept of foresight, and I think as we have more people engaged in the concepts of servant-leadership, and continue to take an empirical look at what servant-leadership means, I believe we can put it to better use. My hope is that we'll do that very much from a global perspective.

MC: Mary, in your work in leadership throughout the globe, what insights have you come to regarding how servant-leadership is understood in other parts of the world?

MM: In traveling to several different places in the world and having an opportunity to address aspects of servant-leadership with students who are in different systems I've asked people, "When you hear the term *servant-leadership* what comes to mind from your cultural context?" It's very interesting. Some people from different countries will focus on the word *servant*. I had one group explain, "Well, that would be like if you're the slave or if you were the hired person at the house that has to do all the work and serve everybody else." Then we also talk about the concept of leadership and in many cultures that is a very loaded term, which surprised me when I first started the conversations in different countries, because we're so comfortable with it here. We have a doctoral program, we have undergraduate, graduate, at the university it's a key principle of Jesuit education, it's just part of our fiber. In other countries it raises all kinds of concerns. As a matter of fact in one location I was asked not to use the term because in that country it created a concern about whether we were making an effort to overthrow the government by teaching people about leadership roles. So, instead of calling one whole area of this new model "Community Leadership Tracks," we now call them "Community Service Learning Tracks," because there was sincere trepidation about the term *leadership* and how that would be perceived.

On the servant part, the group of refugee students studying in Kakuma Camp came to a realization from conversation and then from reading about servant-leadership, that it did in fact have a very different connotation than what they first thought. As part of the admission process Dr. Mark Beatty had given us a quote by Julius Nyerere, the past president of Tanzania, and in that quote Nyerere poses the obligation that people who have access to an education are actually obliged to go back to their community and make a broader difference. So in the admission process we had the students address whether or not they agree with that quote. If they agreed, how might that come to life for them in their own role? So in this segment of a class on servant-leadership we used some of their responses from the admission interview to talk about the reality of servant-leadership tied into their hopes for when they went back home to serve their home community, and, importantly, today, when they left class. What could they do to help make the life of someone else better? They're going to be part of a very small population of people—of eighty thousand people who live in the Camp, thirty-two were selected to study—so what do they do today and tomorrow to be of service to their community matters. On that they could just take off on the conversation about what their hopes were wherever they found themselves living. So I think servant-leadership has very powerful, significant implications for people even in very dire circumstances.

We know around the world right now the average length of stay in a refugee camp is eighteen to twenty years, so some of the people won't go back home. Some of the people who will be the students in this program are actually born in the camp or have been on the run coming in early on their life, so this thought of making a difference today, even if we are in the camp, was very significant. We're in the context of people living in a circumstance they haven't chosen, this thought of, no, this approach could be so helpful and how, how do we just realize we are here at this moment and we can be of service to other people. Even a small action on our part really can be felt in different places in the world. And in different places in the world as people come into greater understanding—I think they always understood servant-leadership from the inside—but now to have a name to call what they want to do, this entity of servant-leadership, it gives people a parameter, a framework to go forward, which is really exciting.

MC: You've worked now for a number of years on different boards here in the United States, and certainly Greenleaf's initial work was for boards. Talk about servant-leadership from your perspective as a member of a board, of working on boards, how do you see it applicable, how do you see it actually experienced?

MM: For boards of directors in the context of servant-leadership there is tremendous value and opportunity. Some of our corporate structures, our fast pace of meeting quarterly deadlines, expectations of shareholders, can put tremendous pressure on a company, even the most ethical people within that company. Certainly there is great pressure for CEOs, presidents, people who are genuinely trying to do their best to keep an organization moving forward at a pace that's necessary in today's world, but without losing sight of the people who are both being served by that company and the employees who are helping the company get there. For boards of directors to have an understanding and an appreciation of the concepts that form the framework of servant-leadership can be of immense help. Even taking the perspective around empathy and listening, a board of directors can be a great help to a CEO. Boards help a CEO notice those moments that become too rapid, where the challenges are not providing an opportunity for that CEO to have a moment of reflection to determine if we going the right direction. Boards hold a mirror up about—a link back to the stewardship concept—is this company actually being a good steward of our world, our country, our environment, of the people who have trust in us? So from the perspective of a board of directors, I am always so grateful to have read Greenleaf's work, to have had a chance to intersect with people who are studying and really trying to implement the principles of servant-leadership, because it makes a big difference in how we pose a question, in how we can help our fellow directors take a deep breath and be sure we are asking the depth of questions we need to ask and are listening with a heart and a mind that keeps the mission of this company at the forefront?

The principle of foresight is crucial for boards of directors. There is this drive to be ready for what's coming down the pike. Highly competitive environments create their own set of challenges around ethical decision-making. They also can be a very rich source of ethical decision-making. But that principle of servant-leadership engages the question, Will people actually be better off from having been served by this board of directors, in how that board supports the CEO and has their eye on the mission of the organization? I think it's part of the reason we see more companies actually adopting a philosophical premise around servant-leadership.

MC: Is there a particular leadership challenge you've faced where your understanding and practice of servant-leadership proved to be an asset?

MM: I think it would be more difficult to think of one where it wasn't an asset. I came out of a career in nursing. At a cellular level servant-leadership is found in that profession. Early on I didn't have the terminology about servant-leadership but the reality of serving others, helping nurture them back to their best state of health or to a peaceful death was paramount. Those lessons have been a great help as I moved into higher education and work on boards, on a board of trustees for a medical center, for example, and certainly in working as the dean of a very vibrant school. If people aren't healthier and freer and wiser, oh, we've just made a terrible mistake, because there is such collective wisdom available out there.

I can feel it when I'm not engaged at a servant-leadership level and again, that's not to say that I'm a servant-leader, because I don't think it is the individual's right to say that. But as an individual this mission, this quest toward servant-leadership tells us what could make the biggest difference. And when I'm not doing it, I can feel it and sometimes somebody would walk out of the office and I'd just think, I wish I could have a redo. I wish I could rewind that tape. There were other ways to address the issue that would have made the person, open up other solutions. I love the quote by Mary Anne Radmacher: "courage does not always roar, sometimes it is that quiet voice at the end of the day that says I will try again tomorrow." The bar is high because the outcome could be so tremendous. So when as a leader I've had chances to get a glimmer of it, I add that moment to that toolbox. I've got to find ways to do that more often because generally the human spirit is so incredible and the people we work with, they want to do their best on behalf of many other people, so when we find ourselves being the one in a position that could help open that door, it's a vital asset. And then on the days when I fall short, I hope I can have courage to try this again tomorrow and do a better job. Servant-leadership is tremendous way of life.

MC: How have you changed over the years, how have you developed related to this idea of servant-leadership?

MM: This striving to develop oneself as a servant-leader for me personally has made a difference. I think I realized early on as a critical-care nurse how good it is, and in fact I remember vividly coming in to work—I worked a lot of night shifts—and I came in and most of the people were in their eighties and nineties. They were on respirators. I remember saying to my colleague, "You know, there has to be a better way to leave this world." And we had bells on the door. Family members would have to ring the doorbell to come in; the nurses, physicians, we could come in and out, but families who should have been at the bedside had to actually ask permission to come in: I couldn't stand that. One of the early initiatives was how do we change this? How do we get the right people at the bedside who can actually help in the spiritual context, who can truly nurture the one who is either going to die or recover? So, in the context of servant-leadership—again at that time I didn't have the terminology for it—how do we look at something in the system we know isn't the best for people and get that shifted around. So part of the journey has been an awareness even at a very personal level of caring for someone in a situation who needs nursing care, and then taking that from the servant-leadership perspective to a policy level, to actually shift things for the good of many people. That experience in critical care is what made me start a hospice program. An incredible experience with a great group of people. There are times in people's lives when things feel so out of control: for a family member who is about to lose a loved one, for a person who is terminally ill who needs to find a way to say good-bye to everybody. In those moments servant-leadership involves a sense of listening deeply, of empathy—not sympathy, truly empathy. Those things have stayed on the journey with me, and I hope they do until I'm the one that's ready to move on and needing somebody to help facilitate that part of my life.

In our professional and personal lives we encounter incredible opportunities to be stewards of what is healthiest and what we can contribute to a situation. So it might be stewardship in the context of what could happen in a family or in health care or in higher education or in a corporate setting. These linkages, how they intersect, have been tremendous lessons for me. The current work that I'm doing with refugees around the world is just rattling my brain cells. I'm amazed by the human capacity for resilience, for forgiveness, and how people in truly dire circumstances can still want from a cellular level to give something back, to make something better for people. So I've got a lot left to learn. I hope I get some time to keep learning it. But that personal journey, I think it's that mirror that you hold up and you know instantly if you did something selfish, because it will just yell back, and servant-leadership provides a framework, an umbrella, to help just do a little bit better every day. That's the personal journey.

MC: Tell me about the ten characteristics of servant-leadership from a cultural perspective?

MM: With regard to the ten characteristics related to cultural applications, I'm really intrigued with the area of conceptualization. Sometimes the conflict that we encounter is so pertinent to the area of conceptualization. In just taking some time to truly see if there is an understanding of what we're talking about, not that it has to be agreed upon, but is there a shared understanding of what we are actually engaged in, that has become so significant in the cultural aspects of working with people from many different countries in the same setting. One of the things we did recently was to get used the concept of a greeting. So, how do you greet someone? How do you say hello or make someone feel welcome? And it was fascinating. A student from Somalia told the story of first arriving at the refugee camp and seeing two Sudanese men, in retrospect he realized greet each other, but he thought he was going to have to break up a fight. And he said what he observed was two people come up to each other, and first there was a handshake and then there was violent beating on the shoulders, and he said he didn't know what he should do, should he break it up? And then of course the Sudanese students in the class had a good laugh because that is their greeting, meaning, "I haven't seen you for so long, I'm so happy to see you." So as a community of learners, how do we help support each other? How do we become servant-leaders to each other in the struggle to acquire new knowledge?

From a cultural perspective it is important to first understand where we could have cultural misunderstandings so that someone doesn't think, "Well, that was rude." Another student told the story of how in one culture clicking is the sign for "yes." Tongue clicking means, "That's great. Let's go on." And in another culture one student described it as, "If I ever clicked to my father there would have been a police case." Tongue clicking in that culture is considered rude, and very negative. In one classroom in the culture where clicking was acceptable, a new teacher came in and said, "I want to be sure I'm starting where the previous teacher was in this curriculum, and is this right?" And the students clicked. And the teacher stormed out of the room and went to the headmaster and said that was the rudest class he had ever encountered and he would not go back. And the student who was relaying this said, "You know, the students were like, What did we do? What was wrong?" So in the broader context of servant-leadership, if we truly want to be wiser ourselves as well, what do we pay attention to? Are we willing to ask questions to be sure that our concept or our conceptualization is similar? Can we really listen deeply at a point that brings empathy? It's so easy to say and it is so hard to do. There was a situation where our refugees had been asked to tell a little bit about their story, their life story, and it was moving along at an academic kind of a pace. We had done a section on communication, how communication can be data, factual, all the way down to feelings and beliefs. And then looking at this issue of story in relation to who are we becoming as a group, a new community of learners comprised now of seven countries who are sometimes at war with each other, and now we're in a small room learning together. The students—and this was another place where servant-leadership was so helpful, helping us ask ourselves: Do we have the courage to listen deeply? And once we have listened, do we have the human capacity to extend empathy? I kind of just stopped people and we referred back to the servant-leadership characteristics and to some of the base principles of communication and said, "Maybe we need to just step back for a minute and see, with permission from the group, does somebody want to tell the story different than just the key learning points so people will have a better understanding of what has really happened to create a turning point?" And one young man got up and told a very powerful story about his life, his family, the poverty that he had experienced, the life circumstance. He became very emotional and he sat down and my first response inside was, You know, maybe this moves it too fast. Maybe we aren't really prepared to hear the story. And then I just thought, again, and not at an academic level about servant-leadership, but trusting that people will determine if the pace is too fast. And when he sat down another student said, "You just brought us into your family, so now we are a new whole. We are going to be a family who learns together." The moment was so powerful. His vulnerability brought us all to a different point that could not have happened if people weren't willing. Understanding servant-leadership takes us to a different place if we can care about each other in that way.

MC: How does a servant-leader best deal with conflict?

MM: I think a servant-leader, in relationship to the dynamic of conflict, can actually get to where conflict can become a friend, because if we're engaged in meaningful work—substantial work that could actually create transformational change—there is going to be conflict. I'm actually in awe of people who believe you don't even have to go there, that there are just ways that you can be more gentle in the approach; so I'm not saying this is right, it's just in my own personal approach to it has been more that it's okay for conflict to arise, as long as we can stay within the parameters of respect and the mutuality of learning. Back again to the ten characteristics, there's so much there that can take us over the hurdle of conflict, or through the conflict, to a healthy resolution that really does make all of us wiser.

When I read Larry Spears's article on the Myers-Briggs connections between servant-leadership and the different categories, the different types that emerge with the Myers-Briggs, I thought, that could be a wonderful asset as we go into the situations where we anticipate we might encounter conflict. When people feel strongly about things this might create a conflict moment, but if we can understand more about the personality dynamic and have superimposed on that or interconnected with that the characteristics of servant-leadership I believe we will find very interesting outcomes. I've worked with people sometimes who I love as people but in a leadership role who at the end of the day still want everyone to like them. But there are times we just acknowledge what's bigger than everybody in the room is the issue at hand, and let's work through that and if we're a little upset with each other or a lot upset with each other, let's just know we will get through it and there will be another day we'll be holding hands, as partners again. In servant-leadership, gentleness comes to us, and we don't have to be a battering ram. I'm still working on and trying to learn from gentleness.

MC: If you were able to have a conversation with Robert Greenleaf today, what would you talk about?

MM: If I could talk to Robert Greenleaf today . . . wouldn't that be fun? I would love to know more about the emergence of the terminology of *servant* and *leadership*. At a cellular level, what did it mean? I would love to know what he would have done in a global world that is with us like this [*snaps fingers*] because of the Internet and Skype and Twitter and everything else that we encounter.

MC: What books intersect with servant-leadership for you?

MM: *The Talent Code* is a book that considers years of study on where are there hotbeds of talent, often in places you would never expect them to be. So I've been thinking about this idea of talent hotbeds where we don't expect it, and the thread throughout is that there was somebody or some group who encouraged, supported, provided some environmental net. And Gladwell's book *Outliers* provides an intersection where Gladwell studied geniuses and found that some geniuses, IQs of over 140, end up laying on a couch doing nothing, while others are Nobel Prize winners. He makes this profound statement: no matter how smart we are by IQ, if we don't have somebody—it doesn't even have to be our direct family—but somebody who recognizes there is potential, we do not reach the talent latent in us.

Thinking about the refugee camps, in reality we want home countries to be at peace in order to let people get back home, and yet we see it is not going to happen for some people, at least in our finite thinking right now. So what could happen from an education perspective if we're truly trying to address how people become healthier and wiser and freer? If we could do a better job as servant-leaders, if we could make that happen, what kind of talent hotbeds are sitting in these desolate areas that could make an incredible difference. There is not a doubt in my mind we have geniuses in the camps. They are there. If they could intersect with people in a different way, how could we create talent hotbeds there in the middle of the desolation? At a foundational level, I think that is what servant-leadership is. And I think as a world we have the capacity to generate greater health, wisdom, and freedom. Do we have the will and do we have the understanding and can we create an environment where talent hotbeds can emerge?

I believe we can.

Chapter Nine

Raymond Reyes

Interviewed by Michael R. Carey

Dr. Raymond F. Reyes currently serves as the associate academic vice president and chief diversity officer for Gonzaga University in Spokane, Washington. He has also served as the interim director for Gonzaga University's Center for Global Engagement. Prior to these administrative appointments he was an assistant professor in the School of Education at Gonzaga University. For the College of Arts and Sciences, he has taught undergraduate courses in sociology, religious studies, and philosophy. For the School of Business he has taught a graduate seminar for the MBA program on tribal leadership. All of these courses have issues of human rights, equity, and justice at their heart. He has thirty-three years of experience in Indian Education and professional development training. Reyes has conducted leadership development throughout the United States, Zambia, Mexico, Colombia, and Canada. His areas of scholarship and expertise are institutional diversity planning, implementation and assessment, optimizing organizational performance through intercultural competence and multicultural literacy, human development and learning, culturally responsive teaching, and Ignatian pedagogy. He is a founding board member of Gonzaga University's Institute for Hate Studies. He has served as a visiting professor at the University of Pretoria in South Africa, teaching doctoral seminars for the Department of Economic and Management Sciences, and is currently actively involved with Gonzaga University's study abroad programs in Zambia, Africa.

Michael Carey: What are your thoughts about servant-leadership and morality?

Raymond Reyes: My sense of morality and servant-leadership has a lot to do with the fundamental assumption or belief that my role is to bring out the best in people. I think it's a moral imperative on my part, personally and professionally, that I honor the *entelekheia* in the other, that diamond-essence is what Jean Houston calls it. So for me that's the beginning point for a sense of morality and how I interact with others.

Houston Smith once said that reason is too short of a ladder to reach the lofty heights of truth, and many times people see me as being unreasonable with my expectations of myself and others when it comes to servant-leadership and what it means to be a leader with such esoteric, abstract, ideological standards that are unimaginable in ever achieving or acting in a meaningful way, in a real way in the world. And I've been accused of being an idealist, and rightly so, because then the challenge becomes, if you're going to fly those kites, how do you drive the nails? How do you integrate yourself and keep yourself grounded in matters of practicality so you can have the potential of realizing these high ideals, this high standard. For me—and others that I admire, because I have not mastered or achieved these ways—I aspire to know that my foremost identity is spiritual and not physical. So number one is being able to see ourselves as spiritual beings having physical experiences. You're not a physical being having spiritual experiences; it's the other way around. So servant-leaders always have a perspective, a room with a view, that allows them—and I'm trying to learn this too—to see a larger context. The larger context reveals that this is not the end of the world, that our current experience has total beauty and symmetry to the whole pattern and design of everything else. In order to have that perspective, we have to have the discipline of being able to, as the old country-and-Western song goes, know when to hold them and when to fold them, when to be quiet and retrospective and when to reveal and engage. Such discernment has the quality of having the desert years in your life, we need time for sabbatical, we need time for removal from the chaotic pace of life, quiet time, and whether it's early in the morning prayer time or going for a run—I like to run—a person needs some time every twenty-four-hour cycle where it's your time, it's so you can sit with what the Platonics call, being pregnant in soul, you can have that fertile void, you can have that time to yourself. You need that; that's essential. We don't have to be religious or spiritual about this: it could be taking your dog for a walk, it could be playing pinochle, it could be praying in the morning at four thirty, it could be running, it could be riding your bike, it could be listening to classical music in your car while you're going to work—anything that is, that you declare, you intentionally declare as, "This is my sacred time to reconnect, with the big battery charger in the sky, or in the earth, to renew the sense of spirit and offer the clarity that will be required to live from this lofty height of being."

The other thing I see in servant-leaders is a sense of humor. I mean you can't take yourself too serious. The word *silly* in Old English used to be *siliġ*, it meant blessed, sacred, or touched, and so to dare to act your shoe size and not your age, and to dare to be vulnerable. As they say, dance like there's no one looking and love like you've never been hurt and work like you'll never get paid. Just to have the authenticity, the pristine curiosity of a three- or four-year-old, I mean, to me that is what sustains a leader to these high, lofty spiritual ideals of what it means to be a servant-leader: the silliness and playfulness of a three- or four-year-old, the wisdom of our desert fathers in terms of finding sanctuary with our own personhood and having time alone, the ability to have perspective and have a room with a view or be able to see that 360-degree vista of this moment compared to all the other moments, and how it is part of a tapestry of being that we can appreciate by virtue of what they say of a Monet painting: if you get too close to the painting you can't appreciate or see it; you have to get back to be able to appreciate its beauty.

From somebody I admire, Parker Palmer, I want to remember one of *my* favorite lines: to enjoy the rapture of being alive. There's nothing wrong with being alive. I try to enjoy the rapture of being alive. Get a kick out of who you are, look in the mirror in the morning and say, "You're a character." Like your own company, not in terms of ego, but in terms of revelation and saying, "My goodness, what do we have today." And going from the known to the unknown with that rapture and joy.

MC: When you think of servant-leader responsibility what comes to mind?

RR: *Entelekheia* is the Greek idea that we each have a sense of potential and essence we have yet to discover, and it is in human relationship that that is revealed and we actually have revelation with and for, not only for our selves, but for others; and that in relationships, I think, the moral imperative is to create the conditions that allow for servant-leadership to emerge so the common good can benefit from the grace and gifts that each person has, much like an acorn is the *entelekheia* of an oak tree. For me the moral imperative in leadership and in relationship with others, whether it's professionally or personally, is to optimize their human being-ness, their sense of personhood. Truth, love, beauty, all come into play through being mindful and vigilant to the idea that that person represents something—the active presence of God in all things. I need to be mindful of this, and seek to find out how I can I bring that out. This is also the sense of morality that drives why one would want to be fair, why one would want to be truthful, why one would want to be loving, compassionate, all the noblest things we talk about when we talk about being human.

MC: What is your understanding of servant-leadership with regard to race and gender?

RR: How we lead is who we are. And who we are is the sacred interaction of our biography and our biology. And so what leaders need to know about race, ethnicity, and gender and social class and religion and all the human difference below what I call the human, the blue dome, the earth, is to first know your own cultural identity. I believe that it speaks to what a leader needs to know about diversity or multicultural education or intercultural competency or intercultural literacy. To me diversity is really about Personhood 101. One of the first things that is important and essential in this literacy regarding human difference and how it plays out in the workplace and also as a leader is the idea that we see things how we are, not as it is, and it is through our lens of socialization and history and collective experience going back generations that we unconsciously are who our ancestors have been, and need to have a conscious realization and appreciation of who we are in that deep sense, that indeed we are all multicultural beings and it's amazing that it takes a lifetime, sometimes people are fifty and sixty years old before they get a full comprehension of their story, their history, their story, her-story. And so that's alpha point. Alpha point is to know your sacred story: Who are you as a multicultural being? And how does that legacy, that historical legacy of your biology and your biography influence your value system, your behavior, your thought process in terms of decision making, and the quality of relationships. We know that all behavior is learned and that culture is that living, breathing curriculum that incarnates our sense of humanity.

The second thing I think servant-leaders need to know about diversity and race and ethnicity, culture is that I could argue the roots of all human conflict come down to the other three Rs that we often have difficulty talking about. I mean, you look at the history of this planet and the conflicts that have occurred, they come down to conflict over race, religion, and resources. I believe if we are truly going to be about peace and service, we need to understand the root causes, or the epistemology, of those things pertaining to race and religion and resources. Servant-leaders need to understand the dynamics and nature of prejudice, discrimination, and bias. What are the sociological, psychological underpinnings that perpetuate, consciously or unconsciously, these kinds of behaviors?

The third element is, I believe, is "Who's who in the 'hood," is how I call it. Intercultural competency as it pertains to step one—"I know my story and I know who my people are"—or as the South Africans would say, I am because we are, I am because we have been, I am because of the cultural legacy and ancestral roots behind me. Second, I understand the nature and dynamics of prejudice, discrimination, bias, and oppression, and third is, I want to know other people's stories. What are other people's stories? You can't know everything, but how can I create relationship as a resonating chamber to understand, meaning know the similarities, understand the differences, so I can hear where the other person is, and how she or he comes to this moment? Finally, you are responsible for what you know, so act upon what you care about, out of respect.

So many times I talk about the intercultural literacies and competencies as being relationship, relevance, and respect, and that in traditional American education we often talk about reading, writing, and arithmetic being the traditional three Rs. And I'm suggesting that the three Rs that can resolve the roots of conflict—race, religion, and resources—are relationship: relationship, relevance, and respect. Relationship to self first: Who am I as a multicultural being in relationship to the other? It's not enough to know about the power of relationship, but to care about what you know and make it relevant. So it's that idea of questing for common ground. We know we are different, we all come from multiple perspectives, we have shared histories that come from different vantage points in terms of power and privilege. How do we reconcile that? And then most importantly, creating empathetic moments that give us, not altruism, but the ability to hear the call for respect and to act upon what we know out of respect. To me, that's what servant-leaders need to know about diversity and multiculturalism. And I always like to say that PC does not stand for being politically correct, it means promoting consciousness, or in other ways, creating positive choices. With awareness we create choices to act differently, and diversity for me is about a constant vigilance to be aware so I can make better choices in how I manage the mission of an organization and how I self-manage myself as a trustee leader for others.

Let me give you an example very quickly. Out here on the road—and you see this in a lot of communities—you're driving and you see this sign and it's flashing and it says twenty-five miles an hour. It tells you how fast you're going. And I think to myself, why are they telling me that . . . I can see that I'm speeding, but I make it a game now. Right out here in front of Gonzaga

University they have this thing and it fluctuates. Somebody in front of me is supposed to be going twenty-five and they're going thirty-five or forty, and I slow down, but I'm still speeding so I slow down, and I want to see theirs say twenty-five miles an hour. So it becomes a game, you know, but a game of conformity, and a game that allows me to understand that with awareness, the awareness of constantly giving me immediate feedback, I can change my behavior and I can be lawful. Silly as it may sound, human relationship does that. Here, again, I affirm the idea of bringing out the essence in other, the diamond essence in other, bringing out the goodness essence in others, or seeing the Good News in others and not being misguided or ill-informed by the difference that I might have an allergic reaction to: if I'm Catholic/Jewish, if I'm male/female, if I'm gay/lesbian/straight, if I'm Indian/Mexican/black/white, whatever it may be, and it's an invitation to really have greater awareness. Hence, to make different choices about how we're going to interact and the quality of the relationship and optimize the creative intelligence of the organization. Again, many people talk about the business case for diversity. I want to believe beyond compliance and the economic imperative, there's a moral imperative that one would want to have their workforce interculturally competent.

MC: As a servant-leader how do you work with opposing views?

RR: First, I believe that people do the best they can do, even though it might not be compatible or friendly to my viewpoint. And so the best way that I have learned to address and interact and have relationship with people who may not have the same ideology I have, or interpretation of the mission of the organization, is to try to find what common ground we have, because I actually believe that every position has an opposition. So it's a grace of God to have multiple perspectives, or in Gandhi's terms, informed dissent. So how can I cultivate and nurture informed dissent? The operative here is *informed*, and who defines what is informed dissent.

Underneath the opposition, because I think any conflict is the result of an unmet need or an unhealed wound, is a concern, an interest, or a need, whether it's about what I believe, or it's about an interpretation of the mission. As you do the archaeological dig—in relationship this is labor-intensive and it takes time—you need the patience to go and understand what the need, concern, or interest is, and what drives that as a quality, a value, what people value. Beneath that is the essence of the person.

And so always trying to quest and say, for example, at a place like Gonzaga University, let's take Catholic social thought and the issue of sexual orientation, or Planned Parenthood and abortion. You know, you have a position, you have the opposition, and underneath it you have a concern, an interest, or an issue related to pro-choice, pro-life, whatever it may be. Sexual orientation, same thing. What that represents for people, and what are the concerns, the interests, et cetera. And beneath that is a value or a quality, depending on, here again, what the concern or interest is, and I think my role and duty as a leader is to try to reveal for the other person and for myself, what is the quality underneath. And I think that's the aquifer that nurtures the stuff at the surface that gets in the way of clear thinking and clear communication.

And typically what I find is that the quality or the value that is driving the concern or the interest or the need is something that we both have in common, only it's being experienced differently, whether it's fidelity to the Bible and what the Bible says about homosexuality, for example, and what it means to "be good," but then the quality is to be good, and then my sense of to "be good" is to be inclusive, to see the total human being, and my interpretation of the Bible might be different, but here again, the quality is this goodness of fit with what does it mean to be human, you know, that we want the truth but the interpretation of something give us another whole manifestation of behavior and ideology at the surface level.

And then beneath it all is this essence, and so I think that the method to interact with people that have a different ideology or philosophy than I do is to take the time to get beneath the behavior that I many times have experienced as the symptomology of their passion for what interests them, what their concern is, what their need is, and try to resonate beneath that what the character or the quality or value that is supporting that position that creates the opposition, the common ground.

And that presupposes the common good in trying to figure that out. But I think that the primary beginning point is to believe that everybody is trying to do the best that they can, putting a positive interpretation on the other's behavior. In the Ignatian tradition, it's the principle of presupposition, that I am going to put a positive interpretation on the sentiment, behavior, feelings of the other. And it's a difficult one. It's a challenging one because many times we just want to say, "My way or the highway." We want to believe that we are the ones with the roadmap to the Holy Grail and no one else has or knows what we know. And it's a difficult challenge.

MC: Tell us more about your understanding of *entelekheia*.

RR: *Entelekheia* in the moral imperative is, pedagogically speaking, how you do something and what becomes of what you do. For me, it operates from the idea of love. I know that's an abstract notion, but love, for me, is goodwill in action. Love is a gift. Love is unconditional, you don't have to do anything to receive it. Love is an emotional response to a need. So the idea of approaching somebody in a moral way—the method—has to do with my understanding of the human notion that we all want to be loved and we all want to love. I believe that. I assume about everybody I work with—transcendent of gender, race, sexual orientation, religion—that this thing, this DNA of love, this spiritual DNA we all have is transcendent of our human difference and becomes the common ground and basis for morality that can be inclusive. My presupposition is that as human beings, we all have a need to be loved and we all have a need to love. From there that becomes the method. One of the operatives is: do no harm. I will do no harm, or try to do no harm. I want to be coresponsible for what I say and what I do and how it affects others, and understand that I am imperfect in an imperfect world, but I also have the ability and the responsibility to self-correct in midflight when I catch myself, either with sins of omission or sins of commission that will inhibit the *entelekheia* from emerging in that person.

MC: Can you tell me of your experience of Greenleaf's work?

RR: I was introduced to Robert Greenleaf's work many, many years ago, and I think—no, I know, the thing that really resonates with me is that the principles of servant-leadership are a clear blueprint for how a leader can incarnate the followership's sense of potential. For me the purpose of life is to honor ourselves, honor our ancestors, and ultimately honor God: she/he/it, the Creator, however we define that. And a leader is uniquely positioned to do that for others and for themselves. Robert Greenleaf's work lays out a whole method and raison d'être for doing that. What else is the purpose of life? When you think about the Christian ideal to treat others as we would like to be treated, or to love others, to love your neighbor as yourself, or the idea of cause and effect and karma, or the idea of the principle of interdependence, what goes around, comes around, what better way to work with the order of life and the universe than to be a servant-leader? It makes sense outside the organization, in the community, at home, in your own family. In fact, if everyone adopted that as an orienting way of being in the world, the promise of minimizing dysfunction would be greater. Servant-leadership is truly living out what it means to be human and taking words like empathy and compassion and respect and truth and love and imbuing them with a sense of practicality and lived experience. Servant-leadership goes hand in glove with what I believe shows the greatest promise for the greatest good, not only for myself, but for others.

MC: Greenleaf spoke about ethics and servant-leadership. What do you believe about ethics?

RR: The connection between individual, workplace, and global ethics is so intimate and so seamless there is no difference. They're all the same, because I believe it all boils down to Martin Luther King's notion of the beloved community, and in the beloved community he talked about different types of love. There are three different types of love and I will expand it to four different types of love. He said there's God love, and you can look at this through that prism, through that lens of individual, the workplace, the work culture, and the global society. He said that God love is the height of love, God love is about our purpose and our divinity in our relationship with God. This means we understand our destiny and that each one of us has a purpose. The second type of love, self-love, is about the skills and the abilities we all have, and it is through prayer and ritual and ceremony, or spiritual exercise, or religious discipline that we learn how our gifts and abilities will honor the purpose that we've been given. The third type of love, love for others, involves our relationship with others, agape love, unconditional love, or as I've often said and talked about in my teaching, the idea that love is a gift, and it's timeless. Anthony de Mello once said, "Does the light say I will share my light with the good people in the room and deny the light to the 'bad' people in the room? Or does the rose say I'm going to withhold my wonderful fragrance from the evil people and share my beautiful fragrance with the good people? Or on a hot day, does a tree say, I'm going to share my soothing, refreshing shade with the good people and withhold it from the 'bad' people? No." I think that's what we're called to do in this other love sense, transcendent of what we believe, whether we have issues regarding human difference or not, we are called to understand that person is a living curriculum, a part of our journey to spiritualize our consciousness, to master the love and the lessons of love and service. And so for me when I think about the connections between the individual and the workplace and society at large, or the global society, I hope to ground it in the notion of the beloved community Martin Luther King often talked about.

The symbol of the cross or the medicine wheel is the vertical relationship with God and the horizontal relationship with others. Going down even further is the fourth notion of our first mother, the mother earth: to have a love relationship with the environment and with the planet. If we're right with God and we're right with ourselves and we're right with others and we're right with the earth, then whether we're talking about the individual level or whether we're talking about the work culture or whether we're talking about the broader global context, everything is going to be good. All things will be good . . . we will find the potential for balance and harmony. That's the beauty of being imperfect: there are multiple opportunities to master the lessons, and in the process hopefully the journey is rewarding and joyful. To me, love is the heart and soul. Love creates the interdependent synergy of these four dimensions.

MC: What do you see as the causes of dysfunction in organizations?

RR: You know, organizations would be okay if there weren't any people. One of my favorite bumper stickers is, "Life is a metaphor for group therapy." I believe, with John Bradshaw and Virginia Satir and Milton Erickson and others, that 99.9 percent of the planet is dysfunctional. We are! Why? Because our lives are the midwife for soul. We are here to incarnate a sense of the divine, and what better way to do it than to be dysfunctional? Now I also believe that sin comes from life—you know, S-I-N, self-inflicted nonsense—and that in this thing called life we reveal our dysfunction. For me the causes of dysfunction relate—and there's a multitude of reasons for this, given our family experience—to the need to be loved and the need to love. The older I get and the more I experience different cultures and different places on this planet, the more I am convinced that if this innate spiritual DNA quality is subterfuged, is sabotaged, is somehow killed for any reason at any point in our formative process, then we create a maladaptive response. Anne Wilson Schaef, who wrote *Addictive Organizations* and *When Society Becomes an Addict* and other books, talks about the interface between one's family history and what we've experienced in our first twelve years on this planet and then how we enact those experiences in the work culture. So many times you don't know who you're dealing with because you truly don't know their history. But, to me, the root of all dysfunction is the need to be love and be loved. From love we find the ability to consciously live and not be playing old tapes and projecting old relationships onto somebody who is sitting, standing in front of us in the workplace. I know that that's a pretty limiting definition of human dysfunction, but I am also a spiritual/religious junkie and have spent much of my life reading and studying different religious traditions, both in the formal sense as well as tribal, ceremonial life, and I've come to what I'd call a safe generalization that most of these traditions have in common: that life truly is about learning how to love. Learning how to love and then, once you learn how to love, stepping into service. Life is about love and service.

I know people want highly complex, multidimensional assessments, evaluation, and analysis of what constitutes human dysfunction, but I'm here to tell you that as many times as I've been around the sun—and I'll say it's been over fifty and counting—that life is truly about learning how to love. Once you learn how to love—and it's always a process, *i-n-g*, always in progress, a work in progress, never arriving—we are then called to step into service and do something with that love. When that is somehow compromised or repressed or suppressed, that's when you get into these aggravated dysfunctional responses because I actually believe that we either act upon our feelings or act them out.

I also believe our emotional life is our spiritual report card and that human dysfunction is another invitation that says, What are you going to do about who you are? We get multiple invitations for that sort of transformation, and transformation indeed occurs in human relationship, and what better way to establish creative tension that will midwife a new way of being and knowing in the world than dysfunction? Learning to be the alchemist. I think we're all called, if we're about transformation and about improvement and progress, to take responsibility for knowing that we are the alchemist in our lives, and potentially the alchemist for others, too, if it's mutually consenting in nature, to be able to use dysfunction—i.e., make lemonade out of a lemon—for the benefit of all. To me that is the role of dysfunction.

So I guess dysfunction is a blessing in disguise. It is the grace of God masked in regalia and costumed in things we cannot even imagine. In Greek the word *imagine* means a moment's intuition into reality. So what is dysfunction? It is an image of God. It is God incarnate inviting us to be who we really are, to get to the other side of the illusion and cut through our prejudices and preconceived notions and our judgments about the other, to do what Anthony de Mello said in the book *Awareness: The Perils and Opportunities of Reality*, that all human beings have difficulty doing three things, which is what dysfunction presents to us: We have difficulty including the excluded, we have difficulty responding to hate with love, and we have difficulty admitting we are wrong when we're wrong. What better way to be humbled by the three things that all human beings have difficulty doing than having to confront, to interact, embrace, reconcile, and love, ultimately, not only our dysfunction, but the dysfunction of others? Hallelujah! Let's hear it for dysfunction!

MC: How do you use servant-leadership to deal with the darker moments of life?

RR: Carl Jung once said that we don't become enlightened by imaginary figures of light, but illuminated by our shadows. Fear to me is the darkroom where negatives are developed and when I have doubt and fear in my heart, it's a reminder that I have to embrace my shadow. The brighter the light, the darker the shadow. And I've realized in my life that I haven't always been the altar boy that I used to be when I was twelve years old, and that I have done some things and said some things that have not been good for myself or for others, and likewise have created many times doubt and fears in my heart. But I also want to believe that I want to know as I am known by God, and I know that there's at least one being that exists that knows me in my full sense and still loves me despite what he/she/it knows. The doubt is a reminder to get back in touch with God's love for me, and there have been times in my life when I have experienced the presence of God and I have felt God's love for me; not all the time, it's not like a running faucet that's going, it's not like the river out here flowing all the time. I have to remind myself that it's there. Fear and doubt come to me when I have taken my grace for granted and I have run on automatic pilot for an extended period of time and I haven't been taking time for myself, I haven't been integrated, I haven't been healthy, and so it's an early-warning sign to say, "Raymond, wake up, be vigilant to who you really are, and remind yourself of God's love for you." To servant-lead myself is to know myself the way God knows me and to embrace my light as well as my dark, my luminosity as well as my shadows, because all things come from God.

MC: You are one of the best people I know with regard to dealing with conflict. What is the role of servant-leadership in dealing with conflict?

RR: When I am in a moment of conflict . . . my immediate reaction, to be honest with you, is to react. I burn hot. I'm a passionate person. I really hold strong convictions. So . . . when there's a conflicting situation going on I will use that as a wake-up call, first—and this sounds silly—to breathe. Just to breathe. To breathe. Because sometimes I can actually feel—I guess this is it with conflict. I want my head to be connected to my heart. The older I get the more I realize that if your head is not connected to your heart you can hurt people. I've done it before in my life. I have hurt people. I've been disrespectful and I've hurt people because I have worshiped at the altar of reason and logic and will do the frontal assault on whatever is going on. It's like putting fire out with gasoline. You will not address, heal, or reconcile conflict if you react. So my challenge is, is when I'm in a meeting—and believe me, I have plenty of opportunities here—I have to remember to pause and not be impulsive and to breathe. And the breath down deep is a physical reminder that whatever I say and whatever I do, is a prayer to the other person, and that that prayer will be connected to my heart as I say something, because in a lot of tribal languages relationships can be prayerful and that the word *prayer* translated in English from many tribes means "practice relatedness, listen to the goodness." As a servant-leader I want to be able to pause and breathe deep enough for that opportunity, to create the space for that opportunity to happen. But more importantly, and this is what I want to remember when I inhale, is that the word *communicate* in many tribal languages means, "Something holy passes between us." We use the word *communicate* in English. If you ask a group of people the first word that comes to mind when you say the word *communicate*, most often they'll say talk, *listen*, *dialogue*, et cetera. But in tribal languages the word *communicate* means, "Something holy passes between us." So I inhale the good air—Why? Because air is the first power of creation. There are four powers of creation in a lot of tribal belief systems: air, fire, water, and things from the earth. And as I talk right now with you, I am using air through my earth body through the power of creation to express what is in my heart and my mind to you.

So when there is a conflicting situation and things are heating up in a meeting, I want to use that as a wake-up call to remind myself that relationships are prayerful. The servant-leader leads by example, and it is good to remember, you cannot give what you don't have. If you want peace, you have to surround yourself with peace. In my younger years I'd want to react and as I told you, my initial reaction is often to react, but now I want to interact. I want to interact and I want the best way to deal with aggression—many times there are aggressive remarks that happen in these types of meetings, to be able to say it's not personal, that's the first thing because then I don't feel that I have to defend myself, and then the second thing is to remember my role as a servant-leader is to create the space of inclusivity. I want to create the space that allows people to incarnate their voice and their sense of the truth in institutions that are wired, by the way, to suppress voices, to create autism in others. And my role is to create more space, not to shrink the space. So when I react, I shrink the space; when I interact I allow for a larger circle to occur to include the excluded, as Anthony de Mello would say. And the other part is it offers me an invitation to admit that I'm wrong when I'm wrong, which is an act of humility. And that is how I deal with conflict. I try to take total responsibility for everything that happens to me and what I create. No blame, no victimization, or guilt. I am the director, producer, editor, screenwriter, and casting agent of the psychodrama that I create in any meeting that I'm in. And that's difficult to accept. But here again when there's conflict and somebody says something, you know, "Incoming. Here it comes." It's a wake-up call to breathe and to remember that that breath is sacred, and that what I say can help or can hinder and it is my total responsibility—I can't take responsibility for what that person says, but I have sovereignty and self-determination over what I say and how I interact. I want to choose, consciously, to interact with love and compassion. The default setting is that person is doing the best that they can do, and I have to believe that. When I believe, I can act from a place of love, not the place of ego that says I have to defend or explain or promote or coerce, but simply be present and vigilant to that person's truth.

MC: How do you balance leadership with collaboration?

RR: Many times people believe there is a dichotomy between, on one hand, a leader needing to make strong decisions that are definitive and clear and, on the other hand, a leader inviting collaborative consultation with the followership. And I don't believe in oppositional thinking when it comes to those two ideas. I think that good decision-making *is* collaborative consultation with the followership. In fact, the quality of the servant-leader is directly related to the quality of the followership and ultimately the quality of any decisions that are made that affect everybody. I believe it is a question of time and patience. We live in a culture where time is money, and hence many times it's prudent for a leader to be autocratic so it appears when the bottom line is at stake to make a decision and engage in a top-down relationship with those that we manage. But ultimately what goes around comes around, and if you want to dance that way you will have to pay the fiddler. And going back to the idea of dysfunction in organizations, we do have passive-aggressive behaviors many times that are expressed from feelings that come to people when their voice has been suppressed or not respected or not acknowledged, and so I think that in the long run it's a good investment of yourself when you listen to others. Strong decision-making is listening to the voices of others, understanding that it is the creative synergy of all these voices that comes up with collective wisdom that will spawn the best policy that will be for the many, not for the one.

Chapter Ten

George Zimmer

Interviewed by Michael R. Carey

George Zimmer is an American entrepreneur, the founder of the Men's Wearhouse, a men's clothing retailer that has more than 1,200 stores across the United States and Canada, under the brands Moores, Men's Wearhouse, and K&G Superstores. Men's Wearhouse is a perennial Best Company to Work For according to Fortune *magazine. Known as a driven leader and a marketing genius, Zimmer's leadership style has revealed some of the tougher sides of servant-leadership while producing strong and enduring results in the corporate setting. He has become a household name because of the excellence of his company, and the name recognition of his commercials for Men's Wearhouse. He believes in people, and embodies a leadership model in which the highest priority needs of others are served. "I am a servant-leader," he said. "It was ingrained in me by my parents."*

Michael Carey: How does your sense of morality as a person affect the way you deal with situations and individuals within an organization?

George Zimmer: Well, I believe personal morality and professional morality should overlap. Some would describe it as the Golden Rule. I prefer to describe it as the juxtaposition of serving self and serving others. I see that we have to make that delicate balance work both personally and professionally.

MC: What are the difficulties of applying that within the organization?

GZ: Number one, we have to respect the fact that all individuals have a self-interest and we have to be able to respect their self-interest while at the same time encouraging them to balance their self-interest professionally with the collective interest in a business organization.

MC: Given that response, how do you deal with the reality that in such a large organization as yours, not everybody is coming from the same sense of a common morality? They may all have very clear self-interests but how do you deal with the fact that not everybody may be plugging into a kind of corporate common value?

GZ: That's a good question because you're right; a lot of people are more selfish than others, so it's up to the leaders of the organization to promote collective interest. You rarely have to promote self-interest, people have a natural resonance with their self-interest. So leadership has to remind and model what collective interest is and how collective interest and self-interest are not in competition but can be collaborative in terms of a rising tide lifts all boats.

MC: You just said that you look to leadership to provide the model for that kind of raising it to a higher level. Can you think of some examples of how that has been something that you've tried to do in your experience? How have you tried to get that sense of community or the bigger value inculcated in the employees or in the people that you work with?

GZ: When a leader is modeling the behaviors that he would like the organization as a whole to have you can do that in two ways. One way is to make sure that decisions that affect you personally are made in such a way that others looking at that decision will see that you yourself are walking the talk and not just talking the talk. An example would be compensation. In the ten years since Men's Wearhouse has gone public, I've been drawing a salary and bonus which is approximately 10 times that of the average store manager in our organization. No one need feel sorry for me, but it's not the 100 to a 1,000 times that we more commonly see today—the CEO's multiple of personal earnings to the average employees' earnings. But in our case here at Men's Wearhouse I've actually been giving away more money annually in college scholarships to children of Men's Wearhouse employees, and this is personal money not corporate money, than I've been taking annually in salary, bonus, and options which I do not receive. So I can stand up in front of the organization and say that I've been working for free since we went public. That's a way of personally modeling the idea of the balance of self and others.

The other way that the leader can promote this notion is by simply incorporating this idea into whatever remarks we make when we're addressing corporate gatherings. This would include not only training classes but at holiday celebrations where I get a few minutes to speak to everybody. I make sure that what I say includes the notion of collaboration.

MC: George, in your experience, both as you were working with a smaller company and now with a larger company, how do you deal with conflicts within your own work group, within the larger company?

GZ: Humorously, I don't deal well with conflicts, most people don't, and we could all do a better job. Of course, the degree and intensity of the conflict is what really determines our response. I really don't have a panacea or magic wand for how to deal with conflict, because conflict by definition is very personal and each human being involved in the conflict brings their own intensity to the situation. What I've tried to do in my professional as well as personal career is evaluate the intensity of the opposition and recognize that when there is intense conflict or disagreement it usually has an emotional component that has to be diffused before the intellectual ideas can be discussed and resolved more amicably.

MC: Do you have any ways that are typical of your approach to try to diffuse that emotional?

GZ: We have a training program which has been in place for many years and one of the original components of our training program was what we call the three key principles. These are really not original ideas that we invented but just ideas that our training people have brought together as a simple and effective way to communicate to large groups how emotional intelligence plays a significant role in business decision-making. These three key principles are to listen attentively. It's very important when one is listening to really put the same energy into listening as one puts into one's own words. We find that most people need to be reminded to listen as carefully as they speak. What this does is not only clears up misunderstandings, but the person who is being listened to can usually distinguish when somebody is really listening as opposed to superficially listening, where you can tell that the other person is forming their own response before you've actually had a chance to finish. What we try to do is talk about really listening well.

Then we talk about having a lot of authentic caring/compassion/empathy because ultimately if you want somebody to engage in honest dialogue they have to believe that you really do understand where they're coming from and what their point of view is. The more they believe that you understand that, the more willing the other person is to modify their own thoughts to meet you halfway, so to speak. So I would say that those are among the most important things in trying to avoid conflicts.

MC: Let's shift a little and talk about, and your website reflects this, the connection between individual ethics, workplace ethics, and global ethics.

GZ: Well, I believe individual, workplace, and global ethics all should be based on the same set of values so that there isn't really a difference between the ethics. What is different is the environment in which the ethics or values are going to be applied. In business we're often talking about issues concerning compensation. Which really are not issues in the global marketplace but nonetheless reflect the same underlying values. To follow up on my earlier answer, if the basic value is to balance appropriately self-interest and collective interest, then we can see that in the workplace in terms of individual compensation tied to personal achievement as opposed to collective goal achievement. At the global level we can see that reflected in the United States trying to work out treaties with other countries concerning greenhouse emissions in which our economy is going to be restricted to some degree to enable the entire world to participate in the industrial experience.

MC: How do sympathy, empathy, and respect play into relationships with individuals within your organization?

GZ: Well, *sympathy*, *empathy*, and *respect* are words which, to me, suggest the level of authenticity. I believe that to be an authentic human being you have to be in touch with the emotional part of life, with your feelings. Often in a professional environment we believe that we need to suppress or repress our feelings to be more science-like and more rational. I believe when we adopt that strategy we deny the authenticity of our humanity. I believe the nexus of being compassionate, being empathetic, and being respectful is the true expression of what a human being has inside as potential. Therefore, when we're in business, we've got to bring those qualities to the table alongside the more rational, scientific qualities.

MC: As you were working your way through your career, just what you described there, did you encounter experiences that were the opposite of that and how would you connect up some of your early experiences of the opposite of what you just said as helping you clarify what you wanted?

GZ: One of the advantages we've had at Men's Wearhouse is that we've never had to reinvent ourselves in a significant way. Because from the day this company began, thirty years ago, we've always had the ideas of being a complete human being as part of our business experience. The reason why this company was able to start that way is because I went to college in the late sixties during the counterculture revolution, which was really a student intellectual movement in which students were challenging the paradigm of the times which basically was about science and reason. Students were saying that was only part of the story and that we needed to balance our more traditional achievements with our essential humanity. Because I was able to experience that during those turbulent sixties, I was able to bring those values into the business model from the very beginning. So we really never had to deal, internally at least, with the old paradigm taskmaster, headmaster ideology.

MC: One of the things I value about what you said at the Greenleaf Center was that you're focused on profit as well. I want to talk a little bit about how in many companies, those two things (the essential humanity of being compassionate, empathetic, and respectful as well as scientific) would be viewed as contradictory. Talk about how it actually helps profit or it helps the company to prosper?

GZ: One of the jobs of a leader of an organization and business of a CEO is to create a business that is vibrant and that provides continuing opportunity both financially and nonfinancially for the employees in the organization. There is a myth, a new-age myth that making profit is negative or that profit itself is a four-letter word and, of course, it's a seven-letter word. What I have found frustrating is that I seem to meet many businesspeople for whom profit is the primary goal, and I meet an equal number of businesspeople who believe that the corporate culture is the primary goal. I believe that the appropriate balance is to create a business model or an economic model which respects increasing shareholder value at the same time that the other stakeholders in the business, the employees, the customers, the communities in which we do business experience an increase as well. In fact, I believe in all stakeholders having value not just the shareholder. So to me, it's an intersection between maximizing profits and maximizing employee experiences and customer experiences.

MC: What do I need to understand about the impact of gender, class, race, and ethnicity on a person's ability to be a competent leader?

GZ: Gender, race, ethnicity, these are all real issues in modern-day business. There are laws that govern behaviors as it relates to these subsets of being a human being. In a perfect world none of these subsets would matter. In a perfect world it would make no difference whether you were a white male, or a black woman, or a gay person. But we do not live, at this time, in a perfect world. And so we all do bring to everything in life internal biases. Because of that I believe that we must recognize that a woman in business is going to have certain preconceived notions that others will have concerning her abilities and she needs to factor those into her style of doing business. In a similar way any minority class has to be aware today that people are going to have biases and prejudices. What I believe is the best way to address that is with humor. That rather than trying to say directly something about the bias, if someone can think of a humorous way to bring the bias up without directly speaking about it, it creates a relaxation that I believe enables people to get by the biases easier.

MC: What do you see as the causes of dysfunctional thinking and behavior in organizations, in your organization here, or a store, or whatever it is?

GZ: Dysfunctional thinking, in my opinion, is caused primarily by two human frailties, fear and greed. Fear of course is something that we have hard wired into us for environmental survival reasons, so we can't ask for fear to be eradicated from our systems. But we must be able to use our consciousness to have the appropriate amount of fear and not allow fear to become a driver of our decision making. Similarly, greed or excessive self-interest can become out of control. A person has to know when their own self-interest is satisfied and when they need to be now thinking of how the collective interest needs to be satisfied equally. What I find in life is that when one is able to focus on collective as well as self-interest that what oftentimes is the outcome is that both go up, self-interest and collective interest. Because when we're creatively looking at the whole, we're often able to come up with solutions which drive better outcomes.

MC: In your experience, how does a leader deal with dysfunctional thinking or behavior in the organization or the store?

GZ: There's really no panacea to fixing another person's dysfunction. It's very difficult to fix one's own dysfunction, and to fix somebody else's dysfunction is really impossible in real-time. The way I believe a leader should approach those problems is to be patient and continue to model the functional thinking and over time when one gets good breaks in terms of outcomes we can create that "aha" experience in another person where the light switch goes off and they finally get it. But it requires great patience because again, in real time we rarely get that conversion in another person, and so you have to be prepared to work with dysfunction on an ongoing basis.

MC: In speaking of servant-leadership in the past, you talked a little bit about even getting to a place with people where you were counseling them out of working in the store. Maybe you could relate some of that, not merely in dysfunction but just in general the lack of fit between an individual and the organization.

GZ: The most difficult and challenging decisions that I make in business, whether it's today in a billion dollar public company or thirty years ago in a small start-up, are when the decision is made to terminate and separate from an employee. What we try to do at the Men's Wearhouse is speak to the employee in terms of why we believe this partnership has not succeeded. It usually can be tied back to the fact that an employee who was not properly positioned will not be able to generate the enthusiasm, spirit, and energy that is required for anybody to do their best. If you are not fully engaged in what you are doing, if you do not enjoy what you are doing, if you do not periodically experience what you are doing professionally as being fun so that you're sometimes feeling guilty about getting a paycheck because you enjoy it so much, then it's unlikely you'll be able to tap into your natural passions sufficiently to do the job as well as it needs to be done. So what we try to do when we separate with employees is help them find other areas that they can be involved in where their passion will bubble to the surface. Sometimes it can be within the organization in which a job change is appropriate but oftentimes it requires them leaving the organization and getting into some other line of work.

MC: How do you keep an integrated leadership view or perspective of situations within the organization? You've been touching a little bit on that, but how do you as a leader not get thrown off into a segmented view of things? How do you maintain a real sense of integrated vision as you go through the day-to-day situations you have to deal with?

GZ: One of the things I love about being in business is the ability to put together an integrated plan. The problem that I believe we have politically, not just in the United States but in any political sovereign entity, is that it's very difficult to create an integrated strategy. What happens in politics often is that we come to compromises which are neither fish nor fowl but something in between and quite often it results in ineffective solutions to real-world problems.

In business, on the other hand, because it is not ultimately a democracy, it is possible for the leader of the organization to create a better integration of all the different facets of the business and get everybody pushing in the same direction, which is why I believe it is easier to be successful in business than it is politically. The great challenge of our times, I believe, is how do we create that same integration in our political ideologies as successful businesses have been able to create over generations.

MC: How do you maintain a sense of personal self-integration so that you're able to see how things will fit together?

GZ: All of us have our strengths and our weaknesses. When I use those terms, *strengths* and *weaknesses,* I probably should be more specific because they suggest positive and negative and I don't mean them in that way. What I mean is that if you are a typical male then you are going to be typically more aggressive and less nurturing. That doesn't mean that you are weak and it neither means you're strong. What it means is that is your nature and you need to try to become aware of your nature and then provide the appropriate balance that you and uniquely you requires. In the case of George Zimmer who tends to be a typical, competitive, aggressive male, I've selected as my wife a very loving, kind, and generous woman. I feel that having that type of home life gives me the ability to be more balanced and more integrated as a business leader.

I think that women who find themselves in leadership roles in business and who may be natural nurturers may, through their self-awareness, learn that they have to balance that ability to nurture with a masculine sense of assertiveness at appropriate times. I believe that we all have the personal challenge and responsibility to try to be as aware of our own natural instincts, natures, and biases as is humanly possible and then work over a lifetime, because this is a lifetime project, to become more fully balanced and therefore, more fully the complete human being that we all have inside.

MC: It sounds like you're a very decisive leader, somebody who's making sure that this integration is taking place. How does a leader balance the need for strong decision-making with the responsibility for collaboration, even dialogue with those who do the work of the organization and those who are served by the organization? Greenleaf spoke of foresight and persuasion, please speak to those.

GZ: One of the myths of leadership is that the leader is certain of his or her decisions. It's a myth, and any leader, when they get honest, will freely admit that we make many decisions, sometimes very important decisions, in which we are simply making a probability call and we're not certain but yet because we're the leader we need to project confidence about the decision. So the first thing to understand about decision making is that we're rarely certain and we usually are just making our best guess. Having said that, one of the strategies in effective leadership in business is that we must try to persuade people as opposed to coerce people. But unlike politics, we do in business have the ability, when persuasion does not work, to fall back on coercion. Although it's an inferior solution, and usually reflects a creative inability to come up with the language to persuade, what makes companies more successful than political entities is that at the end of the day we can coerce when we can't persuade.

MC: How do you balance, as a leader, a sense of real dialogue among your key team with a sense of the integrity of your own vision? Servant-leadership is foundationally about listening, can you say more about listening?

GZ: The way to balance through collaborative dialogue competing ideas is by allowing people the space to fully express their own ideas and, following up on my earlier response about listening carefully, when we listen carefully even in committee meetings we are more likely to be able to find those areas of agreement than latch onto those areas of disagreement. Again, it is not a perfect universe and so this works more often better but it is not a perfect solution and there are times that occur regularly when a group of men and women cannot come to agreement, and in business ultimately there is somebody in charge who then makes the decision. What we try to do in business is once a decision is made it is easier to get those that disagreed with the decision to support the decision 100 percent than it is in nonbusiness situations, where people are more reluctant to follow the leader's or the collective decision for partisan reasons they are more likely to sabotage the collective decision. In business that does happen, but it doesn't happen by the same person more than once.

MC: Before we started filming, we talked a little bit about the ideas of the renaissance and holding two contradictory thoughts together. Please talk about how you see the renaissance as a metaphor for what you do as an effective leader.

GZ: Well the Renaissance in Italy, 500 years ago signified a rebirth of humanity and it signified a new direction that the world was going to take, which was an integration between an old paradigm and an emerging new paradigm.

I believe that this is a great metaphor for business today because today what business needs to do is be able to hold polar opposite ideas simultaneously in a mental space so that the integration of these two ideas can emerge. An example would be the balance between spirit and science. We need to use science, which is best symbolized in business through the computer. We need to be able to take the science of numbers as it relates to our businesses and integrate it with the spirit of the workers in a business and the other stakeholders in a business, because ultimately we will get better results by integrating spirit and science than we will by relying on one or the other. The same could be said for competency and intuition. In business we want to have men and women who are competent but we also want men and women who are able to tap into their intuition.

Abraham Lincoln said, during the Civil War, "Send me lucky generals." What exactly was he suggesting? He was suggesting that there is some quality that winning generals have which transcends their military, strategic cognition, and their rank, and their class at West Point. There is something about certain generals that transcends the battlefield diagrams. That was what Mr. Lincoln was looking for. I believe that is what we should all be looking for not just in our business leaders but in our own lives as well.

MC: Greenleaf says, "The best test of leadership is; do those served grow as persons; do they while being served become healthier, wiser, freer, more autonomous, more likely themselves to become servants; and what is the effect on the least privileged in society, will they benefit or at least not be further deprived?" Obviously, you've got a connection to the ideas of servant-leadership. I'd like you to talk about your own sense of what servant-leadership is. How do you understand the statement of Robert Greenleaf?

GZ: Robert Greenleaf, who I never had the pleasure of meeting, started writing about servant-leadership almost fifty years ago. *Servant-leadership* is a term that we've adopted at the Men's Wearhouse as one of our core foundational strategies, and like Mr. Greenleaf suggested we believe that servant-leadership has two primary components. One is, if you are really a servant-leader than what you are trying to do is share your wisdom, experience, knowledge, that which you could hold as proprietary to yourself but to share that in a nonproprietary way with those that you are entrusted to lead, so that over time they will be able to become servant-leaders themselves. If one is really interested in the long-term viability of any organization than that would seem to be a prerequisite for leadership, because ultimately all leaders move on and if a business or any organization is going to prosper over generations then this notion of servant-leadership must be passed on from generation to generation

But the other aspect of servant-leadership, speaking to the issue of whether the least fortunate in the organization are deriving a benefit or are only the senior people in the organization, at the Men's Wearhouse we have a great example of how that idea played out inside this organization. About twenty years ago we put one of the first employee stock ownership plans that the United States had into effect here. Because at that time we weren't familiar with the philosophical basis for ESOPs (employee stock ownership plans), we were persuaded to put a 200 thousand dollar salary threshold into our original ESOP. Of course what that did was it made the employee stock ownership plan top heavy. The more money you made, up to 200 thousand dollars, the bigger your cut of the pie was at the end of the year. After about ten years, I decided that that was not servant-leadership-like in that the lower-paid people, the least fortunate people, the tailors and little people in our organization were not only getting lower annual wages but a significantly lower share of the employee stock ownership plan. So we reduced the threshold to 100 thousand dollars. At that time there were only a handful of people who objected to that reduction, obviously they were the ones earning six-figure incomes. We thought that was good, but believe it or not about five years later we made a further reduction in our salary threshold to 50 thousand dollars. So today our employee stock ownership plan has, I believe, one of the lower thresholds of any such plan in existence. Fifty thousand dollars a year, which is the approximate salary of an average store manager is now the threshold above which increased annual earnings are not reflected in your share of the profits. And so we believe that, as Robert Greenleaf espoused in his writings, and if he were alive today that would probably bring a smile to his face, we've taken this wonderful idea of employee stock ownership plan in which the workers can own the means of production, invalidating Karl Marx's ideas, and made it truly democratic.

MC: George is there anything that I haven't asked that you have a really good answer for?

GZ: I've spoken this morning about the need to be creative. I believe that creativity is a direct function of your ability to hold competing ideas simultaneously in one's mind and detach from personal bias. When we made the first television commercial in which I appeared as spokesperson eighteen years ago, during the commercial I was thinking of an ad lib that I wanted to say at the end of the commercial for emphasis to reiterate and remind the viewer that I really believed in what I was saying. I kept flashing in my mind's eye on that scene from Bill Murray's movie, *Stripes*, toward the end of the movie in which standing on the parade ground this rag tag platoon said that in response to the question as to whether they were part of the United States Army Bill Murray responded, "That's the fact Jack." I wanted to say that but knew that it would be inappropriate in a television commercial. But because I was open to spontaneity and making a mistake I was able to say, "I guarantee it," and that has become one of the significant American icons now in business and came from just a casual ad-lib eighteen years ago. So if anybody is wondering whether or not there is value in being open-minded my answer is, "I guarantee it."

MC: What kind of things keep you up at night being a leader, what are the things that you worry about?

GZ: I have two college kids and two in diapers right at this moment. So when I get home from work and I do go home early, I eat dinner with my children every night, which I did not do with my first children, and I find when I get home that I am not worrying about business matters. In fact my real job begins at 5:30 in the evening when I get home. Although I don't necessarily sleep without interruption because of my age, I do not have trouble falling asleep, I just have trouble remaining asleep through the evening.

MC: How do you recognize leadership in your employees? What are the traits that you look for that sort of shine?

GZ: One of the important jobs that all leaders have is identifying and selecting future leaders. So the question has always been asked, "How do you identify future leaders?" Well of course there are many components that go into being a successful leader, but what I have found is that it is far easier to identify people who have the intellectual abilities than it is to identify the people that have the emotional abilities. So what I look for when I'm trying to identify new leaders is I look for the emotional intelligence far more than the intellectual intelligence. As Dan Goleman said in his book, *Emotional Intelligence*, about 80 percent of our success as adults both professionally and personally is derived from our EQ rather than from our IQ.

Another key principle is to ask the other person for their suggestions as to what would best solve the problem or issue at hand. A third key principle is to follow up attentive and careful listening by putting into your own words what you think you've just heard the other person say. By doing that, we find we eliminate much of the superficial disagreement, which can ultimately evolve into argument, and really focus instead on what is essentially the issue at hand. In addition, we believe it is important to ask the employees for their suggestions as to what would be the most effective solution for the problem being discussed.

We assume that people are understanding things and so we don't say it because we don't want to be redundant, and you know so I sort of am redundant and a lot of people I think sometimes turn off to you. It's particularly troublesome at home where you don't have the legal authority to be king.

MC: That's good, it's a humbling experience. I have to ask, your name is Zimmer, but do you have some Italian heritage?

GZ: My mother actually was an orphan. So one of the great things when your mother is an orphan, she never experienced this herself because she was the orphan, but when you're the child of an orphan and not the orphan, then you have your parents and yet you have the mystery of not knowing your lineage so you can be whatever you want to be on that side of your family. You know, I discussed that with my mother, and she of course was bothered by being an orphan and not knowing her real parents.

MC: About four years ago, I found out that, I had grown up thinking my dad's name was Robert Carey. And about four years ago my wife who does genealogy, discovered that he was born Abraham Lieberman.

GZ: And changed his name?

MC: Changed his name before I was born.

GZ: To Robert, I mean he just changed his whole name?

MC: Oh yeah, that was just the beginning of it. So I grew up thinking, you know, he was an Irish Catholic from New York and . . .

GZ: He was Jewish.

MC: And I never knew his parents or my cousins or anything. He lied to me. And so what happened was my wife was able to actually make contact with my extended family, and I have twenty-one first cousins on my father's side. They had a reunion back in New York about three years ago, so we went back there. And it's like a whole new world I did not grow up thinking, you know, of. So my daughter is getting married in about three weeks, and we've got a whole contingent from New York coming to the wedding.

GZ: It's interesting, my thought as you were speaking about that was, you know how my wife is somewhat flabbergasted at the existence of anti-Semitism. She's not Jewish and, you know, she has never been exposed to it, and now that she's married to a Jew, you know, she's trying to understand why anti-Semitism would exist. I said it really all goes back to the myth that was perpetrated about Jews killing Jesus; it really all starts from that. And, of course, now she understands that Jesus was a Jewish rabbi. And so, you know, she says, well how if Jesus was a Jewish rabbi could . . . and I said it just shows you how powerful spin is. Because, you know, the people who write history are the winners.

Chapter Eleven

Corazon Aquino

Interviewed by Shann Ray Ferch

Noted by political leaders throughout the world as a global servant-leader, Maria Corazon Sumulong "Cory" Cojuangco-Aquino (January 25, 1933–August 1, 2009) was the eleventh president of the Philippines and the first woman to hold that office. She was the first female president in Asia. She led the 1986 People Power Revolution, which toppled Ferdinand Marcos and restored democracy in the Philippines. She was named Woman of the Year in 1986 by Time *magazine. A self-proclaimed "plain housewife," Aquino was married to Senator Benigno Aquino Jr., the staunchest critic of then President Ferdinand Marcos. Senator Benigno Aquino Jr. was assassinated on August 21, 1983, upon returning to the Philippines after three years in exile in the United States. After her husband's assassination, Corazon Aquino emerged as the leader of the opposition against the Marcos regime. In late 1985, when President Marcos called for a snap election, Aquino ran for president with former senator Salvador Laurel as her vice-presidential running mate. After the elections were held on February 7, 1986, and the Batasang Pambansa proclaimed Marcos the winner in the elections, she called for massive civil disobedience protests, and Filipinos enthusiastically heeded her call and rallied behind her. These events eventually led to the ousting of Marcos and the installation of Aquino as president of the Philippines on February 25, 1986, through the People Power Revolution. As president, Aquino oversaw the promulgation of a new constitution, which limited the powers of the presidency and established a bicameral legislature. Her administration gave strong emphasis and concern for civil liberties and human rights, and peace talks with communist insurgents and Muslim secessionists. Aquino's economic policies centered on bringing back economic health and confidence and focused on creating a market-oriented and socially respon-*

sible economy. Aquino's administration also faced a series of coup attempts and destructive natural calamities and disasters until the end of her term in 1992. Succeeded by Fidel V. Ramos as president in 1992, Aquino returned to private life, although she remained active in the public eye, often voicing her views and opinions on the pressing political issues. In 2008, Aquino was diagnosed with cancer, from which she died on August 1, 2009. Her son Benigno Aquino III was elected president and was sworn in on June 30, 2010.

Shann Ray Ferch: Thank you, President Aquino, for your presence here today and for this interview. What happened to make you the leader of the Philippines?

Corazon C. Aquino: Well, circumstances prevailed. First my husband was assassinated. And then, of course, we had been living under a dictatorship. And at that time, I was never considering myself as a presidential candidate. But as the opposition, I suppose, looked around and searched for the best possible candidate against a dictator, a number of them were convinced that it had to be somebody the opposite of Marcos—if possible, the complete opposite of Marcos. So I suppose they thought of me because, first, I'm a woman, he's a man. I've never been a politician, although I have been a politician's wife. I had never voted for Marcos. And the fact that he had incarcerated my husband—of course, we were against his dictatorship. And we were, both my husband and I, working toward the restoration of democracy. So circumstances perhaps required that the opposition present somebody who would be the opposite of Marcos, and in addition to that, somebody who could unite the opposition. And it was the perception that I would be the candidate that could best unite the opposition. The fact that a number of the politicians who had presidential ambitions had indicated to me that they would give way only to me was perhaps a sign that a number of them could be united if I were the candidate.

SF: Did those indications come personally to you?

CA: Oh, yes, they came to me. And then, of course, some of them had said that on whatever media was available then.

SF: What do you think were the great harms the Marcos's regime brought to the Philippines?

CA: Well, first of all, he had promised us, promised the Filipino people, that in exchange for our freedom, he would give us bread. He would address our economic needs. But, unfortunately for us Filipinos, he not only took away our freedom, he also took away our bread. So it was, of course, very difficult for most Filipinos. Although in the beginning, most Filipinos were willing to give him the benefit of the doubt. And the first year, second year, third year, you hardly heard any opposition. It was only toward . . . I suppose when my husband decided to run in the elections for Parliament, where he was able to have a forum for voicing out his stand against the dictatorship. And also, his fellow opposition leaders were able to go out and campaign because Marcos had called for elections for Parliament.

SF: For many servant-leaders faith is a crucial foundation. How did your faith help you deal with martial law and the different types of injury martial law brought into your life, such as your husband's incarceration? How did your faith help you deal with that?

CA: Well, I'm just grateful that I did have the kind of faith that I did, and there was nobody I could turn to, my husband being in prison. And there was nobody who could really help us. So it became very clear to me I had to surrender all these problems to the Lord, and ask Him to guide me. There was no alternative to that. And in fact I am grateful, and I thank the Lord for making me the kind of person I am—realizing my inadequacies, of which there are many, and going to Him who could help me in everything.

SF: And at that time, I would imagine, some people divided away from you to avoid being associated with Marcos coming after them?

CA: Oh, yes.

SF: And some people probably stayed close from their courage. Can you tell me about that?

CA: Oh, well, in the beginning, as they say in the Bible, "In adversity, you get to know your friends." And, of course, prior to my husband's incarceration, many people thought that he would have a good chance of becoming the successor to Marcos. And, in fact, I remember once I was in the supermarket, and I was waiting for my driver to come bring the car, and there was this woman, a friend of ours, an acquaintance, who was on the other side of the street. And she rushes to me, and says, "Cory, please don't forget me when Ninoy becomes president." And I said, "Oh, well, sure." Then just so many months after, we had martial law. And, oh, people were just so afraid to come to our house. And I could count on my fingers the number of friends that continued to be loyal and who truly were concerned about Ninoy, about me, and about our children. But I was glad that in my children's case, the young people did not allow themselves to stay away from my children. And they continued to be good friends. They were not afraid, and they just wanted to show my children that they would continue to be friends. But it was good for us to know. I remember my husband telling me, he had one visit with Marcos. He was taken there maybe five years after his detention. And I think my husband had told him, "Well, I'm luckier than you in the sense that I know who my friends are." And, in fact, he was telling Marcos that if we were on opposite sides, I wonder who among these people you can trust.

So it was very clear to us then, yes, we don't have the many friends we used to have, or that my husband used to have, but still the ones who chose to stay with us really were exceptional. And I'm really grateful they continued to be there for us.

SF: Love may be the true cornerstone of servant-leadership. There is such love for you in the hearts of the young people, and also it's been part of your leadership to try to encourage and develop the young leaders of the nation. Can you tell me about that some more?

CA: Well, as you know, I became president because of People Power, because after the elections—Marcos had manipulated election returns, and so he had been declared the winner. But I had called for a big rally. And I had asked people to come and to listen to my proposal of having a nonviolent protest movement. I was asking them to boycott the products and services of Marcos-controlled or Marcos-owned enterprises. And initially, the opposition leaders were telling me, "You know, Cory, after elections, nobody calls for a rally. And especially after one has been declared the loser."

I had been going around, specifically here in Makati (in Manila), because they had had big problems here about safeguarding the ballot boxes. And so I went around and I was looking to see how the people were. And they were calling out to me, "Cory, what else can we do?" And you know, it was not just one, but several of them had told me this. So I would say, "Yes, what else can we do?" And I felt a certain obligation to them, because I had asked them to support me, and to try to work for the restoration of democracy. So, that same day, I called for a meeting of the opposition leaders, and I told them what had happened, and I said, "I'd like to call for a rally." And so this was when they discouraged me, saying that nobody calls for rallies. But I cannot just, you know, ignore what these people were calling out to me. And so, like I was their little kid and they were telling me, "Okay, so where do you want the rally?" And I said, "Well, I'd like it in the Luneta," which is the biggest open space here in metro Manila. And they said, "Oh, what if we just have it in another area?" This is in front of the post office that they were suggesting to me, and they said, "If we get ten thousand, or twenty thousand, it'll look so huge. So let's just have it there." I said, "No, no. I really want to know once and for all whether people still want to work for the restoration of democracy, or whether they have given up. So let's have it in this big park." And I said, "If nobody comes, or very few people come, then we will know that they don't want any more of this, and so we can go back to our private lives." But, of course, the unexpected happened, and estimates ran from half a million to more. And it was just amazing, considering that we did not have any sophisticated sound equipment.

And what we had told the people was to bring their transistor radios because my speech would be broadcast on the Catholic radio station, so they would be able to listen from whatever place they were. That was on February 16, 1986. And I told the people, "I will be visiting ten cities in the Philippines to ask for their support in this nonviolent protest movement." I was only on my third city, in Cebu province in southern Philippines, and news came to us that there were military who had—well, actually had plotted against Marcos, but they had been discovered. So they were retreating and going back to their military camp and the police camp to, I guess, protect themselves from whatever Marcos was going to do to them. So this was the beginning of People Power. And they asked Cardinal Sin to call the people, and Cardinal Sin appealed to the people to go there and to, in effect, protect the military. And I was saying this was the first time perhaps in world history that the civilians were called upon to protect the military. And, of course, the rest is history. The People Power Revolution took four days—actually, a little less than four days. But it was the first of its kind, and it was a very peaceful revolution and we were able to oust a dictator.

SF: When you saw that first moment and when you made the courageous decision, "Let's put it in a larger setting, a larger forum," and then you saw the 500 thousand and more people—what came into your heart?

CA: Of course, I was overwhelmed. And so it gave me the courage to continue, because if they were willing to make such a sacrifice of going there, then the least I could do was to carry on with what I had been proposing to them. And it was just fantastic, something that nobody had expected. Because as the veteran politicians had told me, nobody calls for a rally after the elections, especially after one has lost.

Oh, may I point out that the Catholic Bishops Conference of the Philippines gave us tremendous support, because they issued the statement saying that this was the most fraudulent election ever, and that it was highly immoral. So the people were not expected, or did not have to, recognize an immoral leader. Or a leader elected through immoral means.

SF: Beautiful. So after that initial rally, and when you're starting to go to the cities, was the country still under martial law at that time?

CA: Oh, yes. Although officially, or on paper, Marcos said he had lifted martial law.

SF: Was there a threat that you might be imprisoned for your work?

CA: Anything could happen.

SF: And how did you develop—you mentioned that Ninoy had been reading Bonhoeffer, and Martin Luther King, and your own—

CA: José Rizal.

SF: José Rizal.

CA: And Mahatma Gandhi.

SF: Gandhi, yes.

CA: Well, he was reading so many. He had also—I remember you mentioning Victor Frankl—

SF: Yes.

CA: —and he had also told me about all the books he had read. Because he had so much time in prison. And it was really more a question of me getting him as many books as he wanted. And so whenever our friends would ask, "What can we send him?" I said, "Well, could you just send him books?" and, "Which books?" I tell them, "Look at *Time* magazine, and look at whatever's on the best-seller list, both under fiction and nonfiction, and he would appreciate that. Like, one of his lawyers, one of his chief lawyers, was a Protestant, and very well-read on the writings of Christians. And so he was the one who introduced my husband to Bonhoeffer. And I suppose who introduced him to Victor Frankl. But then my mother-in-law was a very religious woman, so she had sent him *Imitation of Christ.*

SF: Thomas à Kempis.

CA: So it was, as I said, maybe God's way of . . . and in fact, my husband had written that, that in the past he had been so busy because of his being a public official, and he was also very much concerned that he succeed in his political ambition, that he forgot to thank God for all the good things that had happened to him. So it was in prison when he finally realized that he had to ask for God's forgiveness. He found God in prison.

SF: You came into this position where the opposition was uniting around you and against Marcos. In light of this, how did you come to your own love for nonviolence?

CA: From the very beginning I've never been into violence. And also, when we were living in the United States, my husband had gone to Nicaragua to find out exactly what had happened there, and he was convinced that no way can we Filipinos resort to violence. Because what good will the restoration of freedom be if you will have so many widows and orphans crying and in pain because of having lost their husbands or their fathers?

When my husband was assassinated, and when in fact around two million people joined us in the funeral procession, later on some of the leaders of the opposition were saying that I missed my golden opportunity. I said, "What do you mean?" Well, they said that at that point I could have asked people to do anything, and they would have done so. And they said, "You should have led them to Malacanya, and we could have taken over." And I said, "Oh, no. That is not my way." And what guarantee do we have: First, how many people would be killed? And then, would we in fact have succeeded? I mean, these are all unarmed people: violence was never my thing. And even during the campaign, some people were also saying, "Why don't you go to Malacanya and challenge the dictator?" I said, "No, no, that's not my way, and we will just have to do it this way." Nonviolence is a slower way of doing things, but in the end, the results will be more lasting than if you are able to accomplish things in a hurry.

SF: In America and throughout the world, you are an icon of world peace, human rights, the abolition of war as an instrument of policy. How do you try to continue these processes in the world?

CA: Well, let me say that because we do have many problems in the Philippines, perhaps the problems in the Philippines are occupying top priority with me, and while it is true I continue to be involved in the work in other nations, in other people who have suffered loss of their freedom, I try to concentrate on what we can do here in the Philippines to help our poor brothers and sisters. And so last year I launched what I refer to as a People Power, People Movement. I felt it was time that we should not just confine People Power to politics, or to political activities, but that People Power should be used to help people get together and to help them in the alleviation of poverty. So I sought out twenty NGOs, or foundations, throughout the Philippines to commemorate the twentieth death anniversary of my husband. And the idea was for the Aquino Foundation to put their projects or their programs in video and in print so that others who would like to replicate their successful projects would have an easier time of doing so. And my role principally was to be a convener, to bring these people together, to let them know that they are all together in improving lives here. And we have the foundations. We have small NGOs, but each one definitely has a role in the building of a better nation.

SF: There tends to be a great deal of cynicism just as an operating force when people feel like things aren't going the way they might want them to go. And your leadership is completely the opposite of that consistently. Servant-leaders are courageous and hopeful. How do you maintain hope and courage, and stop cynicism? You're emphasizing the life-giving nature, the appreciative elements rather than the deficit-based elements.

CA: Well, because we have enough of the negatives. And I keep on appealing to media that perhaps you could balance it, bring 50 percent of the bad news and 50 percent the good news. Because I am convinced that it cannot be all bad news. And people should know that there are still good things happening in our country, and that there are many good people here, and it would be worthwhile to emulate what they are doing for our country. And fortunately, it's really the bad things that get into the limelight. And I remember reading, I think it was an American magazine, and they were saying, "Well, it's like this, suppose there is a school, and somebody gets this incurable sickness, and that person gets sick and dies." And so everything is focused on that. And, in fact, the story goes that all students are not able to go to school because of this incident. But you know, they fail to say that it was really a very unusual case, just one out of that entire student body, and yet the attention was focused on that one sad thing. Of course, I agreed they should report on that, but not to the extent that you forget that 99 percent are still able to go to school, and were not affected by such an ailment.

I guess in everything there should be a balance, and we should, throughout the world, know that we have both a good and a bad. But even if the bad news is more, attracts more attention, still we should do our best to also bring forth the good news.

SF: In leadership across different sectors there's a conception that a person has to be ultimately powerful to make things happen. And then power is held in certain ways, often subversively or dominantly. Yours isn't held that way. How do you envision power, and how do you lead with power?

CA: Well, of course, power is a gift from the people, and so you owe the people. And you have to be responsible enough that the power should be used in order to improve their lives and not just your life. And also, it's good to remember that power is temporary, and that you may be the most powerful person here in the Philippines today, but who knows what will happen in succeeding days? And in the same way that when my husband was senator, I would like to believe that he was one of the most powerful senators then. Of course, many people thought that he would eventually become president. But then there he was, and then on the same day he gets arrested and detained, for seven years. So I think for all of us who have been entrusted with the responsibility of leading, it is important for us to remember that this is temporary, and it's not yours permanently. But you will have to render an accounting. I think that should be first and foremost, that in the end not only the people but, I guess, when you face the Final Judgment, you will be asked how exactly you used that kind of power. So I suppose consciously or unconsciously that was part of my prayer, that I not abuse the power given to me, and that I try to use it the best way I can in order to address the needs of the people.

SF: The changes in your husband, the transformations that he underwent during prison, what was that like for you personally as his wife?

CA: Well, some changes I could see; other changes I could not. Like when he went on his forty-day hunger strike, he was telling me, "You know, Cory, try not to worry too much, because if I go, then that means my sufferings will be over." But I was telling him, "Well, you know, just make sure that you don't have a death wish, and let's just continue praying so that God will guide you and guide me in the best way to do this." And for him, later on, he would tell me that his life really had changed so much because of that, that he was able to not have anything to do with food. He limited himself to water, amino acid tablets, potassium, a little bit of sugar, and salt tablets. So he lost forty pounds in forty days. And, of course, it was a very difficult experience for me. Also, seeing him become weaker and weaker. And the military had allowed me to visit him every day because he was having difficulty just walking from his bed to the bathroom. And so my oldest son and I would help him up and bring him to the bathroom. But, as I said, I didn't see all the changes; but certainly, later I could see that whereas before he was completely a politician, with all this suffering that he had undergone, and all these prayers, he no longer was aiming to become president, but in fact, he was looking to God to show him the way to becoming a better person, and to show him how best he could help the people. Some of his critics would say, "Oh, how can Ninoy forget about being a politician? He's been a politician almost all of his adult life." But I could see that. And also, he would tell me, "I hope I will be released from prison if only to make up to you and to the children for all the times that I neglected you because I was so busy with my political life." And, in fact, he told our youngest daughter, who was only a year and a half when he was incarcerated, "I hope I can make it up to you." So she was nine years old when finally he was living in the same house as we were. Because prior to that, she thought that we were talking about the possibility of her dad being released, and she said, "So, Mom, where's he gonna live?" And I said, "He's gonna live here." "Where? Where is his room?" Because she was sleeping with me all the time that my husband was in prison. I said, "Here," and she said, "But this is not his bed." It was really something so new for her. And so when we got to Boston is the first time she had a father living with us. And Ninoy was just so happy he was able to be with us. And, as I said, he really tried his best to make up for whatever neglect in the past.

SF: That's a very lovely aftereffect of suffering. What's your view of suffering in leadership, and the way you approach it?

CA: Well, to be a leader is to be prepared to take on whatever sacrifices or whatever sufferings you will have to go through. I mean, leadership is not a gift without strings, okay? So you really have to devote most if not all of your time to seeing that you are in fact leading your people toward the right direction. It carries with it so many responsibilities. And, of course, a leader also has to worry about making the right decisions. But that's what a leader is about. You have to take risks. At the same time, it is important . . . and the suffering was more in my husband's case than my case . . . that we prayed a lot and asked the Lord to help us as we were confronted with different trials, so that we could arrive at the right or the best possible decision.

SF: You went to Assisi, and can you relate what you discovered there?

CA: Yes. After my presidency, I had a chance to visit Assisi, and as we were going around, the guide said, "You know, St. Francis would always ask the Lord for more sufferings." So when we got back to the hotel, I said to God, "I don't think I'll ask for more sufferings. But if more sufferings come my way, I will not complain." And, in fact, that has been my prayer to the Lord, that I hope there will be no more suffering, but if suffering does come, please help me. And I used to think, or I like to think, that there was a quota for suffering, and that all of us had served in quotas. And I felt I had filled up mine. And I remember when we were living in Boston, I would write haikus. You know, the Japanese way of writing verses? And in one of them, I had said, "The worst of my life is over, I hope. And may the best please come soon." And I had shown it to my husband. I said, "I hope the worst is over." And he said, "No, Cory, I'm afraid it's not." And I said, "My goodness, what else will happen?" You know? Then one of my other haikus was, "In pain and sorrow, I have never been alone. Many thanks, dear Lord." And I have been so grateful that in my greatest difficulty and my greatest pain, there was always someone who would help me. There would be my children, or there would be friends. It would have been disastrous, I think, if I had been all alone. I mean, of course, you believe that God is there. But since we are still in this world, you still want human beings to talk to and to relate to.

SF: What was it like to grieve Ninoy's death, and unite your family, and three years later, step into presidential leadership?

CA: Well, before my husband left Boston to return to Manila, he had explained certain scenarios to me. And he was telling me, "Well, Cory, try not to worry too much. Maybe when I return home, I guess I'll probably be arrested at the airport and taken back to the detention center where I was. Or I might be confined at the heart center, because I have gone through a triple bypass. Or better still, they might think I am no longer a threat anyway, they might agree to make me go under house arrest." And I said, "Oh, that would be wonderful," I was thinking. And then he added as a last thing, "But then if Marcos makes a mistake and has me killed, that could be the best thing that will happen to me." This is what Ninoy said. And I said, "Ninoy, how can you say that?" And he said, "Well, I've always wanted to die for our country, and this would be it." And so when my husband was assassinated, of course my children and I were all crying. And I told them, "Well, I have to tell you what Dad told me before he left." I hadn't told them before. And I said, "He said that he has always wanted to die for our country, and he got his wish." And later on, my children told me, "Well, Mom, it helped when you told us. That was what Dad wished for, and that at least his sufferings have ended and he really was able to the very last moment of his life to do something for the Filipino people."

SF: In your own leadership, then, without Senator Aquino, your husband, with you, comes this huge responsibility to recover a nation that's been destroyed by the Marcos regime. Can you tell me about the loneliness and the responsibility?

CA: I had almost three years before the presidency, I mean from 1983 to 1986. And in the beginning, I was just telling the opposition leaders that I would support them in the activities, and principally that entailed my going to the protest marches, and giving speeches occasionally. The first big decision I had to face was in 1984, a year after my husband's assassination, when Marcos called for elections to Parliament, and the opposition was divided. Some of them were saying, "Why should we go into this again? He'll just cheat us again, as he did in 1978." And then there were others who were saying, "No, no. Let's take advantage of this, because then it gives us at least a chance to speak out openly, and we will not be arrested," because after all, Marcos had said, you know, "This will be a time for open discussion," or whatever he meant by that. Anyway, I was really very much troubled by that and I kept praying. And in fact, I was saying, "Ninoy, I hope you can appear to me in a dream because I'm having so much difficulty." Both sides really have very convincing arguments, either for boycott or participation. But in the end, I was convinced that it had to be participation. And initially, when people were asking, I said, "You know, why don't all of us make our own decision about this?" And, "Why do I have to make it public?" But people kept telling, "No, no. People are waiting." Or, "A number of people are waiting for you to tell them how you stand on this issue." So, finally, I had to do that, and I requested a Catholic radio station if I could read my statement, and they could broadcast it.

SF: Would that be broadcast to the whole country generally?

CA: Nearly. But anyway, it was the only way I could deliver the message. And after that, oh, I really received some terrible mail. There were letters telling me that, "You're so naive," and "How can you believe this is the best option?" And somebody even said, "Ninoy must be turning in his grave. You didn't seem to learn anything from him." Oh, really some very painful things. And I said, "Well, anyway, I am convinced this is the right way." And later on, in fact, one of those who had written to me had the nerve to ask me if I could endorse him. He decided to participate after all. He was running for mayor in Mindanao. And I'm saying, well, I'm not really such a charitable person in that respect. So when he came and asked me that, I said, "Wait a second. Didn't you write to me and tell me how naive I was, and how Ninoy must be suffering because . . ." So I said, "No, I can't endorse you." And he said, "No, Ma'am, I never wrote you that." And I said, "Isn't your name so-and-so?" And he said, "Yes, but maybe somebody else wrote that." And I said, "Oh, look, let's just forget it, and just get somebody else to endorse your candidacy." It was like that. And during that time, I was not a candidate myself, but I campaigned. I must have delivered at least sixty speeches. I went throughout the country, and where we had candidates who had asked me to help in their campaign, I did so. And it gave me a chance also to tell the people what exactly had happened during martial law. Because most of them were in the dark. They didn't know, well, maybe they knew Ninoy, but they weren't too clear about exactly what detention in a military camp is all about. So I told them that, and I was saying, "I don't want what happened to my husband to happen to any of you. And also, I don't want your children to suffer the loss of their father." And, "All of us, I hope, can work together to bring about a change, and to restore democracy in our country." So I would be saying the same speech everywhere. But anyway, since most of them had not heard it, I suppose I was no longer nervous facing crowds. It was before that, when my husband ran during . . . well, he was running from prison, and we had to substitute for him. It was my youngest daughter who was seven years old who didn't mind giving speeches. And she gave, I counted, seventy speeches. And she would . . . friend of mine who was a radio announcer was present when I introduced the candidates for the opposition, and he volunteered to teach my daughter how to give a speech in Filipino. And I asked her first, "Do you want to do it?" And she said, "Yes, I do, Mom." And so she went all over, and she was a hit because how many seven-year-olds do you have who can speak like that? And in fact, the women who would listen to her really were always in tears. And her speech was quite simple. She said, "I'm Kris Aquino, I'm seven years old, but for almost six years, my father has not lived with us because he has been in prison. So please help us; help my mom, help my brother, and my sisters, so that we can be a family again. And give my father the opportunity to serve you once again." And then she would recite the twenty-one names of the candidates of the opposition, which she could easily do. And so she, in fact, we were really impressed because she made it to the front page of *Time* magazine and the *New York Times*. And so I was telling my husband, "She beat you to it." She also beat me to it!

SF: Beautiful presence. In Ninoy's letters to his children, and in your prayers for your children, and just the way you carry yourself, there's a deep tenderness for your children and your family, which is also communicated to the nation and to the world. Tell us, tell me about the tenderness that you two have for your children.

CA: Well, again, I had said that when I got married, I was determined to be a good wife and mother. And there was no problem there. And my husband also agreed that one of us should be with the children. Because we had seen how many children of public officials really craved for attention, and I guess needed parental supervision, et cetera. And so we were determined we would give them that, and we would make sure they grew up to be responsible citizens. And I remember during martial law, it was my second daughter who was being interviewed by a foreign journalist, and I heard the journalist ask her, "So, you must miss your dad a lot, and it must be very difficult for you." And she said, "Oh, yes, I really miss my dad, but it would have been worse if it were my mom in prison." And the journalist says, "Why do you say that?" And she said, "Well, every day, as far as I can remember, whenever I would go home, I knew she'd be there. And so I knew whatever problems or whatever thing, whatever I needed, I could immediately tell her." And so it made me feel good that whatever I did was not only appreciated, but I guess made an impact on the lives of my children.

SF: You said for a loving marriage, it takes people that can bring out the best in each other. How did Ninoy bring out the best in you, and how did you bring out the best in him?

CA: Both Ninoy and I were opposites in a sense. He was an extrovert with a capital *E*, and I, I enjoyed my privacy. But I realized because of martial law, there was a reversal of roles since he was confined in his tiny, tiny room. And he had no access, of course, to the outside world. I had to be his spokesperson, his eyes and ears also. So I would report to him whatever his lawyers and his political associates would tell me. And because he had an ongoing trial, I would attend the meetings with his lawyers. And it was also very good education for me. They were teaching me all about, well, not only the laws, but telling me how impossible it was for us to win because Marcos could change the rules at any given moment. So in his case, because before, he could solve almost any problem. And I also felt whatever problem I had, I could just bring to him, and he would find ways and means of addressing that problem, or the two of us could easily look for solutions. But this time, both of us were powerless to do so. And so the two of us naturally had to turn to God. And while I was prayerful before, I was not as fervently prayerful as I became, okay? Because before, what were my problems? Really nothing. And very inconsequential compared to the enormous problems that were brought to us because of martial law. Ninoy, in his case, he had written in his diary, "Well, I was a nominal Catholic, and the only reason I would go to Mass every Sunday was to avoid a quarrel with Cory." So because I had made it a rule every Sunday, all of us go to church, and we go to church together. So that's what he had written in his diary. But, later on, he had all the time in the world. He had become so prayerful. And in fact, he would ask me, "So, Cory, you pray the Rosary every day?" I said, "Yes, of course." "How many do you pray in a day?" And I said, "Well, three." At that time, there were only three major mysteries, unlike now, there are four major mysteries. "Three." "Is that all?" he said. "Yeah, well how many do you pray?" And so he said, "Well, once I think I prayed fifty Rosaries." And I said, "Oh, well, Ninoy, you don't do anything, you know? You're just here, so you have all the time in the world." But I suppose all the prayers . . . and he was forever reading the Bible. Prior to that, neither one of us really was into Bible reading. But in prison, oh, he was just reading the Bible. In fact, I think my oldest daughter was telling me, "You know, Mom, for my first year in college, you put down the occupation of your father, so I put down senator. And then now, the way he talks to us about . . . I think I'll just say preacher, because every time we visit him, he tells us about what he has read, not only the Bible, but all these other religious books that he has read." So we were seeing that the years of his imprisonment were very difficult, but they gave us the greatest learning experiences. If we had not gone through those difficult times, oh yes, I guess I would go to Mass, and I would pray, but there would not be that fervor, or that intense consciousness of really surrendering yourself to God. So while . . . as I keep on saying, "I hope there will no longer be more sufferings," but I think that if one were not suffering, would one pray? Because if things are going well, then you think, "Do I need the Lord?" But when things look hopeless, or you feel so helpless, then there's no other recourse. And I feel sorry for people who do not pray, or who do not believe that there is a God. And I am grateful to the Lord that He did not allow us to despair. In fact, He made us better people. As I was saying, I was glad that neither my husband nor I felt hopeless or helpless at the same time. It would have been tragic if both of us were feeling so low. And there would be times when I'd visit him, and oh, he would say, "Oh, Cory, does anybody ever even remember me?" And I think this reminded us to resign ourselves, that this will be forever. And he'd say it might be forever. And I'd say, "No, no, Ninoy, of course not." And I'd tell him that I'm sure things will change, and whatever good news I could get, which was very few and far between, I'd just tell him, "Look, this happened." Then there would be days when I would feel really bad, and I'd say, "Oh, I wonder if this will ever end?" And he'd say, "Yes, it will . . ." So it was good. God made . . . I believe God made it possible for us not to be feeling low at the same time, so that one would be able to comfort the other.

SF: You have one of the rare marriages the world can emulate, and—

CA: Oh, it wasn't a perfect marriage!

SF: I understand, but it is one that has another sort of icon of love, where two people even switch their ways of being in order to be more whole, you know?

CA: Yes.

SF: And learn from each other in doing that, and then maintain that deepened sense of love during pressure, and during suffering, versus something that fell apart during the pressure.

CA: That's why I really feel so blessed. Of course, I've been thinking, "Would I ever have married anybody else?" I don't think so. And not that nobody ever looked at me, you know? Because I am vain enough to think that there were others. But none of them ever measured to my husband's qualities. And I feel blessed that we found each other, although it was inevitable that we would meet each other, because we both come from the same province, we both come from political families. And so it would have been almost impossible for us not to meet.

SF: And so I have to ask, how did you fall in love?

CA: Well, we met when we were both nine years old, okay? Of course, no love then [*laughs*]. Then I was in the United States from age thirteen to twenty. We met again when I was about sixteen or seventeen. And then he wrote to me. But I was looking for somebody who was five years older than me, because my father was five years older than my mother, and they did have an ideal marriage. And I thought, "Yes, I need somebody who is at least five years older." So I wasn't paying attention to him. But after my junior year, when I came home for vacation, that's when I fell in love. And I felt, yes, he's the man for me. But before that, I was still hoping, as I said, looking for a man five years older than me. But I never met that man.

SF: What was it that inspired you when you did fall in love?

CA: Oh, yes. Because my husband perhaps is the most entertaining person that I have ever met. He read a lot. And as I said, he could outtalk anyone. And when we were living in Boston, most of our friends, they were Filipino doctors. And they were just amazed at his knowledge of medicine. And they would ask, "Ninoy, were you ever in medical school?" And he said, "No." But he was just so knowledgeable about so many things. And, well, it was to his credit that whatever he read, he retained. He really was, maybe not a walking encyclopedia, but close to that. And so I was lazy in doing research. And you know, I knew that so long as Ninoy was there, I'd be able to ask him anything and everything. And when we were living in Boston, he was telling me, "Cory, why do you keep on reading those best sellers?" I said, "Ninoy, this is my only time finally that I can relax, and I like to leave the world of politics and all these other difficult things, and only just let me be." And when I became president, I said, "Oh, why didn't I listen to Ninoy and read all those books that he was forever bringing me from Harvard?" But well, anyway, that was it. But whenever we would attend a dinner given by one of his Harvard associates or a professor, I'd just keep quiet, because oh, my goodness, I was just in awe of all these learned people talking about everything. And so after the dinner, when we would go home, then I'd ask my husband, "So, can you talk about what he was saying?" And I'd ask him to amplify whatever it was. So again, he'd say, "That's what I'm telling you. Read other books than what you're reading." And I'd say, "It's okay. Anyway, I'm sure they appreciate that some of us are just listeners, because all of you want to talk at the same time." [*Laughs*] It was good for me to be in that kind of environment also. And certainly, I knew that I knew so little compared to all of these people.

SF: Your presidency at the same time was defined by an intelligence that people could adore and follow willingly and joyfully. Can you talk about the nature of that? I mean, you have this . . . I was talking to one of the people . . . Monchito, recently, and how a woman approached you just on the street to embrace you and kiss you on the cheek. And it reminds me of when I was in South Africa, and the love for Mandela is so physical, and you can feel it in the people. And you feel it here for you, and it's very inspiring. Can you talk about the nature of that?

CA: Well, I'm very grateful to the Filipino people that a number of them still care for me, and certainly let me know that they're willing to help in whatever way they can. I suppose some people tell me that I'm credible because I'm sincere. And I said, "Well, I don't say something that I don't mean." Although, of course, I'll tell somebody who's unattractive, "Well, you look very good!" [*Laughs*] But I won't go beyond that. But I suppose you can say that at the start of each day, I pray to the Lord and tell Him to guide me, and to help me every moment of the day. And it's not a long prayer; it's just I ask for His help. And early on, I would tell my husband, "Could you tell me in a dream again, or tell me what it is that I can do?" But I suppose, somebody was telling me, I think God was telling me, "Look, it's about time you thought for yourself," or something like that. But anyway, I was just so happy and so relieved that I was able to finish my term of six years, because when my husband was preparing to leave Boston to come back here, and I think an American journalist had asked him, "So Mr. Aquino, why are you going home? Isn't it dangerous for you to do so?" And he said, "No, it's very important for me to go home because I want to be able to talk to Marcos, and to ask him to start returning our country to democracy." And the journalist said, "But aren't you afraid of the danger?" And he said, "Yes, of course. But as a leader, I should be with my people, especially in times of suffering." And he was. And then he said, "I will never be able to forgive myself, knowing that I could have done something and I did not do anything." And that stayed with me, and even if it were such a monumental task to challenge the dictator, at a certain point, I said, "I have to do as Ninoy did."

SF: How about world leaders? The world needs servant-leaders. Please tell us of one or two world leaders that you have a great appreciation for?

CA: Well, Nelson Mandela would be the top of the list. And I met him in South Africa in 1997. Anyway, aside from being the great person that he is, oh, he's just the most charming person also. And when I met him in Cape Town, he said, "Oh, Corazon Aquino!" And he said so many nice things about me. Then he tells my two daughters who are with me, "You really know how to choose the right mother." Of course, how does one feel when Mandela himself says that? And so we had a chance to talk and I had told him that I was involved in NGO activities. And he had said, "Well, how do you propose to go about this?" I said, "Well, initially I'll just be working with NGOs in the Philippines. But I felt we could all learn from each other." And he had said, "Well, I hope you will not forget South Africa." And luckily, the people who had invited me to South Africa, the Kaiser Foundation, when I told them that, they said, "Well, maybe we can work on something." And so when I came back, I asked my former secretary of Health, Dr. Alran Bengzon, to think of some program where we could invite health workers from South Africa to come here, and also health workers, I think, from Thailand. So they arranged for a one-week seminar. And so Philippine medical workers and Thai medical workers could, in fact, pass on to the South Africans what we were able to do here successfully. And so I was glad that we were able to do that. And even now, we work closely with the Hansider Foundation, and Hansider Foundation helps a number of other NGOs in the region. And I was suggesting to them that perhaps we could go to different countries and inform them what we are doing in our respective countries so that others who would like to replicate successful projects would not have to go through a trial-and-error method, but could in fact just follow what the NGOs have done. And I told him, "Well, I'm volunteering. If you need my help, I can go to other countries and tell them." So I'm waiting for them to tell us about that. Because I was saying that First World to Third World sometimes is difficult, but I think Third World to Third World could, in fact, understand each other better, perhaps would have similar problems and would be able to address those problems better. And another person . . . a world leader? King Baudoin of Belgium. I was just so impressed with his holiness. I have, maybe, well, Mother Teresa, I also was fortunate enough to have met her a number of times, but King Baudoin was just somebody so special, and I felt so fortunate I was given the opportunity to meet with him and his wife, Queen Fabiola.

SF: Your leadership is often seen as united with the deep leadership of Christ. How does your love for Christ influence your leadership?

CA: Well, not only my leadership, but I guess my whole life. And especially where suffering is concerned. It gives me much consolation that, my goodness, what is this that I am suffering compared to what Our Lord has suffered. And I was so glad that they did make a movie, *The Passion of the Christ*, which certainly moved me, and I guess must have moved millions all over the world. So I cannot think of myself as being separate from the good Lord. And my whole day is dedicated to Him. I mean, I say that in the beginning of the day, and at the end of the day, I address myself to the Lord. So I pray that those who do not believe in Him hopefully will be given that grace, to go to Him so that their lives will be that much better, and that they will be able to handle whatever problems or trials come their way.

SF: Another unique aspect of your leadership around the world is politically, it's not often that you see politics founded on prayer. So I was listening to one of the interviews yesterday when some of the media were interviewing you, and you ended with, "All parties concerned, really, we need to pray." And that's a different approach for the world. How do you think of prayer as foundational?

CA: Well, I suppose some people make fun of me when I talk like that. But that's what I believe in, and it's worked for me as I suppose it has worked for others. And I will continue believing in the power of prayer, and I will pray that more people will do the same thing.

SF: Your government was one of the strongest postregime governments the world has seen. And how were you able to effectively resist seven coup attempts, when you think back to that?

CA: Well, thanks to the help of the people. In spite of the coup attempts, the people were for me. They never, you know, showed preference. Maybe a few showed preference for the military rebels, but the great majority stuck by me.

SF: Finally, what is your view of Filipino leadership, and what do you hope for Filipino leadership?

CA: Well, leaders are the same, and different at the same time. And I am not one to say that my leadership is the best kind. And also, different times require different kinds of leaders. So perhaps in the transition from a dictatorship to a democracy, perhaps my kind of leadership was necessary at that time. But, as I said, it really depends on the circumstances, on the times, and on the world situation. But I just hope, and I pray, that we in the Philippines will always try to get the best leaders possible.

SF: Do you have any recommendations or thoughts for the more Western, especially American, leadership these days?

CA: No, I think it's improper for me to give advice, especially unsolicited advice.

SF: Thank you so much.

CA: You're welcome.

SF: Also, a few gifts from us to you.

CA: Oh, thank you.

CA: And I have something. This is for your daughters.

SF: Thank you.

CA: And that's my sign for the letter *L*. It stands for *Love* and was the name of the party. And these are cards for your wife.

SF: Thank you. Your time is a gift to us.

CA: So, thank you very much.

Chapter Twelve

Shann Ray Ferch

Interviewed by Larry C. Spears

Shann Ray Ferch's collection of short stories American Masculine *(Graywolf Press), named by* Esquire *as one of "Three Books Every Man Should Read" and selected by* Kirkus Reviews *as a Best Book of the Year, won the Bread Loaf Writers' Conference Bakeless Prize, the High Plains Book Award, and the American Book Award. Sherman Alexie called it "tough, poetic, and beautiful," and Dave Eggers called Ferch's work "lyrical, prophetic, and brutal, yet ultimately hopeful."Dr. Ferch is a National Endowment for the Arts Literature Fellow and has served as a panelist for the National Endowment for the Humanities, Research Division. His book of creative nonfiction, leadership and political theory,* Forgiveness and Power in the Age of Atrocity: Servant Leadership as a Way of Life *(Rowman & Littlefield/Lexington), was named an Amazon Top Ten Hot New Release in War and Peace in Current Events, and engages the question of ultimate forgiveness in the context of ultimate violence. His book of poems,* Balefire, *appears with Lost Horse Press. He is the winner of the* Subterrain *Poetry Prize, the* Crab Creek Review *Fiction Award, the* Pacific Northwest Inlander *Short Story Contest, and the* Ruminate *Short Story Prize, and his work has appeared in scientific journals internationally as well as in some of the nation's leading literary venues including* Poetry, McSweeney's, Narrative, StoryQuarterly, Northwest Review. *and* Poetry International. *Dr. Ferch serves as the editor of the* International Journal of Servant-Leadership *(2005–present). Shann grew up in Montana, and spent part of his childhood on the Northern Cheyenne reservation. He lives with his wife and three daughters in Spokane, Washington, where he teaches leadership and forgiveness studies in the internationally renowned Doctoral Program in Leadership Studies at Gonzaga University.*

Larry C. Spears: Shann, when did you first encounter the term *servant-leader*?

Shann Ray Ferch: The first time I encountered the term *servant-leader* was when I was hired at Gonzaga University to teach a Leadership and Psychology class nearly twenty years ago. I knew I needed to find something on leadership, since I was trained not directly in leadership studies but in clinical and systems psychology. So I went to the library and actually, the first book I found was *Servant Leadership* by Greenleaf. I'm not sure exactly how it came into my hands in the search, but I remember finding the title and thinking, *I wonder what that's about?* Then I started reading the first forty or fifty pages, which ends up being Greenleaf's original essay, and I immediately decided, *This is the book I want to use for the class.* I was immediately intrigued by the philosophy underlying servant-leadership.

LS: Many people, once they have heard the term, *servant-leader,* in retrospect begin to look at people in their earlier lives who acted as servant-leaders for them. I'm wondering if there are one or two stories of people in your life who were servant-leaders to you before you had heard the term.

SF: The first one that comes to mind is my grandma, who loved dancing and who earned the nickname "the Great One" from our family members because she had a vibrant, joyful, loving spirit and a great amount of communal power. She was a central community figure in a town of eight people in Montana: Cohagen, a town serving the surrounding ranching community, and she was the postmaster, a unique person, and a strong woman. She had many talents. The post office was attached to the back of her house and people would come in, and more often than not, she just invited them farther in, and they'd end up sitting in the kitchen and talking, and she always had coffee and all kinds of baked goods ready on the table. Great cinnamon rolls. My brother and I went to live with her every summer when I was a young boy, and her husband, my grandpa, was pretty stern for a lot of years until he realized that these young boys he thought didn't work hard enough were going to do all right. Then he opened up a little more. She was openly wonderful with us from the beginning.

I loved being around her. There was always good conversational engagement, and gladness in the air, and a lot of dancing and a lot of music. I think the part about her servant-leadership that really helped was you felt safe in her presence, and you felt wisdom in her presence, a natural wisdom, not downloaded into you but more just what happened and how she lived and moved. You could ask her any question you wanted and she'd have a quality answer. The way she lived her life was with great joy and great respect for others and the grace and ease that comes across from being in the presence of a well-lived life.

People who have been servant-leaders in my life include my grandma and also my father and my mother, and my father-in-law and mother-in-law, and my wife, and each of my three daughters. A story about all of them is going to be impossible, so let me start with a story about my father-in-law. He had a special way of servant-leading people and still does. In the beginning, the way he led me was, strangely enough, through power. I was afraid of the power in the beginning, but below the power he also carried an ultimate and immanent depth of love and care. In the beginning I think I projected onto his power, Oh, this is bad power and this person is going to dominate me or try to dominate me. But very soon I noticed, He isn't about dominance at all; he just happens to be a powerful person, probably due to various factors in how he has chosen to live his life.

One of the moments that showed me servant-leadership and legitimate power was when I was in a work setting with him. He was the CEO and one of the female workers had talked over him inside this larger group setting, and he had said something pretty sharp, like, "Hey, I'm talking here." And the person just quieted down and the work went on, but when the meeting was over and people began to disperse the woman went directly to him and said, "During the meeting you offended me. You said something rude to me and I felt embarrassed." I happened to be seated off to the side. So here's a worker talking to the CEO like that, and in my own way of looking at work I was thinking, Wow, that takes a lot of bravery to talk to the CEO so directly and in fact, forwardly. I also felt nervous and thought, It's probably not going to go well.

His response to the woman was, "You're right. I was wrong to treat you that way. I apologize for doing that and I would like to ask your forgiveness." They had a really nice conversation then, and I thought, That's a lot different than what I'm used to in leadership.

A second intriguing element of his leadership came after the rest of us had dispersed, and this was maybe twenty-five minutes later, when he came walking up to me and said, "Do you remember when I was sharp with so-and-so in the meeting?"

"Yeah, I do," I said.

"Well, that was wrong of me," he went on. "That's not how I want to handle things, and I'd like to apologize to you. I'd like to ask your forgiveness for treating her with rudeness and a sharp tone of voice. For being disrespectful to her as a person."

Many different types of thought hit me. Just being around him, I encountered thought and action I had not been used to at all. Such as people in power being willing to admit their own weaknesses, people in power being able to listen well when other people bring them a problem or a difficulty, and then people in power finding a strong peaceful resolution that can lead to a deeper place, without saying, "Okay, now, everybody, this is how we should do it." His actions helped everybody think about what to do with their own weaknesses or when something comes up as a conflict or a character issue. Through servant-leadership, he embedded a certain type of culture.

Another way I learn servant-leadership is through my children, especially their beautiful responses, and so I'll just tell one of those. I was with my youngest, my five-year-old Isabella, and asking her, "Hey, Bella," and I had my hands on her face and I was looking into her eyes, "Bella, why do you think I love you so much?" I said. And she simply looked up and into my eyes and said, "Because God made you to love me."

My wife and daughters servant-lead me all the time.

LS: To the question, "Who is a servant-leader?" Greenleaf said, "The servant-leader is one who is servant first." And in "The Servant as Leader" he wrote, "It begins with a natural feeling that one wants to serve, to serve first. Then conscious choice brings one to aspire to lead. The difference manifests itself in the care taken by the servant first, to make sure that other people's highest priority needs are being served. The best test is, do those served grow as persons? Do they, while being served, become healthier, wiser, freer, more autonomous, more likely themselves to become servants? And what is the affect on the least privileged in society? Will they benefit or at least not be further deprived?" How close does that come to your own definition of servant-leadership, and are their differences between your understanding and this one when it comes to servant-leadership?

SF: Greenleaf's definition of servant-leadership has given me pause many times, because when contrasted with other leadership theories, servant-leadership involves a complete reversal of power and a restoration of the communal idea of humanity: people working together in a good direction. Greenleaf reverses what we normally think about power. So Greenleaf is often questioning the moral and communal integrity of the person we normally think of as the leader. Maybe that person came to leadership with too much self-absorption, too much ambition. Maybe that person came to it because of a certain need to assuage or soothe their own power drive. I know in leadership, narcissism, ambition, and ego are a brutal triad, and certainly Greenleaf had tremendous strength of thought to build ultimate questions in order to challenge that triad. So, in looking at the idea of servant-leadership and the fact that the best test of a servant-leader is that people around the servant-leader become more wise, more healthy, more autonomous, more free, and better able themselves to become servant-leaders . . . the fact is the question is so authentic, it scares any sane person because it is difficult to fathom and it means if a person actually would like to be a servant-leader, the answer to whether or not they are being one is not in their hands; the answer is in the hands of the people that person is with, the relationships both cursory and in-depth formed by that person. Servant-leadership reverses almost all traditional conceptions of leadership and puts the power or the relational dynamic or the follow-through, the effects and impacts or the ability to measure those effects and impacts, in the hands of those around us and takes it out of our hands. We cannot control the dynamic of a given system, nor can we control the beloved other. So, for example, I can't bend my wife's arm behind her back and say, "Tell them I'm not defensive anymore." I'm either not defensive and then she can openly say, "He's not defensive," or I still need to work on myself and gain a deeper sense of self, other, love, and care. When we take that to the workplace or to nation-states, from the individual all the way up through the family to the organization and the world, people around us get the opportunity to say whether or not they are becoming, in our presence, more wise, more healthy, more free, more autonomous and whether or not we are an encumbrance or a liberator to them in that process.

So how close is Greenleaf's definition to my own? I'm humbled by his definition so it sounds strange talking about, "Well, what differences might I consider?" When I went to the Philippines and Colombia and South Africa and looked at servant-leadership, it was very different than looking at servant-leadership in the U.S. In the U.S in general, not always, but in many spheres of influence, an individualized leadership ethos is the standard versus a collectivist leadership ethos. So there's great emphasis on individual responsibility, on who's to blame and who needs to take responsibility and who needs to change. I see a particular focus on individual aspiration. In the Philippines, Colombia, and South Africa, more circular rather than linear cultures, I notice a more collectivist sense of aspiration: "How can we collectively move together?" We have the collective idea. I think when we look at Greenleaf's definition we have, for example, "others become more autonomous," but it might be nice to also have, "others become more collectively responsible."

LS: Throughout Greenleaf's published work he wrote about a number of characteristics of servant-leadership, and in 1992, I pulled those together as a kind of a "top ten list" of servant-leader characteristics, based upon a reading of his work and actually going through and ticking them off. Those ten that I've identified that he spoke most frequently about in various writings were: listening, empathy, healing, awareness, persuasion, conceptualization, foresight, stewardship, commitment to the growth of people, and building community. Would you share your thoughts with us on one or two of these characteristics?

SF: The ten characteristics of servant-leadership, so beautifully laid out by you Larry, are so beautiful in my opinion because they quietly and with great endurance and force deconstruct typical patriarchal, postcolonial society. Not that fatherhood or masculinity isn't necessary and imbued with the capacity for excellence, or that Western thought and logic and reason isn't a superb contribution to human life, it's just that such things can be wrongfully used. The ten characteristics help us realign and ask eloquent questions of one another: What does it mean to be together? What does it mean to actually be servants to one another? Not servant meaning "slave," but servant meaning what you do when you love someone. I want my children to do well in the world. I am invested in their emotional, physical, and spiritual well-being. I want the people I'm around to experience life at its most ultimate. I want the organization I'm in or the nation I'm part of to be in humble and mutually meaningful relationship with other organizations and with other nations. I want that kind of servanthood, not the kind where a person is dominated or enslaved or subsumed by the power of another person or by the inappropriate influence of another person or another entity, organization, or nation. So when I think about the ten characteristics, they hold many elegant pathways to help us live more fully as human beings with each other and live in ways that we can answer to the great questions and the great problems of humanity. As for a few characteristics to focus on, how about foresight, healing, and building community?

When I think of foresight, I think of foresight differently as a clinical psychologist than I would if I were trained in another field. As a clinical psychologist, foresight not only can be trained, but should be trained. When we lack foresight, we should want to be held responsible for lacking foresight. That's a difficult concept, especially in our current setting in America where it's so easy for us to be irresponsible across the spectrum: in relationality and organizational ethics and financial responsibilities, in the way that we handle ourselves with other countries, in the way we handle ourselves with each other. So being that America has some difficulties in that setting—not to speak of other countries, but just to look at our own country—I think we lack foresight and the results are devastating. There are areas of America that have very strong foresight; generally those are elusive, a little bit hidden, a reflection of what foresight is in general. Yet they exist, so when I think about it from the perspective of a psychologist, I think, Okay, how can we train ourselves toward greater foresight?

I'll give a small example. John Gottman and his research on relationships out of the University of Washington—profound research over THIRTY years which resulted in major discoveries about relationships and what breaks us down—shows foresight about relationships in a very small space that ends up being significantly impactful over the next two and three and ten and fifteen years. So for example, he can predict at a 95 percent rate within five minutes how likely a couple is to divorce or to go toward what he called negative sentiment override, a level of negative interaction in which the relationship is oriented toward dissolution rather than unification. In his thirty years of longitudinal research with thousands of couples, he and his team also discovered that 80 percent of men (or those with a more masculine trait emphasis) who divorce all share one character quality, and that 80 percent of women (or those with a more feminine trait emphasis) who divorce share a different but mutually aligned character quality. This would be very important knowledge for all of us in personal life, in business, in relational interactions across the board, and in fact in the basic way we relate with others. So what is it?

Those 80 percent of men who divorce don't receive the influence of the feminine. And those 80 percent of women who divorce have contempt for the masculine.

Such an imploding dynamic in human relations becomes an obvious and almost immediate foresight: men who relate well receive the influence of the feminine, and in fact love the feminine; women who relate well affirm the masculine, and in fact, love the masculine.

Gottman's work presents an underlying systemic way of looking at the world: if I am one type of person I'm generally going to attract another type of person. If I don't receive the influence of others, I attract contempt. If I am full of contempt, I attract people who are defensive and who put up a wall in their interactions with me. The same principles are reflected in organizational life, national policy, and global interactions. If I'm cynical I tend to attract cynicism. If I am depressed or angry at the world or difficult to relate to, I tend to find friends and colleagues of the same ilk. Similarly, the person who is humble or graced with common sense or self-responsibility, tends to attract these qualities in others. In other words, we attract to ourselves the same level of maturity we have attained. In psychological understanding, this is the devastating fundamental foresight that you marry an equal level of dysfunction as yourself.

Unwritten psychological truths fall under the wing of foresight. We all understand some of these, such as: the only person in the world you can change is yourself. But then there are unwritten rules not as easily detected but which I've found come from the central essence of foresight, and these are all very helpful in the life of leadership. For example, when you change yourself, others around you have to change. That's an interesting notion, and a very powerful one. So, for example, if in my relationships with others I get more defensive or more fortified or more rigid or more severe for the next thirty days, three years, or thirty years, it's somewhat predictable how people will respond to me in the early days of my descent: probably with something like, "What's going on?" "Gee, I don't like this very much." "Wow, I wish this person wasn't as difficult to be with." The outlay is going to be somewhat predictable. I'm going to make people irritated and, eventually, different types of responses beyond irritation will come my way, like anger, frustration, and attacks on my character. Finally, my relationships will be characterized by complete alienation and subtle or overt violence against legitimate relational intimacy. There are certain consequences if I change myself to become less fully human.

If I change myself to become more fully human, the result is not generally what we think. It doesn't mean my life suddenly goes over into the right way of being. Why? Because the people around me will wonder if I'm really going to change, or whether this just a phase I'm going through? So generally, changing to a greater way of being or a more ultimate way of life or a more fully human expression of character as a leader, as a person, as a servant of others, is going to get resistance at first, because people need to see if the change is actually going to happen. We call this integrity. Integrity is also the difference between what we call first-order and second-order change. In first-order change, the system changes for a bit and then pops back to the same shape it was in before; in second-order change, the system changes for the long term, we see the changes, and experience the changes because eventually they are more fully embodied, and then the system begins to realign itself into a better and more fully realized sense of human development.

So, foresight is incredibly powerful. Greenleaf had a wonderful grasp of foresight and the rather robust responsibilities associated with foresight. He believed not only are servant-leaders responsible to have foresight, they are responsible to create collective responsibility for foresight so that the entire family, organization or system has the kind of foresight necessary in order to guarantee, or at least give us a much better chance at, experiencing our way of being in the world in its more full or true expressions, in its most ultimate forms. If we just extrapolate that out, the question becomes: Can we actually gather ourselves to the kind of foresight we need for things like the current state of the globe, the environment, the financial overdraw, the volatile ways we relate to each other, the nature of apathy, lack of responsibility, and enmity?

Our lives depend on the answer.

How did Gottman come to understand foresight? How did he become capable of predicting the nature of such valuable relational fulcrum points? First, he discovered that people attract to themselves their own level of maturity and their own level of immaturity. That's foresight. Then he started to break that mutual dysfunction and function down, even to the level of behaviors, patterns of action, patterns of inaction, resistances, energy, drive, the myriad ways people relate, and then he even analyzed people's patterns of interaction all the way into facial expression, the types of words people use, the thoughts driving those words, the thoughts driving those facial expressions, the interior that would be the engine behind such thoughts. So we're getting down into consciousness, the way people are with each other consciously and unconsciously in the depth of their being or the depth of their soul, we could say, and how we try to relate to others. So a fortified, defended, protected, fearful, angry, troubled self is going to attract that kind of person on the other side of them. And a self that embodies contentment, grace and ease, discipline, responsibility, and community building, a person who asks and grants forgiveness and is capable of change and atonement and capable of loving and serving others, is generally going to attract such qualities in others. I think we can kind of map that out a bit when we look at each other. Life is not normally linear, one-two-three, or solely behaviorally determined. Life has so much mystery. The mystery allows us to see something ultimate happening that goes toward ultimate good or ultimate truth or ultimate beauty, those beautiful Jesuit and classical terms that help us understand the world, and then we can also see critical mass has been reached at a certain level and the system has surrendered in a good way. The community, or the system, has broken over into a deeper expression. Foresight, a deepened form of personal awareness, leads us to that gorgeous, imaginative, and expansive surrender.

So back to Gottman, how did he do that? Obviously, a lot of reading and mentoring, and a lot of science and a lot of research, but there's one thing that reminds me often of how with foresight, if we want more of it, we ought to get trained in it. Gottman realized that relational foresight had a lot to do with a person's face—we can see certain crucial elements in person's facial expression, we can see what is driving people and their emotions and their spoken voice and the thoughts driving their voice. So Gottman went to France and studied under a facial expression expert for a year in order to improve his foresight regarding facial expression. Most of us would not think of doing that. His journey still shocks me and makes me think, Okay, who can I study under regarding leadership foresight? Who can I find to mentor me? And then if we take that out into other characteristics of servant-leadership—who would I study under regarding being a servant-leader who heals, who is a healer? Who would I study under regarding being a servant-leader in any of the ten characteristics? And how might I surrender to the learning? How might I listen deeply enough—listening being the first characteristic of servant-leadership—to change in ways that not just me, but a critical mass of servant-leaders can be a part of building a movement that would be healing-oriented in the family, in organizations, and among nations?

LS: What are your thoughts on the differences between knowing and doing, or understanding and practicing, when it comes to servant-leadership?

SF: The differences between knowing and doing, or understanding and practicing, in servant-leadership become pretty profound in our day and age, especially when you consider we so often live in a fast-paced, please-give-it-to-me-now society. But the great works of all nations and all societies and all people have always taken time. I think that servant-leadership is one of those great works, one of the great understandings, and one of the great deeds of any given society, and it takes time. So again I come to it from the perspective of psychology, and also theology. In both perspectives, there's a desire to more closely touch the mystery. When we talk about depth psychology I go to Carl Jung, Viktor Frankl, some of the existential psychologists, and some of the archetypal roots of our humanity. The mystery helps us notice things that are serious and that require our most sustained moral efforts. I believe Jung would say servant-leadership is one of the great archetypes, though the term was not directly available when he was speaking and writing.

I think he would also say that the best servant-leadership in the person and in society, will grasp the fact that there is a deep shadow to leadership. In other words, we can't just say, "Yes, let's all be servant-leaders," and suddenly it happens. Carl Jung and other great thinkers—like Frankl, Dietrich Bonheoffer, and Paul Tillich . . . I think of C. S. Lewis, and his book *Till We Have Faces*, Toni Morrison, Czeslaw Milosz, Marilynne Robinson, bell hooks, and so many others . . . there's going to be a deep knowledge of the fact that leadership involves an attendant long-term necessity to deal with the darkness or the shadow of leadership, and the darkness or the shadow of serving. I think if we just point at those a little bit, we can see the darkness or the shadow of serving might have something to do with codependency or the overwillingness to make sure I don't use any power or that I, in fact, inappropriately give up my power when power is needed most. The shadow of leadership might be the overwillingness to use power, to take power, and dominate with power. Servant-leadership is a beautiful nexus of those shadows and their corresponding light: power balanced by love, and love balanced by power in the terms of Martin Luther King Jr. Servant-leadership involves understanding the darkness of the servant and the leader, ingesting this shadow from a Jungian perspective or embracing it, not running from it, not fleeing or blocking it, and then trying to move together with others to a deeper understanding that would then create a deeper action, a deeper way of enacting and living servant-leadership.

We know from research, it takes three to five years to change character—for a person to surrender enough to change their own character—and by extension in a collective group or an organization, how long does it take for an organization to change from a non-servant-led organization to a fully servant-led organization? I don't know, but it would be at least three to five years. I'm sure it could take much longer. In family systems theory, to change a generational family system, it takes about fifteen years from the point of brokenness, the point of total surrender, to change a family into the fully realized embodiment of deep and healthy change. That's why transitional figures in generational lines are so important: so instead of alcoholism, alcoholism, alcoholism, alcoholism, alcoholism, we get one person then who chooses the emotional well-being required not just for sobriety, but for a new depth of life that has the capacity to change the entire generational structure. And if we look at organizations, instead of overambition, overdominance, overuse of power down through the generations of an organization, we need a transitional generation: servant-leadership, critical density and critical mass, a tipping point into a new and better way of being together mutually and with greater regard for one another, and this necessarily involves great discernment in understanding different parts of the shadow. Again, from Martin Luther King Jr., there is always the need for a balance of love and power because love without power is anemic and weak, and basically ineffectual; and power without love is dictatorship, harms people and is basically abusive. I think we've all witnessed or been a part of both dynamics, overextended love, or overextended power. The two together in mutual balance, love and power, symbolize a legitimate way of life, and that's what servant-leadership embodies.

LS: There's a kind of progression in Greenleaf's writing and thinking about servant-leadership. He started looking at servant-leadership in relation to individuals in "The Servant as Leader" essay in 1970. Two years later he progressed to look at the institution as servant in the essay of that title. And then in 1974, began to look at the role of boards of trustees within organizations and wrote the essay "Trustees as Servants." Could you share an insight or story concerning servant-leadership in any or all of those contexts?

SF: When I think about the different contexts that Greenleaf wrote in, I'd like to focus on "The Servant as Leader," that original essay. That essay is not an easy read, which I think is to Greenleaf's honor, and shows his dignity. I think there's a lot of "pop leadership" out there, popular approaches that are very quick reads and feel like they give you something—and they do—but to me what they give you is something like a candy bar compared to a hearty meal. And so I like the hearty meal, I like something that is sustaining and that is going to get us there over the long haul. Greenleaf's thought does just that. He writes with tremendous depth and layering, and his work can withstand multiple reads as it draws the reader deeper into life. I love that. There are very few leadership writings more robust, in my opinion. Greenleaf provided a large cornerstone in servant-leadership, with great philosophical, psychological, and theological depth. There are other areas for sure in the field of leadership that are profound and powerful, especially with regard to many of the emerging leadership theories, when we think about critical theory and bell hooks and Paulo Freire and we think about relational leadership, transformational leadership, and appreciative inquiry. There are many profound, powerful things moving in society. Servant-leadership provides the inner core of that deeper movement helping us continue to think in a more profound way, to be more discerning, and then to take actions that bring legitimate healing to the world.

So when I think about the original essay and Greenleaf's thought on the servant as leader, the level of thought causes me to approach things differently. And I remember when I started reading it, then started teaching it, and then started being part of trying to help people gather together to heal their organizations, heal the rifts inside of their organizations, and help their organization become not just more efficient, but also more healthy, I also started noticing I wanted to continue to work to deepen this interplay of health and excellence in my own life, forever. I remember suddenly coming upon the idea that this is what I should doing as a psychologist, and thinking, Yes, there is so much theory, existential theory and Jungian theory and systems theory—and Greenleaf's servant-leadership belongs right there with them. As a systems psychologist I see couples, marriages, and families. They loved servant-leadership from when it was first presented to them as a way of life, because it was an obvious reversal of power and it made them remember, *Ah, that's how we influence—that's how we can influence each other with love and care.* So each person in that relational dynamic, whether that was all the members of the family and we talked about the upper structure of the hierarchy, the wife and husband, the partners, the two spouses, when we started looking at that and people started saying, "Okay. So if I'm going to live in a way that makes the other people around me more wise, more healthy, more free, more autonomous, better able to be a servant themselves, that's a different task than just trying to survive in a marriage. Servant-leadership means I am devoted to the beauty, life, and love that exists in my loved ones."

So servant-leadership started to help people in the psychology setting gain a different view of ways of relating and it almost immediately removed the tit-for-tat syndrome, and almost immediately made people realize, Wow, if I'm going to live in a way that that person says of me I've made them more healthy, it changes the whole dynamic. That means I'm going to be searching for what's most meaningful in their life, as one part of it, and then also probably what's most meaningful in life in general, in life above just our own mutual existence. And then that also is going to call me to what I might need to change that hampers or takes away from a healthy, meaningful, and loving progression. Servant-leadership in my family calls me to change my character so that I'm not blocking the progression of health, goodness, beauty, mercy, justice, and love in my loved ones, but rather enhancing these.

So Greenleaf's essay, "The Servant as Leader," became a big part of my psychology practice and also my personal life. If we want to be people who love others deeply enough that they become more healthy and more wise and more free and more autonomous and better able to be servants, then we are in for a profound and often excruciating call. I believe this call emerges from the center of humanity, the nexus of the human and the divine: the call to be a true person, a person who then influences people because the true person is responsible to surrender to their own healing and then to help heal the heart of humanity.

LS: Those three essays form the core of what's considered Greenleaf's most important or significant writings on servant-leadership. But he wrote on servant-leadership in many other contexts as well: with youth, "Have You a Dream Deferred"; in the religious context, "The Servant as Religious Leader," "The Seminary as Servant," "Spirituality as Leadership"; on aging, "Old Age, the Ultimate Test of Spirit," the last essay that he wrote, and others.

The question is, are there any of his other writings that have had a particular influence, maybe even a profound influence on you?

SF: Greenleaf wrote many essays I love. The one I love the most is not "The Servant as Leader," though I love that one truly. The one I love the most is "An Inward Journey," which is a chapter in the book *Servant Leadership*, and that chapter—I think it's the final chapter, actually—is about Robert Frost's poem, "Directive." The arts influence the world with an uncommon and uniquely human and profoundly powerful undercurrent, and I love it that Greenleaf was interested and invested in the arts. He seemed to surrender to trying to deeply understand artistic expression, was artistic himself, and had a very thoughtful and artist's way of looking at the world. He had an artist's eye, in my opinion. And you could see it directly in that essay, "An Inward Journey," where he gives a beautiful, critical look at one of Robert Frost's most difficult and beloved poems. The way the essay influences me is through not just the science of leadership, but the art of leadership. Greenleaf had both. He had the ability to work with the entire development of future leaders at AT&T from a very reductionistic, basically positivistic sense of research that resulted in foresight about who our future leaders will be, and how we might find the best, most humble and wise leaders. This research is generally housed in what we call quantitative science, and the accusations against hard science or science that is oriented toward quantitative understanding is that it is over-linear, tends not to allow for the mystery, tends not to allow for the circular, and is a form of research that makes people feel trapped by an overly rigid design about who people are, what humanity is, and what defines leadership. I don't belief Greenleaf ever foreclosed mystery or more circular understandings, because he was able to be out of the box even while he looked at the quantitative ways that we can develop future leaders. His essays show a very well-rounded picture of humanity. I love, "An Inward Journey," because it is the complete opposite of the linear approach, and it begins to look at Robert Frost's darker poems, or the more intense or the more shadow-oriented poems that Robert Frost wrote. In some of Frost's most famous poems you don't directly see the shadow, but many of his poems in his body of work have such an inherently wise way of looking at the shadow and I think Greenleaf recognized that, so he picked one of the poems which is about how we deal with the depths of darkness that do approach and sometimes consume our lives, when we feel cut off and burned and desolated, or when our experience is that we have been cut off, burned, or desolated.

I think if we look around, we can see a huge sense of lack of responsibility for our world, if we think about violence and deaths due to war going up in the last three centuries from 5 million three centuries ago to 20 million two centuries ago to 120 million this last century. I think people like Robert Frost and Robert Greenleaf sensed and foresaw the oncoming desolation of the current age. In that essay by Greenleaf we see the servant-leader's role inside the desolation of humanity, which I think is felt in the workplace, in our families, in our interior life, and among nations. So when I read that essay and reread that essay, I am brought to a humble place and a contemplative place where we all become more willing to be responsible for each other inside the desolation that exists in society.

LS: Would you share with us something of your own personal journey around servant-leadership?

SF: My own personal journey around servant-leadership became the most significant around the age of seventeen, when I first met the woman who would be my future wife and I was first challenged to be purposeful, or more purposeful, with my life versus just bouncing around and hitting off of things and becoming more hollow. I wasn't necessarily going off the deep end, I just didn't have purpose, a typical feeling for a lot of Americans, especially young Americans. And that had to do with the society I was raised in and my own personal way of looking at the world. So if we look at society and young Americans right now, there's so much media and so much fast, fast thought. Fast thought is nearly always undiscerned. If we look at purposeful lives throughout the centuries, the thought slows down and the willingness to slow down and be deeply embedded in deeper and deeper thought becomes readily apparent.

So, when I found my wife, I discovered a pretty amazing person, full of fire and verve and vitality, and she was already devoted to deep level of thinking, which can equate to a deep level of living. And I remember when she first challenged me, "Let's go back and read the ten major books that have influenced each other's lives." Now, if we were to do that with a cross-section of American young people, I'm willing to say that with seventeen- and eighteen-year olds, it would be very few percentage-wise that would be able to come up with ten books that influenced their lives. When I was seventeen, I could come up with seven, and they were all children's books. And so I was hurting in the reading category. My wife had ten, and each book was a true power. So when we read each other's books, interestingly enough, she had read all seven of mine before I'd even given her the list! I had read none of her ten before I saw her list. So I went about reading her list. I encountered *Candide* by Voltaire, *A Tale of Two Cities* by Charles Dickens, *Les Misérables* by Victor Hugo, and *The Four Loves* by C. S. Lewis, the whole *Lord of the Rings* series, Frances Hodson Burnett's *The Secret Garden*, and Harper Lee's *To Kill a Mockingbird*. These books changed my entire way of looking at the world. So I never went back. I just kept reading.

The next big moment came when we were living in Giessen, Germany, Jennifer and I, and Black History Month came up, and the town had a U.S. Army base. I had some friends on the army base, and I went into the bookstore there on base, and there were three full rows dedicated to Black History Month. Right then I noticed an entire row dedicated to Martin Luther King Jr. I had never read anything on Martin Luther King Jr. As a matter of fact, looking back, I was saturated with quite a bit of what bell hooks would call white privileged supremacist patriarchy, because all I knew about Martin Luther King Jr. were indictments that framed him in a dark light: the accusations of his life with other women outside his marriage, his possible cheating on his dissertation. Harsh judgments I placed on a profound American leader without ever reading anything by him, especially when you consider the primary accuser of Martin Luther King Jr. was a man named Hoover, and Hoover's own life and his own struggles with grave personal hypocrisy were as large as nearly any public figure in American history.

I brought down off the shelf *Strength to Love*, a collection of ten of Martin Luther King Jr.'s sermons. After reading that book I never saw people the same again. The works of Martin Luther King Jr. are interwoven with people like Paulo Freire and bell hooks and Robert Greenleaf in my mind because of that original moment, and when servant-leadership became more present in my life, they all just dovetailed in a natural sisterhood and brotherhood of writers.

LS: Several places Greenleaf talked about the Latin root of *religion*, *religio*, meaning "to rebind." I've met sincere servant-leaders of all faiths, philosophies, and secular beliefs over the years. What are your thoughts, particularly around servant-leadership, faith, and philosophy?

SF: I have great admiration for Greenleaf's look at servant-leadership, faith, and philosophy, and his take of religion and its original etymology meaning "to rebind." My own work and research is in forgiveness and in the nature of ultimate violence and how it is healed by ultimate forgiveness. Profound movements of servant-leadership have arisen in many nations after suffering major atrocities: South Africa and Rwanda and Croatia and Serbia, and here in the U.S. with regard to the atrocities committed against Native Americans. There are profound movements of rebinding. At the site of the Big Hole Massacre in Northern Montana, the descendants of Cavalry troops that committed the massacre and the descendents of Nez Perce people who were massacred gather for reconciliation in a Nez Perce rebinding ceremony that involves rituals of sorrow, honoring the dead, and giving peace. Sacred ceremony engages servant-leadership in a very, very profound way. So when I think of faith and I think of Greenleaf's idea to rebind, I get very excited about it because I know rebinding heals the world; at the same time I know rebinding takes courage and willingness on the part of many people coming together to begin that type of work.

LS: What are your thoughts on faith and servant-leadership?

SF: Any system of thought can get bent so easily. For example, there are bad Christians, there are bad Muslims, there are bad servant-leaders, there are bad people who are atheists; there are great Christians, there are great Muslims, there are great servant-leaders, there are great people who are atheists. There are great people of all faiths or nonfaiths, of all the major traditions, and there are very hypocritical and in, fact horrible people who cause abuse and atrocities. This brings me back to the ground of the shadow of humanity and where does servant-leadership fit in? There are people who claim to be a servant-leader and then pervasively harm others. In fact, I sometimes harm others. Though I claim to be a servant-leader in my family, there are times my family members feel that I have pervasively harmed them and they're right. So what are we going to do with that crucible? It's a great question for all of humanity. What are each of us going to do with the fact that we know we are all hypocrites at some level. For me, as in Greenleaf's work, Christ washing the feet of the disciples is an image I cling to and hope to emulate. The beauty of Christ and his surrender to ultimate meaning even in the context of suffering, breaks me and helps me surrender.

Like Greenleaf, I also identify with the servant Leo in Herman Hesse's *The Journey to the East*. Leo's humility, and how he cooked for others and cleaned, and how he was a singer. Servant-leadership points the way to better understandings of our own hypocrisy and the need for a return to intimacy and integrity. In the ten characteristics, the listening element becomes so foundational. If I really listen to my family members, to my coworkers, and then if I engage in a life that is going to become more whole, more free, more autonomous, more healthy, and better able to serve others, and then if I gather around me, or draw myself toward others who are doing the same, there's a better chance the hypocrisy can be mitigated and healed. We're not talking about eliminating hypocrisy, hypocrisy is part of the human condition—the important part is how we respond to it and what we do with foresight regarding our own hypocrisy and the hypocrisy of others. And that's where I think servant-leadership helps us expand and helps us understand our own darkness, either as individuals or as a collective, as organizations in the workplace, or as nations.

LS: The next question is what is the role of servant-leadership in your own interior life?

SF: I see the role of servant-leadership in my interior life as something that seeks to be quieter and to slow down and to move in ways that have more quietness within them. When I think about the interior of the servant-leader I try to remember to get quiet in the morning, put myself in a bodily posture of humility in the morning, and this generally comes from my mentors, too, women and men who have been beloved servant-leaders to me. From them I learn to value quietness to start the day, humility with the body to start the day, being in a bodily posture of love and affection to my loved ones first, and primarily, but also going forth and giving that to the world throughout the day. I want to physically touch my loved ones every day in good ways. My wife. My three daughters. I want to put my hands tenderly on their faces, I want to look into their eyes, I want to embrace them, I want to hold their hands, especially since my three daughters are young, they make it easy because they are each so lovable! Natalya. Ariana. Isabella. With my wife Jennifer, I want to be there with them physically, to be present. So the interior of the servant-leader for me is about quietness, listening, and being present.

LS: What are useful ways in which servant-leaders can best deal with conflict?

SF: Servant-leaders approach conflict from a listening perspective, with the long road in mind. Servant-leaders know we can't heal major rifts immediately and we shouldn't want to. Rather, servant-leaders engage a long-term conversation and a long-term commitment toward character change, and develop families, organizations, and nations that embrace the longer processes of healing and growth and the endurance needed to have joy and grace and ease involved in the longer process while knowing that conflict tends to surface important dynamics like depression and anger and frustration, even alienation. Servant-leaders have a sustaining source of love and power that directs the self and others through these crucibles of conflict.

I think of Parker Palmer's story in his book *Let Your Life Speak.* He speaks of suffering from depression and an interior conflict he was having, an interior conflict with himself that I think we've all experienced in some form or another. It's excruciating and we don't know how we're going to get out of it. The answers were not coming easily, and he put himself bodily in a position to receive some possible answers, in his case by going to live in Quaker Community, just to be there. Who knows when resolution might come, but the thing that eventually ended up being helpful—because he kept seeking, in a depleted but also in a fierce way—was that he was confronted by the need to surrender instead of the need for an answer, and he started surrendering. He recalls a time when an older gentleman began coming into his room, into the room of his depression, in order to rub Parker's feet. That's it. The older man wouldn't give him advice, wouldn't answer his ferocious need to get an answer—or, in reality, I guess he answered it in a much deeper way, you know, by just being present, and showing care that was deeply meaningful to Parker. That's important. That's foresight also. Showing care in a way the other person considers to be deeply meaningful. Sometimes, paradoxically, it might not even be what the other person seems to want. Yet sometimes that is truly what foresight is about. Perhaps Parker Palmer didn't initially want his feet rubbed, you know what I mean? It was probably a bit uncomfortable. I think Parker even relates that, but eventually there is some resolution, with deep care in it, maybe even deeper than what the hurting person can see at that time, and maybe even deeper than what the person who was showing care could see, but the old man knew something was important in his giving, and that inspires me.

LS: Is there a question you wish you could have asked Robert Greenleaf?

SF: If I had the opportunity to ask Robert Greenleaf a question, I would probably ask him, what would your wife name as your primary weaknesses and how would she speak about the ways you two worked to heal those? And for me, I would ask that question because I notice in my readings of Greenleaf's writings, there appears to be a very nice love between him and his wife. Nobody can really know the interior of a love relationship. However, the one between Robert and his wife seems to be pretty vibrant and vital and enduring. So I think I would be safe in asking that question and I think I would get a wonderful answer.

LS: What excites you most about servant-leadership, and why?

SF: The thing that excites me most about servant-leadership is the focus on listening, the quietness, and the way, if people individually and collectively attend to that type of listening and that type of quietness, things change and others do become more healthy and more wise and more free and more autonomous, and better at serving others.

LS: Do you have thoughts about servant-leadership that we have not touched on that you would like to share?

SF: When I think of servant-leadership, for me—probably because I love the idea of the family as central to our humanity around the world—I would love to see a focus on how to train servant-leaders from the time they are children, and how parents can live as servant-leaders. That's something I feel would help the country and the world.

Chapter Thirteen

Frances Hesselbein

Interviewed by Mary McFarland

A servant-leader of the highest order, Frances Hesselbein is the president and CEO of the Frances Hesselbein Leadership Institute (formerly the Peter F. Drucker Foundation for Nonprofit Management) as well as its founding president. Hesselbein was awarded the Presidential Medal of Freedom, the United States of America's highest civilian honor, in 1998. The award recognized her leadership as chief executive officer of Girl Scouts of the USA from 1976 to 1990, her role as the founding president of the Drucker Foundation, and her service as "a pioneer for women, diversity and inclusion." Her contributions were also recognized by former President Bush Sr., who appointed her to two Presidential Commissions on National and Community Service.

Mary McFarland: Can you tell me about your lessons learned in your work with the Girl Scouts?

Frances Hesselbein: In the 1950s little girl Girl Scouts used to bake cookies and sell them to their neighbors. People loved it so much then the Girl Scouts started having bakers bake them. When I left the Girl Scouts of the USA in 1990, the sale was generating a third-of-a-billion dollars . . . and all of the money stayed in the councils. It meant that little girls and young women were providing the support for their own program. It really is not just a sale; it's a way to learn marketing, and what does the customer value, and keeping your promise: "I will return with two boxes of cookies," and you do. And then comes, "asset management." What do we do with the proceeds, our share of the cookie sale?

MM: Please speak to the importance of ethical leadership.

FH: January 26, 2005, I went to Houston, Texas. Why did I go? Because the University of St. Thomas was going to inaugurate its new president, the first time in university history that a layman was going to be inaugurated as president. And who is the new president? The remarkable General Robert Ivany, a devout Catholic, a great war hero, commandant of the U.S. Army War College at Carlisle, Pennsylvania, with a PhD in modern European history. I'm sure there were hundreds who could have moved into this position. General Ivany was chosen.

Now, I had a call from him. "Frances, I'm going to begin my legacy. And I'm going to have an inauguration with an inaugural address. And I want you to come, and I want you to talk about leadership and ethics."

Now what did I decide would be the title? "Leaders of the Future: Ethics in Action." So the inaugural address was all about leadership, all about the indispensable role, the power, of ethical leadership.

Now, you might say, that's fine, in a university it's sort of cloistered and you're protected, it's easier to be ethical. Wrong. At every level of this society, in every institution, right across the three sectors, the challenges are greater than ever. And I believe in this society and in countries around the world, there is a cry for ethical, principled leadership, for leaders who have a moral compass that works full time. Leaders with values that they don't just frame and put up on a wall. They embody the values. Their people watch. And there's nothing more inspiring than an ethical leader who lives the values and is explicit about the ethics, about the principles we live by in this institution, this organization. And whether it is a giant corporation, the smallest community college, a large nonprofit, a small business, it doesn't matter; ethical, principled leadership is key.

MM: Boards of directors are of paramount importance. What do see as the responsibility of boards of directors?

FH: In October I spent a week in New Zealand speaking to the New Zealand Institute of Management and then to Asia Association of Management Institute including leaders from all over Asia, all over New Zealand. It was a fascinating week, and I did a lot of public relations, on live television, 6:30 in the morning, millions of people watching. What was the one question I was asked? "Mrs. Hesselbein, what is the impact of corporate scandals in the United States?" Now, they knew all my background, they knew all about that marvelous conference, yet the one thing he wanted to ask about: corporate scandals in the United States. It was simple to respond—the corporate scandals represented a small percentage of the principled corporations in the United States.

Recently I spoke to SWIM—they're not aquatic stars, they're Sloan Women in Management at MIT—and they had looked at all the news of corporate scandals. They decided they should serve on boards of directors. But instead of saying, "Well, I'm so bright; I have an MBA from Sloan," they said, "What are the questions we should ask first?" And I think that is the answer to your question. What are the questions we ask before we go on the board, and once we are on the board, do we have the courage to ask the questions that should be asked? Because, if as part of governance, we are responsible for total transparency, total trust, we ask tough questions. Governance in this country—not everywhere, but in these conspicuous cases—they never asked the questions that we are committed to ask. So it was . . . maybe being overwhelmed with the honor, maybe it is director's fees, whatever the reason, it was more of a social experience than a tough, managerial governance experience for some directors. It was the opposite of what the women of SWIM would demonstrate.

MM: You are a person of both courage and spirit. What is the role of the divine in your life and in your leadership?

FH: I have this sense that God has a plan for us, and when we are called, when we listen to that spirit within—however you define it—when we listen, we're given the energy to do what we are called to do. On our website there's an article, "The Whispers of Our Lives," that defines three kinds of whispers that I believe are whispers of our lives—the whispers of the body, the whispers of the mind, the whispers of the heart.

For those of us who feel we are called and are willing to share this, some people, they think it is too personal, it's very helpful to many people if we can say, "I have a sense that I'm called to do what I do." Now, I'm not talking about "Methodist Prayer Meeting." There's a spirit within that calls us, and when we listen, amazing things can happen. I like the words *providence* and *providential*. There is a plan for us.

MM: You have mentioned the secret of life on occasion, Frances, can you tell us a story or two about the secret of life?

FH: Father John Culkin, a Jesuit priest, was the great authority on Marshall McLuhan, and interpreted McLuhan to the country. And he was a great authority on the film, and wrote just remarkable articles years and years ago for the *Saturday Review*. He and my husband John, were two of the first six Robert Flaherty Fellows, and they were fellows who were chosen to be part of this study of the film as an educational tool in honor of the father of modern documentaries, Robert Flaherty.

One time I opened the *Saturday Review*—at this time I had yet to meet Father Culkin—and in the article he described a scene in which a priest asks an eight-year-old, "What is education to you?" And the little boy replied, "Oh, it's how kids learn stuff." But in that article Father Culkin wrote, "It took me 50 years to learn the secret of life. The secret of life is very simple. It is: doing good work, and being with good people, learning to give and receive love. That is the secret of life."

And that was a Jesuit priest sharing a profound concept I adopted.

MM: What is your definition of *leadership*?

FH: First we have to have our own definition of *leadership*. If we can't articulate that, if it isn't just part of us, go back, think about it. I know after much introspection—also known as agonizing—early in my career with the Girl Scouts, I finally developed my own definition. We can quote Jim Collins and Peter Drucker and Warren Bennis and John W. Gardner forever, but what is inside of us that says, "This is leadership to me"? And finally my own definition emerged: "Leadership is a matter of how to be, not how to do. You and I spend most of our lives learning how to do, and teaching other people how to do, yet in the end we know it is the character and quality of the leader that determines the performance, the results."

That is my answer. We define leadership in our way, our own terms, and then we say, "And these are the values, the beliefs and values, of this institution." Now, first we must develop a short, powerful mission statement that says why we do what we do, our reason for being. For example, the International Red Cross: "To serve the most vulnerable." No confusion, translates into every language. Powerful mission statement is the star we steer by.

Then we have the values we live by. All of us know what they are. And we not only plaster them on everything; we live them. So, this is how leaders grow. We can't make leaders. Peter Drucker says, "Leaders can't be made, but leaders are developed." Leadership is a journey. Leaders who are responsible for the development of other people, giving them opportunities to learn and grow and lead, have to be exemplary in their own behavior, in their guidance, in their leadership. If you do not have these clearly stated values, that you live, you will fail.

MM: Greenleaf, in his conception of servant-leadership, places listening as crucial. What does it mean to listen in leadership?

We learn to be good listeners. A great thought leader, Peter Drucker has said: "Think first, speak last." We learn the art of listening. When there is a conflict, instead of thinking, "These are two bad people who aren't getting along," we listen. Often the reason given for the conflict is not the reason. That's the surface we hear. Suppose I am not doing well in my job and I report to you, and your job is "to make my strengths effective and my weaknesses irrelevant," as Peter said. If we are responsible for the work of another person with 90 percent remarkable performance, 10 percent not so wonderful, we ask ourselves, where do we invest? As leaders, we must pour the resources into your great strengths—the 90 percent.

Now sometimes we place a person in the wrong position and conflicts arise because of insecurity. So we listen very carefully, and if this person is failing and in conflict with other people, we say, "This is a person of value," we "repot" them. We find another place for them instead of knocking heads. "You two are going to get along!" doesn't work. So, the most sensitive kind of appreciation of differences, and an appreciation of "Is there something in this institution that causes this, exacerbates it?" We cannot look only at the surface.

MM: I'd love to hear about the servant-leadership influences in your life.

FH: My grandmother was a very quiet, lovely woman. She had ten children; seven lived. She lived way out in the mountains of western Pennsylvania, where her family had been since the 1830s, had a little lumber mill that made barrel staves. She attended a one-room schoolhouse that her father and grandfather had attended. Above the blackboard was this saying—it was perhaps McGuffey I don't know, it'd been there forever. She made me memorize it when I was eight years old. In that one-room schoolhouse, and up there it was: "If wisdom's ways you would wisely seek, these five things observe with care: of whom you speak, to whom you speak, how, when, and where." I memorized it as a little girl, and I realize, today, the only times I've gotten into trouble was when I forgot "wisdoms ways."

Now, Mama Wicks had fourteen grandchildren. When we visited her, I would walk in the door, and she would say, "Oh, Francie," as though I were the only person in the world. And when I talked to her, she listened, she looked into my eyes. From her I learned the power of listening, the art of listening. The messages I received from Mama Wicks made an enormous difference in my life.

My grandmother, John W. Gardner, Peter Drucker, and other remarkable friends added to this understanding. They listened. Always, because my family told stories to the children, I've always had this sense of history about the people who went before me. And from her, and my grandfather, I think early on I had this sense that we are called to do what we do, and when we are called we are given the energy to do it.

MM: I've heard you say women are not a category.

FH: I think I upset people sometimes. I go into a session and it says, A Gathering of Women Leaders and two days later when we leave, we've changed the banner: A Gathering of Leaders Who Are Women. We are not a category!

So when we describe ourselves—"Oh, I'm a woman banker"—No! You're a banker who is a woman. When we place ourselves in categories, we encourage other people to do this. Whatever positions we are in, we're in those positions because of what we bring to the work, not because of our gender. Now, quietly, we know that our gender adds a special dimension to whatever we do, but it's not why we do what we do.

I've been on three large corporate boards, on two of them, the only woman. Now, did I see myself as "the woman of the board"? Of course not. One was Pennsylvania Power and Light, a company that was building two big nuclear power plants, and nothing is more macho than two big nuclear power plants. Now when you walk into a board room and you're the only woman, you do not play a little recording of, "I Am Woman." No! "You know you are there because of what you bring to the table."

This is a very difficult lesson, and a lot people don't agree with me. "No, I am a woman this, or I am a woman that." I have never heard a judge say this: "I am a woman judge." No! You are a judge. Now, gender is important, but it's not why we do what we do. So I think it is very important that our own language does not add to the barriers that are already there. Wherever we go, we make the greatest contribution we can make.

I've discarded all the old barriers. Maybe they still exist, but I ignore them, because if we keep saying, "Oh, there are these big barriers," we give them life and energy. If we ignore the barrier, it disappears. For young women today I believe there are opportunities greater than ever before. And we have to help build this kind of inner security: "I'm here because of what I bring to the work."

Now, for those of us who are older, one question is, "How many younger women do you mentor?" I met twelve tenured university professors who were women, who asked me to meet with them, when I was speaking at their university. They had a concern about younger women leaving after a year or two, leaving the faculty. And I said, "How many of you are mentoring younger faculty women?" They looked at me as though I were speaking some strange language. And I said, "Until every one of you is mentoring a younger woman, you can't complain."

So, not unkindly, one of the professors said, "Well, how many younger women do you mentor?" and I said, "Three. That's all the time I have if I'm going to do a good job." One of them is an African-American lieutenant commander in the U.S. Coast Guard. A remarkable, remarkable young leader. One is a Chinese graduate student. I met her parents in Shenzhen, and after my speech they said, "Please, you must be our daughter's mentor." And I said, "Of course, I would be honored." And I never heard from them when I went back home. Then, six months later I have a call: "Frances, this is Lin. I'm ready to be mentored. I'm at Stonybrook, at the university." So, my second is a young graduate student. And the third person that I mentor is one of the nursing fellows of a distinguished group of executive nurses.

The experience is circular. I find we learn more from them than they learn from us.

MM: Can you tell me about winning the Presidential Medal of Freedom?

FH: This is the Presidential Medal of Freedom. It's our country's highest civilian honor. I received it in 1998 from President Clinton, and I'm still overwhelmed. In the little group that received the award that morning in the East Room of the White House, were Admiral Zumwalt; David Rockefeller; James Farmer—the great civil rights leader who was in a wheelchair, almost reclining, but he got there; and Dr. Robert Coles of Harvard. It was interesting that all of us had done something about diversity and inclusion.

The Marine Band had played and the whole cabinet, about 200 people were present. Each awardee was permitted to have eight guests. We're sitting in the front row and here is a low stage that has been built in the East Room, and there are two lecterns, one for President Clinton, one for Mrs. Clinton. It's about as graceful as anything could be, and we each had a military aide. So the president would say, "Admiral Zumwalt, would you please come up?" and he would go up the two steps, and then Commander Huey, a young Naval Commander would read part of the citation and then the president would read the balance . . . it was so profound. "Mr. David Rockefeller, would you please come up?" And the citations were beautiful.

Finally, it was my turn. President Clinton smiled and said, "Anyone who knows Frances Hesselbein knows she does not permit hierarchical language to be used in her presence. So, I will ask this pioneer for women, diversity, and opportunity, Frances Hesselbein, will you please come, not up, but will you please come forward?" Of course, it was the only joke of the morning, everyone thought it was very funny, and going "forward" I kept thinking, "How does he know that?" It was very profound. . . . I still feel so honored, so overwhelmed. I wear the miniature medal every day.

MM: Peter Drucker has had such a strong presence in your life and work, please speak to the influence of Peter Drucker.

FH: I had used Peter Drucker's works, his philosophy, his books, all of my career. I had discovered him long, long ago and I thought, "He thinks he's writing for corporations, organizations, but I think he is writing just for us." I loved the way he distilled language.

Five years after I had come to New York and those remarkable people had transformed the organization [the Girl Scouts of the USA], I received an invitation to a reception and dinner. New York University President John Brademus invited fifty foundation presidents and some presidents of large nonprofits to the University Club, five thirty p.m.

Now if you grow up in Johnstown, Pennsylvania, five thirty is five thirty. So I get to the University Club. I walk into this big, empty room, and I am alone with two bartenders. I turn around. Behind me is a man. Obviously, if you grow up in Vienna, five thirty is five thirty. And he said, "I am Peter Drucker."

I was so stunned, because I knew in that mob I would never actually meet him, and instead of saying, "How do you do?" I looked at him and said, "Do you realize how important you are to the Girl Scouts?"

And he said, "No, tell me."

And I replied, "Go to any one of our local 335 Girl Scout Councils. You'll find a shelf of your books. Open our corporate planning management monographs and our strategic plan, and you'll find yourself, your philosophy there."

He said, "Oh, you are very daring. I would be afraid to do that. Tell me, does it work?"

And I said, "Wonderfully. And I've been trying to get up enough courage to call you to say, 'May I come to Claremont and have one hour of your time, because we have in place everything you say the great, effective organization must have in place. And I would like to come to Claremont, lay this out before you, and then talk with you about how do we take the lead in this society and just blast off into the future.' "

He said, "Why should both of us travel? I'll be in New York in a month or so. I will give you a day of my time."

Just then Dr. Brademus and his entourage arrived, they swept Peter away, and I looked at my watch and I said, "In four-and-a-half minutes I met Peter Drucker and I have a day of his time."

From then on, for the next eight years, he gave us two or three days of his time. Before he spent that first day with us, he studied us in a very intense way, not at 830 Third Avenue in New York, but out in the field, where our people were, and by the time he arrived in New York, he knew us very well.

So that morning I knew I couldn't keep him to myself, of course, so we brought together our national board and national staff members, and I could tell that when I just looked at our group, I could tell they expected him to say, "You've transformed the organization. You're wonderful." He stood there, thanked us for permitting him to be there, then he looked at our national leadership team and said, "You do not see yourselves life size. You do not appreciate the significance of the work you do, for we live in a society that pretends to care about its children, and *it does not*." Now I'm sitting beside him, and I want to rise and refute it, and I couldn't think of anything to say. Then he said, "And for a little while you give a girl an opportunity to be a girl in a society that that forces her to grow up all too soon."

A year before he died I called Peter and said, "In 1981 you said to the Girl Scout leadership, we live in a society that pretends to care about its children and it does not. Do you still feel the same way?"

Silence then. "Has anything changed?"

So for those marvelous eight years he was incredibly generous. He taught us how to distill the language and he wrote marvelous things about us: *New York Times*, best-managed organization in the United States, and they said, "You mean nonprofit" and he said, "No. I mean any organization." With his inspiration we were mission-focused, values-based, demographics-driven; our house was in order.

Peter Drucker had a wonderful influence upon the organization. At one point he said, "Tough, hard-working women can do anything." That was not exactly the way we would describe ourselves, but anything Peter said about us, we were grateful.

MM: What is the importance of speaking from the heart?

FH: You might wonder what someone who looks like me, who will always be seen as a Girl Scout, why would someone like me be asked to speak to our 200 generals and admirals most responsible for the national security of our country? Also the secretary, the chief of staff of the U.S. Army and their counterparts in the other four branches of the U.S. military. When I read my invitation—"We would like you to come and talk to us about your own experience in the transformation of a large and complex organization"—I was absolutely stunned. I don't exactly look like General Schwarzkopf, but I never had a better audience. And at one point I did say, "Everyone in this room is called to do what you do. For you it is never a job. You are called." And I got a standing ovation. And I think, not because of the example, I think they were touched because someone recognized what they believe. All of them are gifted. They could be very successful in other sectors. They choose to serve their country.

At lunchtime I sat down—with the army you always know where you sit—so here I am, and here's General Shinseki to my right, then the chief of staff, and on my left is a very large, tall, dark man. He was wearing a strange uniform. (There were admirals and generals present from other countries.) Before I can introduce myself, he says, "Are you a Christian?"

Now, think of where we are. I said, "Yes, I'm a Methodist."

And he said, "I thought so. When you said, 'We are called,' I said to myself, 'I think she is a Christian.'" Then he told me, "I am the Defense Minister on a tiny island between Fiji and New Zealand, and we're 95 percent Christian. We have our king. We've never been colonized. And we are Christian."

Now, when I say we are called, I'm not thinking this is a big Methodist call. The spirit within, however we define it, is the message he heard. And I was very touched. But that's what I believe. If we are going to make speeches, we have to speak from the heart.

Chapter Fourteen

Parker J. Palmer

INTERVIEWED BY MICHAEL R. CAREY,
MIKE POUTIATINE, AND SHANN RAY FERCH

Parker J. Palmer is known for his work in education, spirituality, and social change across a wide range of professions, including education, health care, religious life, philanthropy, community organizing, and business. He is author of numerous books, including Healing the Heart of Democracy *(2011),* The Courage to Teach—10th Anniversary Edition *(2007),* A Hidden Wholeness *(2004),* Let Your Life Speak *(2000), and* The Active Life *(1990). Palmer's writing has earned him numerous awards and citations, including twelve honorary doctorates, and has been translated into several languages. His work has been cited in the major voices in the media, including the* New York Times, *National Public Radio, and the* Chronicle of Higher Education. *He travels extensively as a speaker, facilitator, and workshop and retreat leader. A native of Chicago and graduate of Carleton College and the University of California at Berkeley, where he received a doctorate in sociology, Palmer is founder and senior partner of the Center for Courage & Renewal. Special thanks to Mike Poutiatine, Gonzaga University faculty member, for his involvement in this interview.*

Michael Carey, Mike Poutiatine, and Shann Ray Ferch: What is your view of leadership today?

Parker J. Palmer: The major problem leaders have to deal with, I think, is the fundamental brokenness of our institutions, but we seem to be in denial about that. A rational person would think nobody needs to be led toward seeing it or understanding it. It's all around us all the time—on the nightly news and the Internet and in the morning paper, and it's in the self-reports that people give of their own lives. So leaders have to confront a network of mythologies or illusions that we maintain in order to try to convince ourselves that things aren't as bad as they seem, maybe in the manner of a dysfunctional family which keeps pretending that everything is fine here even though Dad is drinking way too much and hitting people way too often. Paradoxically, the best way leaders can help people see this brokenness, I think, is by acknowledging their own. I don't think we are willing to trust anybody on the issue of how broken we are until that person has acknowledged his or her own brokenness. And of course, that's a tricky business for leaders.

There's a strange dance that goes on between leaders and followers. Followers want leaders to pretend that they're totally together and totally in charge—and then they resent them for acting as if they were superhuman, making all the rest of us feel like dorks. So we do this dance in which we project on leaders our need for the very thing we don't have, but we need somebody to pretend that they have it. I don't think ultimately that that's a dance that people really want to do. The problem is that a leader has to take his or her community, or his or her organization, or his or her group, through a rough passage of truth-telling to get to the other side, to get to the place where we can all acknowledge that God ain't finished with any of us yet, that we're all broken, we are all works in progress, and we need each other to help put the pieces together, to help make something better happen in our world.

Think, for example, about religious congregations in the Protestant or the Catholic communities, which are the ones that I'm most familiar with. There's a tremendous need in most congregations on the part of laypeople to have the priest or the pastor be a godly person in some illusory way, and a lot of priests and pastors feel the falsehood of that. They know themselves well enough to know that they're sinners, that they're broken, that they're struggling along with everybody else. Moving a congregation from that place of shared illusions to a place of reality, where people feel safer because the leader has acknowledged his or her brokenness, is a struggling period of time. Sometimes the people rise up and say, "Well, you may be broken, but that means we should get a new leader," and that's a price the leaders sometimes have to pay. This question, like a lot of leadership questions, comes down to a matter of how much the leader values his or her own integrity, because without it, leadership gets reduced to a sham, to putting on a show.

For myself, at age seventy-five, I no longer have much interest in putting on a show for anybody, for a very simple reason. In recent years, I've come to terms with my own mortality in a way I wasn't capable of doing twenty or thirty years ago. I've realized that at the end of the road I'm not going to be asking, "Did I put on a good enough show, and did that show get good enough reviews?" I'm going to be asking, "How real was I? Was I really there? Did I live my real life?" I find those very salutary questions, very bracing questions. In any given moment when I'm tempted to pull my punches or hedge the truth or slip away from something difficult that I feel called to, it's helpful to ask, "How am I going to feel about this at the moment I'm drawing my last breath?" And I'm pretty clear at this point that I'm not going to be asking, "How much did they like me?" Instead, I'm going to be asking, "Did I live it by my own best lights?" I think that's why St. Benedict, in his rule for monks, says, "Daily keep your death before your eyes"—which is not morbid counsel but very life-giving advice. If you keep your death before your eyes each day, you're likely to live more fully and authentically in the moment than you would otherwise.

MC, MP, SF: What can be done to encourage greatness within our organizations?

PP: That's a very interesting question, because if you put this, as I did in *The Courage to Teach*, in terms of academic disciplines it's fairly easy to see what "the great thing" is. I mean for the physicist, it's the mystery of a subatomic particle; for a literary scholar it's the mind of Dostoyevsky or Melville; for a historian it's the dynamics of the Holocaust or the Third Reich. It's a profoundly important and engaging subject that draws the scholar's work forward. So what's the equivalent of that in organizational life? Well, two things come to mind. One is that *we* human beings ourselves are the equivalent of the scholar's "great thing." It's absolutely critical that we see organizations as habitats for human beings. The workplace is where people spend an incredible number of hours of their lives.

I've been doing a lot of thinking lately about how our workplaces do not treat the people who inhabit them as great things worthy of reverence and respect, in the way a great scholar extends reverence and respect to whatever he or she is studying. I think, in fact, that the workplace has become the battlefield of many people's lives—the place where they feel violence done to their identity and integrity as they become cogs in a machine, or deployable and replaceable resources used simply on behalf of some organizational goal or ulterior motive. That's not a life-giving way to be in the world. That's a way that murders the spirit. And if you translate it in terms of the organizational bottom line, that way of treating people gets worse work out of them than you would if you extended them respect at least, if not full reverence. So I think step one is that a leader has to understand that the great thing in organizational life is the people who inhabit that organization, and that the organization, in order to serve its own mission, has to serve its people well. I think some leaders in corporate life understand that, but not everyone does, by a long shot.

But there's another thing that I'd like to say, for which I'll give a homey example. And that has to do with the products that organizations put on the market in the world of business. My dad was a businessman in Chicago for fifty-five years, and he eventually became owner and CEO of the major Midwest distributor of Syracuse china, Reed and Barton silverware, and Fostoria glass for restaurants, hotels, railroads (in the old days) and then airlines. So I grew up in a household where one of the "great things" was a piece of Syracuse china. My dad would hold one of these plates up to the light and he'd say, "This is fine china, because you can see your hand right through it. Now look at this piece of dime-store china. You can't see your hand. The china is not translucent." My sisters and I learned all of these marks of what great china and great silverware were like, as opposed to their cheap imitations. And what I started to learn, slowly on, was that my dad had a reverence and a respect for quality in the product he was selling. And the reason he would not sell anything that in his judgment did not have quality, was that to do so would be to dishonor the people he was selling to. He wanted to sell a product that he believed in.

With that background, it's been very interesting for me to spend most of my adult life hanging around academics and intellectuals who have very little appreciation for material products—as contrasted with ideas—or for art, or music. Among intellectuals, objects, unless they're objets d'art or something of that sort, are often thought of somewhat pejoratively. It was very interesting to grow up with a father—for whom I had immense respect, the best man I ever knew—who had respect for a piece of china or a piece of silverware, and linked that in his mind to good service to a customer, to putting on the table at a restaurant something that would enhance the dining experience for everybody concerned. So I think one of the questions we have to ask ourselves in organizational life is: Are we selling, marketing, something of real quality, or is this a sham? Is this a shell game? Is this one of those products that, as my grandfather used to say, was "made for buying and not for using?" And if so, that crucial "great thing" is lacking at the center of organizational life. So I think organizational greatness involves treating people and things with all due respect, even reverence.

MC, MP, SF: Considering the maturity involved in holding things with respect and reverence, how *do* you mend a broken heart?

PP: The commonest image of what it means to hold things with respect and reverence is that I'm going to have my heart broken apart. That happens sometimes—people's hearts end up in little shards on the floor, and putting them back together is a long process of reconstruction, which maybe never gets accomplished. Some people die heartbroken. But some years ago it came to me that there's another way of imaging the breaking of the heart, which is that it's being broken open to greater capacity. While that's just wordplay on one level, for me it's actually a life experience, and I know many people for whom that's also true. The question of how you turn heartbreak from being broken apart to being broken open—open to a larger capacity to hold more of the world's suffering—is a mysterious matter. I don't have a formula for it.

But I can say a couple of things that have been important to me. One is that I don't know anybody who has gone through that transformation without experiencing profound personal struggles. In my case it was two devastating bouts with clinical depression, which caused me to question everything about myself and my world, to the point that I wasn't sure that I could keep on living. There are lots of people who know exactly what I mean about that kind of inner devastation, where all you can you feel is, "I'm not living anyway—why should I maintain the illusion that I am?" I don't know how I exactly came through to the other side to kind of reclaim my life with new clarity and new gratefulness and new vitality. I can tell you that I spent a lot of time just dwelling in the dark. I can tell you that I found a good therapist. I can name some pieces of that journey, but *how* ultimately it came together I really don't know. I think there's a mystery about that that we can't and shouldn't even *try* to penetrate.

But I also know that in the midst of that very solitary experience, it was very important to have people, just a few people, who knew how to stand at the border of my solitude, respecting the mystery, not trying either to invade it or to evade it, but simply being present to me in a way that helped deliver me from the darkness. We live in a culture where most people either want to invade you or evade you. The invaders say, "Oh, I've got a fix for you. If you'd only read this book, if you'd only go on this diet, if you'd only take this herbal preparation or pop this pill from the Big Pharma, all will be well." So they want to invade you with fixes, which gets them off the hook. Now they can walk away feeling, "Well, he may kill himself, but I did the best I could." They can check you off their to-do list.

That's the invaders. The evaders want to avert their eyes and pretend "this isn't happening." They "never saw it" and they don't want to look your way again. When I was in the midst of depression, it was pretty rare to find people who were willing simply to stand on the border of my solitude and honor it without fleeing from it—reminding me, just by the quality of their presence, that I was still part of the human community, and that there were people who understood at some level what was happening with me. I knew they understood, because the clearest sign that someone *doesn't* understand is when someone says, "I understand exactly what's happening to you."

What fascinates me is that I *know* it's possible to teach people this way of being present to each other without either invading or evading. The Center for Courage & Renewal now has Courage to Teach and Courage to Lead programs going on all over the country in which we gather cohorts of public school educators, physicians, clergy, nonprofit leaders, and others to take them on a two-year journey through eight retreats. During that time they learn how to be present to one another in a way that helps all of them "rejoin soul and role." It's doable, but it's a form of community that's very rare in our culture, and we need to get very intentional about it if we want it to happen. When it does happen, the results are amazing, because it allows people to draw deeply on their inner resources, to attend to their own inner teacher, in a way they can't do as readily and richly when they're just sitting alone in their room. There's something about the electricity of being in a respectful, observant "community of solitudes" that makes a difference for folks.

MC, MP, SF: What is that we can do as individuals to serve people in times of loss and grief?

PP: I liken this relationship to the experience some of us have had sitting at the bedside of a dying person. I've talked with lots of people who've been there, and they talk about two important things that they learned. One is the realization that the person that they were sitting with did not have a problem that they could fix. And so for the first time they thought, I can't be in this room as a "fixer" of this problem, because this is not a problem that has a solution—nobody has a solution for dying. So I have to learn a different way of being here. And I've asked lots of people, "What is that different way? You were doing more than just taking up space in the room. What *were* you doing?" And the only answer I've ever gotten is something like, "I was just being present. I was being fully present. I was trying to be there with my whole self, even if wordlessly." So you learn not to invade, but to be present to this very solitary journey called dying.

The second thing that you realize is how disrespectful it would be to avert your eyes from this—to regard this as something too ugly to watch, too fearsome to watch. Instead, you need to turn *toward* it and hold it in your attentiveness without either invading or evading the person, the moment, the experience. So we have human-scale experience of what it means to be present to another person this way. As I like to say to myself and others, "We're all dying all the time anyway. Wouldn't it be good to learn to be present this way to each other before the last couple of hours?" No one's ever argued with me about that.

MC, MP, SF: How does one keep hope alive in a world where hope sometimes seems to be at a premium?

PP: That's a question that I think about a lot. We're constantly surrounded by so much evidence of evil in our lives, as with the children who are going hungry or starving at this very moment in a world where there's plenty of food to go around. And yet we seem collectively indifferent to massive suffering. So it's a challenging question: What keeps hope alive in the face of all that? And the question that immediately follows on it is equally challenging: If you find reason for hope, how do you engage with the world in the face of evil?

For me, what keeps hope alive is ultimately fairly simple. It's seeing people who haven't been done in by the way the world is. It's seeing people who model hope in their actions, and realizing that I too could do that if I could find a place to stand that's as solid as where those folks are standing. That's why community is so critical to me. Among other things, community means being connected with generative lives of folks who, in whatever arena it is they care about—and it might be anything from the world of business to the world of early childhood care—are keeping hope alive in their embodied actions. Staying close to people like that is so important in a world where the media are, minute by minute, hour by hour, modeling lives of a very different sort—lives of frenzy, of banality, of cheap commercialism, of consumerism. What I'm saying is that we get along with a little help from our friends! I've learned so much from friends who are walking a different path from mine, a path of real service, people who constantly remind me just by the fact that they're walking it that I could walk that way too.

MC, MP, SF: How can we help keep hope alive within our broader community, and in society?

PP: What's needed, among other things, is the paradoxical opposite of community: solitude. If I stop and look at what kills hope in so many people's lives, the answer, I think, is frenzy—the drivenness of a culture that wants us always to be active, always to be engaged, always to be producing, always to be getting ourselves noticed. In solitude, all of that noise and kerfuffle can settle down, the water can become still, the silt can go to the bottom and you can see with some clarity what's really there. And what's really there, I think, is what Thomas Merton called "the hidden wholeness" that lies beneath and beyond the broken surface of our lives. It's there, but you can see it only when you get quiet enough in heart and mind and eye to let it come into view through the madness. So hope requires community, the encouragement and support of other people, *and* my own willingness to take an inner journey in which I become more quiet and perceptive than I usually am so I can see and stand on the ground of the hidden wholeness.

MC, MP, SF: What do you think of the challenge of working to change our systems from within, versus doing so from the outside?

PP: At some point in my mid-thirties, I came to understand that in order to pursue my vocation, I had to liberate myself from large-scale organizations. And starting in my mid-thirties, which is now forty years ago, I began walking a much more independent path—for the past few decades, I've worked independently and have not been on any organization's payroll. But that's not a piece of advice for other people. It's about my own vocational discernment. It's about the struggle to know who one is and what one's gifts are and how those gifts are best deployed in the world. In my case, I began to realize in my mid-thirties that I was spending a lot of time in getting conflicted with the way power was used in whatever organization I was working for instead of using all of my energy to deploy my gifts toward good ends in the world. I was picking fights with my boss, or picking fights with the way the organization was structured, as if "The devil made me do it." I couldn't see my way out of that until one day I said to myself, "If you want to use your energy toward worthwhile ends and stop wasting it picking fights with the logic of organizations, you need to find a way of making a living that's largely outside of the organizations that trigger your pathology!" What's been fascinating to me is that once I started working independently, my work has largely involved serving those institutions from the outside.

As it turns out, it wasn't that I hated those institutions, but that I was not gifted at working and acting within them. I value educational institutions, religious organizations, philanthropies, and certain other forms of corporate life because I love their missions, rightly understood. I just don't belong *in* them, and I can be of more help as an outsider than I can as an insider. And so as soon as I started working independently, I began finding my way back—for example in education—to being someone who's tried to support the best possibilities for those who have stayed at their posts, serving and serving well.

About the Editors

Larry C. Spears

Larry C. Spears is president and CEO of the Larry C. Spears Center for Servant-Leadership, Inc., established in 2008 (www.spearscenter.org). In 2010, he was named Servant-Leadership Scholar at Gonzaga University. From 1990 to 2007 he served as president and CEO of the Robert K. Greenleaf Center for Servant-Leadership. Larry is the creator and editor of a dozen books on servant-leadership, including the best-selling *Insights on Leadership*. A 2004 television broadcast interview of Spears by Stone Phillips on NBC's *Dateline* was seen by ten million viewers. Larry serves as the senior advisory editor for the *International Journal of Servant Leadership* (2005–present). Among several honors, Spears was the recipient of the 2004 Dare-to-Lead Award given by the International Leadership Network. Larry has thirty years of experience in organizational leadership, entrepreneurial development, nonprofit management, and grant writing, having envisioned and authored thirty successful grant projects. He lives in Indianapolis, Indiana, with his wife.

Shann Ray Ferch

Shann Ray Ferch's book of creative nonfiction, leadership and political theory *Forgiveness and Power in the Age of Atrocity: Servant Leadership as a Way of Life* (Rowman & Littlefield/Lexington), was named an Amazon Top Ten Hot New Release in War and Peace in Current Events, and engages the question of ultimate forgiveness in the context of ultimate violence. His collection of short stories *American Masculine* (Graywolf Press), named by *Esquire* for their Three Books Every Man Should Read series, won the Bread Loaf Writers' Conference Bakeless Prize, the High Plains Book Award, and the American Book Award for Literary Excellence. Ferch is a National Endowment for the

Arts Literature Fellow and has served as a panelist for the National Endowment for the Humanities, Research Division. He lives with his wife and three daughters in Spokane, Washington, where he teaches leadership and forgiveness studies in the internationally renowned Doctoral Program in Leadership Studies at Gonzaga University.

Mary McFarland

Mary McFarland is the director of Jesuit Commons: Higher Education at the Margins providing higher education to refugees throughout the world. Prior to her work with Jesuit Commons, McFarland was the dean of the School of Professional Studies at Gonzaga University. As a professor her teaching focus was on health-care policy, nursing education and leadership in corporate and higher-education settings. McFarland's research foci include international refugee educational formation, visionary leadership, and effective leadership strategies during times of corporate organizational transformation. Her career in nursing has included critical care, hospice, adult nurse practitioner, and nursing education. McFarland is a Robert Wood Johnson Fellow, and previously completed a three-year funded project in the Nurse Executive leadership program.

Michael R. Carey

Before coming to Gonzaga University, Michael R. Carey served as a teacher, campus minister, and vice principal at Catholic secondary schools in Los Angeles and Spokane. In 1987, he was hired to teach leadership studies at Gonzaga University. Carey has served in a variety of formal administrative roles during his twenty-five-year tenure at Gonzaga: six years as the first director of the Organizational Leadership program; four years as the first coordinator of the Council for Partnership in Mission; two years as executive assistant to the president; three years as vice president and then president of the Faculty Assembly; and one year as the chairperson of the Mission and Community Committee of the Faculty Senate. Currently, Carey serves as Dean of Gonzaga's Virtual Campus, which supports learning and technology, especially for online graduate programs at Gonzaga.

Recommended Readings

Autry, James A. *The Servant Leader.* New York: Three Rivers Press, 2001.

Baron, Tony. *The Art of Servant Leadership: Designing Your Organization for the Sake of Others.* Tucson, AZ: Wheatmark, 2010.

Blanchard, Ken and Phil Hodges. *The Servant Leader.* Nashville, TN: Thomas Nelson, 2003.

Block, Peter. *Community: The Structure of Belonging.* San Francisco: Berrett-Koehler, 2008.

———. *The Answer to How Is Yes: Acting on What Matters.* San Francisco: Berrett-Koehler, 2001.

———. *Stewardship: Choosing Service Over Self-Interest.* San Francisco: Berrett-Koehler, 1993.

Boyd, Jim. *A Servant Leader's Journey: Lessons from Life.* Mahwah, NJ: Paulist Press, 2008.

DePree, Max. *Leadership Is an Art.* New York: Doubleday, 1989.

———. *Leadership Jazz.* New York: Dell Publishing, 1992.

———. *Leading Without Power.* San Francisco: Jossey-Bass, 1997.

Ferch, Shann Ray. *Forgiveness and Power in the Age of Atrocity: Servant Leadership as a Way of Life.* Lanham, MD: Rowman & Littlefield/Lexington Books, 2011.

———, ed. *International Journal of Servant-Leadership,* 1–7 (2005–2012).

Frick, Don M. *Robert K. Greenleaf: A Life of Servant-Leadership.* San Francisco: Berrett-Koehler, 2004.

———. The *Seven Pillars of Servant-Leadership: Practicing the Wisdom of Leading by Serving.* Mahwah, NJ: Paulist Press, 2009.

Greenleaf, Robert K. *The Institution as Servant.* Indianapolis: The Greenleaf Center, 1976.

———. *Servant Leadership.* Mahwah, NJ: Paulist Press, 1977.

———. *The Leadership Crisis.* Indianapolis, IN: The Greenleaf Center, 1978.

———. *The Servant as Religious Leader.* Indianapolis, IN: The Greenleaf Center, 1982.

———. *Seminary as Servant.* Indianapolis, IN: The Greenleaf Center, 1983.

———. *My Debt to E. B. White.* Indianapolis, IN: The Greenleaf Center, 1987.

———. *Old Age: The Ultimate Test of Spirit.* Indianapolis, IN: The Greenleaf Center, 1987.

———. *Teacher as Servant: A Parable.* Indianapolis, IN: The Greenleaf Center, 1987.
———. *Education and Maturity.* Indianapolis, IN: The Greenleaf Center, 1988.
———. *Have You a Dream Deferred.* Indianapolis, IN: The Greenleaf Center, 1988.
———. *Spirituality as Leadership.* Indianapolis, IN: The Greenleaf Center, 1988.
———. *Trustees as Servants.* Indianapolis, IN: The Greenleaf Center, 1990.
———. *Advices to Servants.* Indianapolis, IN: The Greenleaf Center, 1991.
———. *The Servant as Leader.* Indianapolis, IN: The Greenleaf Center, 1991.
———. *On Becoming a Servant Leader.* San Francisco: Jossey-Bass, 1996.
———. *Seeker and Servant.* San Francisco: Jossey-Bass, 1996.
———. *The Power of Servant-Leadership.* San Francisco: Berrett-Koehler, 1998.
———. *Servant Leadership 25th Anniversary Edition.* Mahwah, NJ: Paulist Press, 2002.
———. *The Servant-Leader Within.* Mahwah, NJ: Paulist Press, 2003.
Hesse, Hermann. *The Journey to the East.* New York: The Noonday Press, 1992.
Jaworski, Joseph. *Synchronicity: The Inner Path of Leadership.* San Francisco: Berrett-Koehler, 1996.
Jones, Michael. *Creating an Imaginative Life.* Berkeley: Conari Press, 1995.
Peter Koestenbaum and Peter Block. *Freedom and Accountability at Work: Applying Philosophic Insight to the Real World.* San Francisco: Jossey-Bass/Pfeiffer, 2001.
Lewis, Ralph and John Noble. *Servant-Leadership: Bringing the Spirit of Work to Work.* London: Management Books 2000, 2008.
McGee-Cooper, Ann and Gary Looper. *The Essentials of Servant-Leadership: Principles in Practice.* Waltham, MA: Pegasus Communications, 2001.
——— and Duane Trammell. *Being the Change: Profiles from Our Servant-Leadership Learning Community.* Dallas, TX: Ann McGee-Cooper & Associate, 2007.
Prosser, Stephen. *To Be a Servant-Leader.* Mahwah, NJ: Paulist Press, 2007.
SanFacon, George. *A Conscious Person's Guide to the Workplace.* Victoria, BC, Canada: Trafford Publishing, 2007.
Showkeir, Jamie and Maren Showkeir. *Authentic Conversations: Moving from Manipulation to Truth and Commitment.* San Francisco: Berrett-Koehler, 2008.
Spears, Larry C., ed. *Reflections on Leadership: How Robert K. Greenleaf's Theory of Servant-Leadership Influenced Today's Top Management Thinkers.* New York: John Wiley & Sons, 1995.
———. *Insights on Leadership: Service, Stewardship, Spirit, and Servant-Leadership.* New York: John Wiley & Sons, 1998.
——— and Michele Lawrence., eds. *Focus on Leadership: Servant-Leadership for the 21st Century.* New York: John Wiley & Sons, 2002.
——— and Michele Lawrence., eds. *Practicing Servant-Leadership.* San Francisco: Jossey-Bass, 2004.
——— and Shann Ferch, eds. *The Spirit of Servant-Leadership.* Mahwah, NJ: Paulist Press, 2011.
——— and Paul Davis, eds. *Fortuitous Encounters.* Mahwah, NJ: Paulist Press, 2011.
Turner, William B. *The Learning of Love: A Journey Toward Servant-Leadership.* Macon, GA: Smyth & Helwys, 1999.

Wheatley, Margaret J. *Leadership and the New Science Revised: Discovering Order in a Chaotic World*. San Francisco: Berrett-Koehler, 1999.

———. *Turning to One Another.* San Francisco: Berrett-Koehler, 2002.

Williams, Lea E. *Servants of the People: The 1960s Legacy of African American Leadership.* New York: St. Martin's Press, 1996.

Zohar, Danah. *Rewiring the Corporate Brain.* San Francisco: Berrett-Koehler, 1997.

Other Books and Other Writings by the Editors

Books by Larry C. Spears as Editor and Contributing Author

Fortuitous Encounters (with Paul Davis), Mahwah, NJ: Paulist Press, 2013.

The Spirit of Servant-Leadership (with Shann Ray Ferch), Mahwah, NJ: Paulist Press, 2011.

Within Your Reach: The Beatitudes in Business and Everyday Life (with Bill Bottum, Dorothy L. Lenz, and George SanFacon), 2010.

The Human Treatment of Human Beings (with John F. Donnelly and Paul Davis), E. Lansing, MI: Scanlon Foundation, 2009.

Scanlon EPIC Leadership: Where the Best Ideas Come Together (with Paul Davis), E. Lansing, MI: Scanlon Foundation, 2008.

Practicing Servant-Leadership: Succeeding Through Trust, Bravery, and Forgiveness (with Michele Lawrence), San Francisco: Jossey-Bass, 2004.

The Servant-Leader Within: A Transformative Path (with Robert K. Greenleaf, Hamilton Beazley, and Julie Beggs), Mahwah, NJ: Paulist Press, 2003.

Servant-Leadership: A Journey into the Nature of Legitimate Power and Greatness: 25th Anniversary Edition (with Robert K. Greenleaf, Stephen Covey, and Peter M. Senge), Mahwah, NJ: Paulist Press, 2002.

Focus on Leadership: Servant-Leadership for the 21st Century (with Michele Lawrence), New York: John Wiley & Sons, 2001.

The Power of Servant-Leadership (with Robert K. Greenleaf, James P. Shannon, and Peter Vaill), San Francisco: Berrett-Koehler, 1998.

Insights on Leadership: Service, Stewardship, Spirit, and Servant-Leadership, New York: John Wiley & Sons, 1998.

On Becoming a Servant-Leader (with Don M. Frick), San Francisco: Jossey-Bass, 1996.

Seeker and Servant (with Anne T. Fraker), San Francisco: Jossey-Bass, 1996.

Reflections on Leadership: How Robert K. Greenleaf's Theory of Servant-Leadership Influenced Today's Top Management Thinkers, New York: John Wiley & Sons, 1995.

Chapters in Other Books as Contributing Author

Forgiveness and Power in the Age of Atrocity: Servant-Leadership as a Way of Life (Shann Ray Ferch, ed.), Lanham, MD: Lexington, 2012.

Leading Wisely in Difficult Times: Three Cases of Faith and Business (Michael Naughton and David Specht, eds.), Mahway, NJ: Paulist Press, 2011.

Setting the Agenda: Meditations for the Organization's Soul (Edgar Stoesz and Rick M. Stiffney, eds.), Scottsdale, PA: Herald Press, 2011.

Servant Leadership: Developments in Theory and Research (Dirk van Dierendonck and Kathleen Patterson, eds.), New York: Palgrave MacMillan, 2010.

The Jossey-Bass Reader on Nonprofit and Public Leadership (James L. Perry), San Francisco: Jossey-Bass, 2010.

The OnTarget Board Member: 8 Indisputable Behaviors (M. Conduff, C. Gabanna, and C. Raso, eds.), Denton, TX: Elim Group Publishing, 2007.

Robert K. Greenleaf: A Life of Servant Leadership (Don M. Frick, ed.), San Francisco: Barrett-Koehler, 2004.

Cutting Edge: Leadership 2000 (Barbara Kellerman and Larraine Matusak, eds.), College Park, MD: The James MacGregor Burns Acadamy of Leadership, 2000.

Stone Soup for the World (Marianne Larned, ed.), Berkeley, CA: Conari Press, 1998.

Leadership in a New Era (John Renesch, ed.), San Francisco: New Leaders Press, 1994.

Books by Shann Ray Ferch

Forgiveness and Power in the Age of Atrocity: Servant Leadership as a Way of Life, Lanham, MD: Lexington, 2011.

American Masculine (as Shann Ray), Minneapolis, MN: Graywolf Press, 2011.

The Spirit of Servant-Leadership (with Larry Spears), Mahway, NJ: Paulist Press, 2011.

Balefire: Poems (as Shann Ray), Sandpoint, ID: Lost Horse Press, 2014.

Monographs by Shann Ray Ferch

Servant-Leadership, Restorative Justice, and Forgiveness (Voices of Servant-Leadership Series), Westfield, IN: The Greenleaf Center, 2000.

Journals Edited by Shann Ray Ferch and Larry C. Spears

The International Journal of Servant-Leadership, SUNY Press, Gonzaga University, The Spears Center, 2005–2014.

Index

Made in the USA
San Bernardino, CA
23 October 2016